MW01008372

The Apocalypse of Settler Colonialism

The Apocalypse of Settler Colonialism

The Roots of Slavery, White Supremacy, and Capitalism in Seventeenth-Century North America and the Caribbean

by GERALD HORNE

MONTHLY REVIEW PRESS
New York

Copyright © 2018 by Gerald Horne
All Rights Reserved

Library of Congress Cataloging-in-Publication Data
available from the publisher.

ISBN: 978-1-58367-663-9 (paper)
ISBN: 978-1-58367-664-6 (cloth)

Typeset in Eldorado

Monthly Review Press, New York
monthlyreview.org

5 4 3 2 1

Contents

Introduction

The years between 1603 and 1714 were perhaps the most decisive in English history. At the onset of the seventeenth century, the sceptered isle was a second-class power but the Great Britain that emerged by the beginning of the eighteenth century was, in many ways, the planet's reigning superpower.[1] It then passed the baton to its revolting spawn, the United States, which has carried global dominance into the present century.[2]

There are many reasons for this stunning turnabout. Yet any explanation that elides slavery, colonialism, and the shards of an emerging capitalism, along with their handmaiden—white supremacy—is deficient in explanatory power. From the sixteenth through the nineteenth centuries nearly 13 million Africans were brutally snatched from their homelands, enslaved, and forced to toil for the greater good of European and Euro-American powers, London not least. Roughly two to four million Native Americans also were enslaved and traded by European settlers in the Americas, English and Scots not least.

From the advent of Columbus to the end of the nineteenth century, it is possible that five million indigenous Americans were enslaved. This form of slavery coexisted roughly with enslavement of Africans, leading to a catastrophic decline in the population of indigenes. In the Caribbean basin, the Gulf Coast, northern Mexico, and what is now the U.S. Southwest, the decline in population during the sixteenth and seventeenth centuries was nothing short of catastrophic. Population may have fallen by up to 90 percent through devilish means including warfare, famine, and slavery, all with resultant epidemics. The majority of the enslaved were women and children, an obvious precursor, and trailblazer, for the sex trafficking of today. But for the massive revolt of the indigenous in 1680 in what is now New Mexico,[3] the toll might have been much worse.[4]

The United States is the inheritor of the munificent crimes of not only London but Madrid, too. When Hernando De Soto crossed what became known as the Mississippi River in the 1530s, he had in tow enslaved indigenes, as he helped to clear the land for what became the future's comfortable U.S. suburbs. [5]

Though disease spread by these interlopers is often trotted out to explain the spectacular downturn in the fortunes of indigenous Americans, genocide[6]—in virtually every meaning of the term, including volitional acts by invading settlers—is the proximate cause of this towering mountain of cadavers. Thus, even when enslaved Africans chose suicide, which they were often forced to do, it would be folly to suggest that enslavers were guiltless. [7]

But within that broad expanse of centuries, it is the seventeenth that stands out conspicuously as the takeoff for London's involvement in the nasty business of enslavement, which simultaneously delivered bounteous profits that set the stage for a racializing rationalization of inhumanity, while setting yet another stage for the takeoff of an enhanced capitalism. A recent study revealed that before 1581 there were no enslaved Africans brought to what was referred to as the "British Caribbean" and "Mainland North America." From 1581 to 1640 there were scores brought to each. But from 1641 to 1700, 15,000 Africans were brought to North America and 308, 000 to the "British Caribbean."[8] Similarly, trade from Dutch forts in Africa amounted to about 700 of the enslaved yearly between 1600 and 1644 but would increase sixfold by the late 1660s.[9] Europeans generally enslaved some two million Africans during the seventeenth century, half of them from West Central Africa and most of the rest from the states abutting today's Ghana and the Bights of Benin and Biafra.

What is euphemistically referred to as "modernity" is marked with the indelible stain of what might be termed the Three Horsemen of the Apocalypse: Slavery, White Supremacy, and Capitalism, with the bloody process of human bondage being the driving and animating force of this abject horror. Decades ago, the Guyanese scholar Walter Rodney sketched adroitly "How Europe Underdeveloped Africa" and, correspondingly, how Western Europe was buoyed by dint of ravaging this beleaguered continent. The slave trade left the infirm and elderly behind—and took the rest. Systems of agriculture, mining, production of metal, cotton, wood, straw, clay and leather goods, trade, transport, and governance that had evolved over centuries were wounded severely. Community was turned against community, neighbor against neighbor. Simultaneously, the agents of this apocalypse profited handsomely.[10]

London was a prime beneficiary of this systemic cruelty. England had a 33 percent share of the slave trade in 1673 and 74 percent by 1683. Of that dreadful total, the Royal African Company, under the thumb of the Crown, held a hefty 90 percent share in 1690, but with deregulation and the entrance into this sinfully profitable market by freelance merchants, this total had shrunk to 8 percent by 1701. This political and economic victory over monarchy by merchants also undergirded the "popular" politics they represented, which eventuated in a republicanism that scored its paradigmatic triumph in 1776. As scholar William Pettigrew has argued forcefully, the African Slave Trade rested at the heart of what is still held dear in capitalist societies: free trade, anti-monarchism, and a racially sharpened and class-based democracy.[11] To put it another way, the weakening of monarchy which was essential to the emerging republicanism was driven in no small way by the desire of certain merchants to weaken the monarch's hold over the lushly lucrative African Slave Trade.[12]

However, the surging merchants so essential to the fomenting of the so-called Glorious Revolution in 1688, which was a kind of Magna Carta for racialized bourgeois democracy, contained aching

contradictions beyond the obvious of being immersed in flesh ped-
dling. In order to undermine Madrid, London in the late sixteenth
century commissioned pirates to hound the vessels groaning with
wealth purloined from the Americas. These swashbucklers found
sanctuary in Jamaica, particularly in 1655, a true turning point that
marked the decline of the ousted Spanish Empire and the rise of its
London-based counterpart. But this was just one more catastrophic
success for the Crown as powerful colonists then began to undermine
a proper colonialism by seeking to break the bonds of "imperial pref-
erence" and trade with any they so chose, including London's fiercest
foes, thus setting the stage for 1776 and a profound loss for Great
Britain.[13] The contradictions did not end there as piracy not only
facilitated the slave trade, particularly after London moved to crush it,
but infused the capitalism that emerged in the republic with the ethos
of the gangster.[14]

Similarly, as the religious conflicts that animated the seventeenth century began to recede—Christian vs. Muslim; Catholic vs.
Protestant—as the filthy wealth generated by slavery and dispposses-
sion accelerated, capitalism and profit became the new god, with its
curia in the basilicas of Wall Street. This new religion had its own
doctrine and theologies, with the logic of the market and its "efficient
market theory" supplanting papal infallibility as the new North Star.[15]
Management theorists have sanctified capitalism in much the same
way that clergymen of yore sanctified feudalism. Business schools are
cathedrals of capitalism. Consultants are its traveling friars. Just as
the clergy in the days of feudalism spoke in Latin to give their words
an air of authority, the myrmidons of capitalism speak in a similarly
indecipherable mumbo-jumbo. To this day, a Reformation—akin to
Martin Luther's of 1517—has been delayed in arrival.[16]

Actually, reducing the present to capitalism is somewhat misleading since today's status quo represents a complex mélange of vestiges
of slavery—the still exploited African population in the United States
and elsewhere—capitalism, and the feudalism from which it emerged.

Moreover, underdevelopment, particularly in Africa, is not only
a product of the depopulation of the halest and heartiest delivered

by the ignominious slave trade. It is the almost casual destruction of Africa, as when Vasco da Gama whimsically bombarded Mogadishu in the late fifteenth century—then continued his rapacious journey—followed shortly thereafter by one of his comrades leaving in his wake a trail of blood along the Swahili coast, not to mention the brutal reconfiguration of what is now Eritrea, leaving tensions and contradictions that have yet to be resolved.[17]

Like a seesaw, as London rose Africa and the Americas fell. As one scholar put it, "the industrial revolution in England and the cotton plantation in the South were part of the same set of facts."[18] (The only friendly amendment to this aphorism would be to include the 17th century so-called "sugar boom" as an antecedent of both.) More to the point, as yet another wise writer put it, "without English capitalism there probably would have been no capitalis[t] system of any kind."[19] As early as 1663, an observer in Surinam noticed that "Negroes [are] the strength and sinews of the Western world."[20] The enslaved, a peculiar form of capital encased in labor, represented simultaneously the barbarism of the emerging capitalism, along with its productive force.

The continent that was compelled to contribute to this process (those now known as "African-American") arguably has yet to recover from the slave trade and the concomitant colonialism that accelerated in the seventeenth century, which in turn has marked this population wickedly with the stain of slavery. Surely, if one seeks to understand how and why it is that so many Africans reside in North America speaking a language with roots in Western Europe, an intimate understanding of the seventeenth century is a requisite.

ENSLAVED AFRICANS CONSTITUTED two-thirds of the total migration into the Americas between 1600 and 1700.[21] These forced migrants can be viewed, metaphorically and actually, as currency, helping to enrich certain Englishmen, aiding their nation's rise from second-class status to global empire. Their arrival in the Americas represented a horrific leap for constructions of "race" that can be said to precede this bloody century.[22]

Of course, there are derivatives of London's extended reach that cannot be downplayed. During the late fourteenth and early fifteenth centuries and continuing into following centuries, Europeans advanced the technology of war-fighting vessels, a boon for the elite of the British Isles.[23] The flintlock musket pioneered in the first few decades of this pivotal century made possible not only the ability of the English—but French and Dutch, too—to impose their will, on Africans not least. The sword bayonet made its appearance during the Thirty Years' War, 1618–1648, and it too was instrumental in the subjugation of entire nations.[24] By the end of this fraught century, some 600,000 flintlocks were being sold in central France alone. Between 1600 and 1750 the rate of successful handgun fire multiplied by a factor of ten. Technological advances—including the invention of ramrods, paper cartridges, and bayonets—made guns cheaper, better, quicker, and more deadly, all to the detriment of those to be enslaved on London's behalf.[25] The development of the astrolabe and the caravel were key to the development of navigation and the encounter with the Americas, as well as the plunder of Africa.[26]

The continuing immiseration that gripped all too many in the British Isles was also a recruiting broadside, magnetically conscripting young men—and some disguised young women—to join the military and wield these weapons against "others." The "English succeeded as colonizers," says one historian, "largely because their society was less successful at keeping people content at home."[27] The wealth generated, in a circle devoid of virtue, allowed for the creation of standing armies that could then compel multiplication of the wealth accumulating in England's coffers, extracted from Africa and the Americas.

It was during the 1600s, driven by seemingly unceasing conflicts between and among them, that European powers developed not just muskets but also countermarch drilling, whereby the front row of gunners fire off their charges, then march to the back of the formation in order to reload. An island monarchy, England had a felt need to develop a formidable navy, which included broadside ships with multiple tiers of cannon and capacity to sail close to the wind. Another innovation that guaranteed rising European power was the building of thick walled forts with angled bastions that often provided defenders with an advantage over far superior numbers.[28]

With no land frontier to defend, at least not to the same degree as continental rivals such as Spain and France, London disproportionately devoted its military expenditure to the navy, which had untoward consequences for Africa and the Americas. Thus, even though the French in 1700 had almost three times more men in service, London was steadily exceeding Paris in colonial conquest.[29]

A problem with London's armed forces was the perceived unreliability of the neighboring Irish. In a sense, the colonial defenestration of Ireland was a rehearsal for what befell the Americas and Africa. But, dialectically, just as this intensified oppression tended to drive the victims of colonialism into the arms of London's antagonists, a pressing issue for England during this entire era was the penchant of the Irish to join the armed forces of Spain.[30] There was a similar tendency operative among traditionally restive Scots, too.[31]

The late sixteenth-century's Anglo-Scot wars prepared the ground for the Act of Union of 1707, which inter alia invited Scots to join in the colonial and enslaving feast, and ameliorated but did not resolve this urgent matter. This attack on London's manpower also intensified the impulse to make up for the shortfall by dragooning Africans. Ultimately, the republicans in North America were to slice this Gordian knot neatly by way of moving toward a new kind of aristocracy—that is, "whiteness"—by which Europeans of various stripes could be accommodated, as against the interests of dispossessed indigenes and enslaved Africans. This concern was facilitated by the practical desire of English colonists in, for example, Virginia, to trade with the then antagonist, the Dutch, engendering a process that led to a new identity: "whiteness" or the leapfrogging of ethnic boundaries and constraints. The influence of the Dutch on events in English colonies, not least in illustrating the value of republicanism, should be underscored here too.[32]

THE ISLES OFF THE WESTERN COAST of Europe had plenty of experience with martial conflict, beginning in the early 1640s.

However, it was not just England that was beset by turmoil. Yes, what has been called the "Puritan Revolution" stretched from the 1640s to the 1660s. There were also a series of revolts in France known as the Fronde, which may have surpassed in havoc and intensity the events there of the late eighteenth century. By 1649 there was a kind of coup that hit the Netherlands. In 1640 there was a revolt in Catalonia that failed, accompanied by another in Portugal against Madrid that succeeded. The next year there was nearly a revolt in Andalusia as well. In 1647 there was a major revolt in Naples. In short, there was a general crisis in Western Europe, inducing strains that were then transferred to the Americas and Africa. The crisis in Europe was resolved in part by transferring the raging militarism westward for conquest. However, dialectically, the riches driven by dispossession and mass enslavement helped to propel colonial merchants, many with close ties to New England, to the forefront in London in the 1640s when civil war rocked England. Finally, these merchants directed a revolt against the monarchy in 1776 that allowed them to further enrich themselves at the expense of enslaved Africans and looted indigenes.

In other words, what was unfolding in Western Europe was in some ways a regional crisis of production as the emerging bourgeoisie strained against the feudal leash, then broke free while retaining the bloodily bellicose backwardness of the previous regime, which facilitated enslavement and dispossession.[33] There was the Swiss peasant war of 1653 and a major Ukrainian revolt during the same period. Bookending these mass uprisings were the rebellions in Ireland in 1641 and 1689. According to the late E. J. Hobsbawm, this represented the "last phase of the general transition from a feudal to a capitalist economy,"[34] a transition fueled by enslavement and colonial dispossession.

Providing a frenzied context was the reality that the year 1641 witnessed the third coldest summer recorded over the past six centuries in the Northern Hemisphere. In 1641 there were more deaths from snow and frost and extreme cold than from violence, which admittedly was extreme, too. There was an accompanying severe drought in Senegambia and Upper Niger from 1640 to 1644. Angola records a unique concentration of droughts, local infestations, and epidemics throughout the second quarter of the seventeenth century with a major drought and famine in the late 1640s, as slave ships began to descend in southwest Africa in droves. It was not just the 1640s that were subject to climate crisis; 1621 saw an "El Niño Autumn" that ruined the harvest in England, and, arguably, helped to instigate migration across the Atlantic.[35]

A quarter or perhaps even a third of the adult male population may have been in arms in the British Isles during this period. Casualties were astronomical, higher as a proportion of population than the catastrophic figures of the First World War. The figures for Scotland in the 1640s were even higher and those of Ireland higher still. This not only created battle-hardened troops well-disposed to subdue Africa and the Americas, but the losers in these conflicts were often dispatched to the budding Caribbean plantations as bonded laborers, and their resultant bumptious rebelling then set the stage for creating enslaved Africans and indigenes to supplant them.[36]

These 1640s' conflicts were another turning point in terms of the apocalypse that ensnared Africans and indigenous Americans. Yet, like a seesaw, as some lost their lives, their freedom, others benefited. Foremost among this latter group was Maurice Thomson, who helped to finance Oliver Cromwell, the "Lord Protector" who deposed the king in London, then went on to rampage through Ireland. Thomson was promised 16,218 acres in the Ulster counties of Antrim and Armagh for his troubles, which included this merchant lending considerable sums of money to support Cromwell's forces in Ireland. This occurred after he had succeeded against the odds as a Virginia planter, taking up a grant at Blunt Point near what is now Newport News as early as 1621. Thomson was also a tireless trafficker in human lives, taking up a grant in St. Kitts to facilitate his growing involvement in the African Slave Trade. The busy Thomson also had a hand in the Canadian fur trade.[37]

As the civil wars in England were unfolding, the Thirty Years' War on the continent was lurching to a close, marked by the Treaty of Westphalia of 1648.[38] This epochal agreement established rules for state sovereignty that have yet to disappear, but the concord also set the stage for European expansion. These sovereigns, including the now battle-hardened England, were able to turn their military prowess outward toward Africa and the Americas. In the process, toughened, albeit defeated, troops were exported abroad to the Caribbean, suitable for wreaking havoc on the indigenous and Africans alike.[39] At the same time, merchants groaning under the wealth produced by plunder and enslavement in the Caribbean were a major force driving the anti-monarchism that led to a beheading of a king in the 1640s. These very same merchants were to triumph in 1688 in the so-called Glorious Revolution, which empowered them further as they weakened the Crown's control of the wildly lucrative African Slave Trade, which ultimately provided the wherewithal for the overthrow of the reign of the monarch again in 1776.

Assuredly, the seventeenth century proved to be decisive, not only to the rise of what came to be the British Empire but also in the secession in 1776 that created a competing power, which has carried the torch of global supremacy into the twenty-first century, with it too being propelled by enslavement of Africans most notably.[40]

Nevertheless, this is not a story of unblemished triumph. This seventeenth-century rise was an unmitigated disaster for those who were its primary victims. Though understandably and justifiably West Africa is viewed routinely as the prime vector of European depredations on the beleaguered continent, hundreds of thousands of souls were snatched from East Africa, with this number accelerating in the seventeenth century, then expanding exponentially thereafter.[41] The early seventeenth century marked the advent of English slaving in the Indian Ocean basin, with some of those manacled shipped to the Malay Peninsula.[42]

The seventeenth century also marked an acceleration of what came to be a genocide against the indigenous population of North America.[43] Though even those on the left, often in a one-sided fashion, hail the point that London's bastard child in North America merits a salute because of its bringing of bourgeois democracy, this was more akin to burning down the house in order to roast the pig. As I have pointed out elsewhere, hailing the arrival of bourgeois democracy should be seen in the same way that it arrived in South Africa—as a means by which to consolidate colonial rule by dint of "race," providing a kind of "combat pay" to settlers. Moreover, 1776 was an attempt to continue the process of moving west through North America, seizing the land of indigenes and stocking same with enslaved Africans, when it seemed an exhausted London was more keen to turn its attention to the jewel that was British India or newer horizons in Africa. Thus, 1776 completed the apocalypse begun in the seventeenth century.[44]

The British scholar Richard Gott has a point when he concludes that "the rulers of the British Empire will one day be perceived to rank with the dictators of the twentieth century as the authors of crimes against humanity on an infamous scale."[45] Of course, a friendly amendment would also include their brethren in North America in this hall of infamous shame. Indeed, the forces unleashed by the rise of London, then New York, proved little less than apocalyptic for Africans and the indigenous of North America.[46]

In North America the colonialism implanted bloodily involved racialization, which meant the denial of the right to have rights, making millions—Africans particularly—denizens of a society but not of it, that is, permanent aliens, a status that has not entirely dissipated to this very day, indicating its profundity. Ultimately, this is a description of what "race" means,[47] a pernicious concept that emerged forcefully, coincidentally enough, in the seventeenth century as colonialism was gaining traction.[48]

This serves to explicate why the eminent Ghanaian scholar A. Adu Boahen has termed the slave trade "an unpardonable crime, a crime unmitigated by any extenuating circumstance."[49] And certainly not extenuating is the racially stained and deformed republicanism and capitalism that is at times seen implicitly as a justification for the genocide.

For, other than Native America, Africa was the primary victim of the apocalypse unleashed with full fury in the seventeenth century. Joseph E. Inikori is doubtlessly correct when he suggests that the African Slave Trade continues to reverberate, distorting African economies and contributing to today's underdevelopment.[50] By way of comparison, imagine if China today began sending vessels to the Pacific Coast of North America, kidnapping the youngest and healthiest; can you imagine the subsequent impact on the United States and Canada?

Inikori has been among those who have pointed to the enslavement of Africans as being essential to the rise of capitalism.[51] Similarly, the construction of the relatively new racial identity that was "whiteness"—and its complement white supremacy—took off as the African Slave Trade itself was reaching a new stage.[52]

Besides enslavement and the wealth it brought, which facilitated development of the productive forces that then delivered military firepower, London was a beneficiary of the decline of competing powers. There are a number of landmark years in this bloody century of ascendancy, and one is assuredly 1683 when the Ottoman Turks were turned back at Vienna, which vouchsafed the security of points west—London not least—and marked the continuing decline of the Ottomans. Thus, by the early nineteenth century, the Ottoman Empire, which stretched from Africa through Europe into Central Asia, was a virtual British protectorate, a reality buoyed by the fact that even before 1683, Istanbul was a cauldron of instability as sultans were murdered, executed, and otherwise deposed in the decades stretching from 1617 to 1703. With the breathing space this provided, London could more readily and easily turn its fuller attention to Africa and the Americas.[53]

THE JESUITS ARRIVED IN THE HORN of Africa as early as 1557, the usual advance guard adumbrating the arrival of armed force, then colonialism. The technological trends that were sweeping through Europe did not leave East Africa unaffected. Firearms first arrived in Ethiopia in the fifteenth century; by the 1620s there were 1,500 muskets in the country; by the 1670s guns were common there.[54] Moreover, as early as 1542 the Ottomans in Yemen were arming Ethiopians, the target of incursions by London's chief European ally, the Portuguese, who already had established a toehold in East Africa.

When the Ottomans suffered a severe setback in 1683, this weakened Africa simultaneously.[55] With the Ottomans at the gates of Vienna in 1683, Europeans were panicking, with the Pope sending an envoy to Persia with the aim of galvanizing an attack on the Turkish rear, which accompanied another plan to persuade the Christian Abyssinians to distract the Sultan with an attack on Egypt.[56]

To be sure, piracy from North Africa that reached the shores of England and led to Christian enslavement in Turkish slave markets did not magically cease in 1683. It continued up to and including the early years of the North American republic. However, it was during that fateful year that a kind of peace was brokered between France and Algeria. Prior to that, London had created a fund of 20,000 pounds for the purpose of ransoming captives, which at the time numbered in the hundreds in North Africa.[57] However, with pressure eased on Western Europe as a result of the setback to the Ottoman Turks and the decline of murderous continental conflict with the Treaty of Westphalia of 1648, London was poised to yoke what had been a present though not dominant trend—slavery—to an ascending capitalism, converting societies with slaves to slave societies. This process took hold most notably in North America, then the United States of America.

More important, a migration from societies with racism to racist societies was required in order to boost the now dominant slavery. Thus, simply ruling slavery illegal without a focused and conscious assault on racism was bound to allow this pestilence to fester and morph, as it has done in the United States since 1865.

One estimate posits that somewhere between one million to 1.25 million Europeans were enslaved on the Barbary Coast between the sixteenth and eighteenth centuries, a figure dwarfed by the number of Africans enchained by Europeans, to be sure. This list included Seth Southall, a future governor of the South Carolina colony who was captured by North African pirates en route from London to North America and held in bondage for more than a year. It is reasonable to infer that such experiences did not make North American settlers more sensitive to the bitter experience of enslavement but instead

convinced them of the necessity of normalizing this violent process, which redounded to the detriment of Africans. Moreover, the
religious cast of the North African experience—Muslims enslaving
Christians—similarly helped to desensitize settlers to the violent process of enslaving non-Christians, that is, Africans.[58] The scholar Jean
Houbert reminds us of the oft ignored point that "settler colonialism"
was "categorically different from non-settler colonialism."[59] How
true. The former often entailed a bloody ethnic cleansing, frequently
amounting to racialized genocide—that dwarfed similar processes
in "non-settler colonialism" not to mention more contemporaneous
versions.

This desensitizing is also revealed by the depredations of the
English Civil War and the Thirty Years' War, which had sent
many fleeing to North America in the first place. Those who witnessed mass rape and beheadings were hardly well placed to display
humanitarianism, especially toward Native Americans and Africans,
which incipient racialization was placing beyond the pale in any
case. Moreover, helping to propel migration to the wilds of North
America was the felt need to elude the distinct possibility of enslavement by Muslims. When New England settlers began to sell Native
Americans into Turkish slave markets, it can be seen as not only a way
to execute "ethnic cleansing" while clearing a tidy profit but also to
sate the seemingly vast appetite overseas for the enslaved.[60]

Arguably, this rough dispossession of indigenous North Americans
would have been even more sweeping but for actions that took place
in sites like Jamaica. There, in late 1676, the authorities sought to bar
the "Indian inhabitants of New England," recently "imported to this
island"; they were deemed to be a "great hazard and danger" to stability, particularly when combined with the already raucous Africans.[61]

To that point, London had been bedeviled by the "Muslim Threat,"
despite myriad efforts to placate the Ottomans. John Smith, who was
to become a kind of hero to settlers in Virginia, had been captured by
Muslims—later escaping—though he pointedly observed that "they,"
meaning his captors, "use the Hungarians, Russians, Wallachians and
Moldovian slaves (whereof they have plenty) as beasts,"[62] a treatment

then doled out to Africans, coincidentally enough, in untold numbers in North America.

Thus London's contacts with the Levantine and Mediterranean Muslims were numerous, and Turks and Moors were to be found on English soil as traders, diplomats, and even as pirates as early as the 1500s. This was not only because Muslims, who had occupied a good deal of Spain for centuries until weakening dramatically in the pivotal year of 1492, were seen as a mortal threat by Madrid and thus a potential ally by London, particularly after His Catholic Majesty's attempt to overthrow the English regime in 1588 had been blunted serendipitously. Then the "Gunpowder Plot" of 1605 unleashed a new wave of anti-Catholicism, with "Papists," thought to be part of Madrid's ubiquitous design, heightening ultra-religiosity. [63]

Helping to propel England, on the other hand, was the simultaneous threat of internal and external plotting, real and imagined, by Catholics against the Crown and the established faith of Protestantism, along with a massive royal debt that was a partial product of seeking to repel this challenge. This led to an attempt in 1585 to colonize what became Virginia. [64] That Paris was deeply in debt at the same time suggests both that London was not alone in its misery but would face rigorous competition for the bounty of colonialism. [65] Singled out as the culprit was Spain, which had flooded Europe with silver, serving to deflate currencies, and then compelled its neighbors to spend heavily—and incur debt—from fighting Madrid-induced wars. [66]

Thus there was a burgeoning Muslim community in Elizabethan London, which may have contributed to religious sensitivity. This openness to Islam was partly a response to nervousness engendered by the Muslim takeover of Constantinople in 1453. This land grab was thought to augur an unavoidable advance and prompted the search for a new route to the riches of Asia, which led to the seizure of the Americas by the Europeans. Surely the parallels between Protestantism and Islam were hard to discount; the former's rejection of clerical authority and belief in the inner light corresponded to the Islamic rejection of intermediaries between the believer and Allah. [67]

LONDON WAS LATE TO THE COLONIAL feast but quickly made up for lost time by helping to weaken the Dutch, early arrivers. London had assisted the eminence of the Netherlands in the late sixteenth century as the sea-bound nation faced an existential challenge from Spain. In response, the cornered Dutch opened their doors for the arrival of Spanish Jews, along with fleeing Catholics and even Puritans from England, helping to form a model of Pan-Europeanism—or a precursor to "whiteness"—that influenced the limited republicanism that was to take hold in North America in 1776.

Indeed, one of the themes of this book is not only how enslaving colonialism forged "whiteness" and a Pan-European concord in order to overawe rebellious Africans and indigenes, but how it also served as a basis for a kind of "enlightenment" to attract Europeans to these war zones. Thus, in the French Caribbean, those who happened to be Jewish enjoyed rights they did not have in Paris, precisely because of the desperation wrought by the ceaseless search for those who could be defined as "white." On the other hand, this trend did not proceed without backsliding; in 1683 the Jesuit denunciation of supposed Jewish dominance of local commerce and of Jewish slaveholders allegedly refusing Christianity to their bondsmen led to a royal order expelling them from Martinique. They were given one month to depart and a similar wave of persecution beset French Huguenots,[68] allowing English Protestants to benefit, as they pioneered in developing "whiteness" and white supremacy and passed on this enriching skill to their rebellious progeny in what became the United States.

Thus, by 1700 there were fourteen Huguenot churches in West London, as these Protestants fled France after Paris forbade their religious liberty, ordered the destruction of their churches, and declared them Catholic. One of this persecuted grouping, John Houblon, became the first governor of the Bank of England in 1694 and a knight of the realm and until 2014 his luxuriantly bewigged features adorned fifty-pound banknotes: this image neatly encapsulated the ties linking Pan-Europeanism, religious liberty, and an ascending capitalism, lessons all developed further by the North American republic.[69]

The self-inflicted wounds imposed by rivals also explain the rise of London in the seventeenth century, a point that U.S. patriots may want to consider today in light of the rise of China.

The decline of the Ottoman Turks was no direct fault of London, which had sought to align with Muslims to check the foe that was Madrid. The continuing decline of Amsterdam and Rotterdam was only somewhat different. As noted, there were those in London who sought to aid the Netherlands in its decades-long conflict with Spain, but this was like fattening a sheep for slaughter, for the gains garnered by the Dutch as it successfully beat back Spain were then seized by London as Amsterdam fell into a centuries-long decline. This became apparent with the Anglo-Dutch war of 1652–54, which weakened the Netherlands in the prime area of controlling Atlantic trade routes.[70] That is, Dutch slavers were undermining the price of English-shipped slaves from West Africa, so a squadron of English warships attacked and captured two West African ports used by the Dutch, then took Manhattan in turn. This contributed to a naval war that lasted until 1667.[71]

A turning point in London's lengthy jousting with Madrid was Spain's ouster from Jamaica in 1655. This had manifold consequences. England could not be indifferent to the fact that this great victory was aided immeasurably by the defection to their side of feisty Africans disgusted with Spain's misrule along with a goodly number of those who were Jewish and understandably apprehensive about what the ongoing Inquisition portended. As this defeat was being inflicted, others who were Jewish were fleeing Brazil, where they had sheltered under the cloak of Protestant Netherlands as Catholic Portugal had surged back into control of this vast territory. That is, after 1654, almost all the remaining Dutch and Jewish merchants fled Recife, with many decamping to the Caribbean; many had begun fleeing South America heading northward as early as 1645. This group then fled to Jamaica, Barbados, and other English colonies, bringing with them the expertise that contributed mightily to a sugar boom, which in turn contributed to an acceleration of the African Slave Trade, so that this bloody commodity could be produced more readily.[72] There was also an influx from Recife to Manhattan, serving to buttress colonialism there too.[73]

As sugar began to boom, the felt need for more enslaved Africans rose. In anticipation of this noxious trend, the Company of Royal Adventurers Trading to Africa had been issued a charter in 1660 in London, accelerating the trade in Africans, which led directly to the organizing of the Royal African Company, under the thumb of the Crown, in 1672.[74]

The taking of Jamaica, however, was not a victory for Africans. It led to an even more voracious appetite for enslaved African labor in order to produce the fabulously profitable crop that was sugar. This, as much as anything else, contributed mightily to the heightening of the already degraded status of Africans, as a by-product and rationalization of their enhanced reputation. Similarly, the Irish and other dissidents who had been conscripted into working in the fields of the Caribbean receded gradually in numbers, as they could now be promoted to be overseers or soldiers to keep this larger group of Africans in check. Out of this crucible emerged the renewed and more toxic racial identity that was "whiteness," which also involved an alliance among Europeans of various class backgrounds, all bound by petrified unity in reaction to the prospect of a slave rebellion that would liquidate them all.

After the triumph of republicans in 1776, these victors were able to forge Pan-European unity as they swept across a continent; the prospect grew accordingly that the poorer among this group could profit from the pillaging of Cherokees (and countless other indigenes) and Mexicans and Hawaiians. This noxious cross-class unity, in other words, metastasized as it traversed North America, where it became unified by the prospect of excluding, if not plundering, those not inducted into the hallowed halls of whiteness, a trait manifested as recently as November 2016.

As the wealth of London's possessions in the Caribbean proliferated, it helped to buoy the North American settlements, then viewed as not as valuable. Ultimately, the unforgiving racial ratios of the

Caribbean helped to induce a "Great Trek" to the mainland—particularly South Carolina—where growing wealth helped to ignite a lurch toward independence in 1776, then an invigorated desire to enchain more Africans—and increased wealth even further as these slaves were compelled to develop land seized from Native Americans.

With the restoration of Charles II in London in 1660 and the companion defeat of the forces that had been arrayed under the now deceased Oliver Cromwell, the commercial class, many of whom had bolstered the Lord Protector—directly supported and aided by the monarch's courtiers—spearheaded the Anglo-Dutch War of 1665–67, which solidified the earlier snatching of Manhattan from the floundering Netherlands. This prize included one of the primary ports on the continent for delivering enslaved Africans. By 1660, New Amsterdam, soon to become New York, had the largest population of the enslaved in North America, a business that had been initiated by Peter Stuyvesant as early as the 1640s.[75] In short, the restoration was not the full reassertion of royal power it appeared to be; it was a dress rehearsal for 1688 when the Crown was further weakened with the rising capitalist and merchant forces flexing their muscles.

By 1664 English slave traders were en route from Madagascar to Barbados. They stopped in Cape Town to try to buy slaves there, which was a signal to the Dutch that their reign at the tip of Africa was winding down.[76] By the end of this tempestuous century, slave traders from British North American colonies had invaded Portuguese settlements in East Africa. This was cheaper in spite of the longer voyage involved than making incursions into West Africa, where until then the Dutch West India Company had a stranglehold.[77] Still, the fall of the Dutch globally was a function of, and response to, the rise of London.

Yet the events at the Cape in the seventeenth century were to encapsulate what Adam Smith was to announce in the eighteenth, which was that "the discovery of America and that of a passage to the East Indies by the Cape of Good Hope, are the greatest and most important events recorded in the history of mankind."[78] Surely, these navigational feats propelled the African Slave Trade, which generated tremendous wealth and even more inequality.

With the coming of London's rule to Manhattan in the 1660s, slavery gained a renewed stringency. That the city was renamed after the Duke of York, a royal who held a controlling interest in major slaving concerns, did not bode well for Africans. Soon major clans in New York had initiated a brisk trade with pirates in Madagascar, which included a goodly number of enslaved Africans. Dutch rule, whereby the Dutch West India Company owned most of the colony's enslaved, fell victim to a "democratizing" impulse in which ownership of these unfortunate souls was spread widely among a population that increasingly was defined, and defined itself, as "white," which, in turn, engendered reactionary anti-African impulses that have yet to be extirpated.[79] The likelihood that the English even sold certain Dutch settlers into slavery in the Caribbean helps to underscore the deeply driven enslaving impulse that gripped these conquerors.[80]

But as slave owning became widespread, it became more difficult to limit slave trading to the aegis of the Crown, and one of the revolutionary demands of the "Glorious Revolution" of 1688 in London was the deregulation of this hateful commerce and the entrance into it of "private" traders.

AS THIS NEW DEPARTURE IN WORLD history was being enacted, featuring Africans as fuel for the enrichment of Europeans, those designated as slaves refused to cooperate willingly. About 1565 the Portuguese built a fort to facilitate enslavement in the Accra area on the Atlantic Coast, despite the opposition of their would-be victims. Eventually, the Africans took the Portuguese by surprise and slaughtered them all.[81] As the Dutch and Portuguese fought in Brazil, Africans allied with one side or the other.[82] Near that same time, Africans in Santo Domingo told the ascending Dutch that they would aid them in ousting the Spanish.[83] Unsurprisingly, the seventeenth century also featured a tidal wave of unrest in Africa, with the infestation of enslavers being a key reason. The forts of the European powers became targets for attack, arson—and worse.[84] "Against our will," complained an enslaver in West Africa in 1663, he and his men were "engaged in an open war" with Africans.[85] That same year the authorities in Jamaica saw fit to pass a law mandating that boats of various sizes be properly secured since enslaved Africans were stealing them and seeking to escape, perhaps even back to Africa.[86] The seventeenth century was London's century, but even what was to be eventually denoted as the British Empire suffered setbacks then at the hands of Africans. Vigorous hostility from North Africans foiled the attempt to establish a colonial toehold in Tangiers,[87] the formation of which would simply have entailed more misery for more Africans.

As the waning years of this century expired, Africans were on the warpath in one of the critical areas where they had been deposited. In Barbados in 1692 the authorities were wringing their hands about a "conspiracy" of the enslaved, who had "been long preparing, contriving, conspiring and designing a most horrid, bloody, damnable and detestable Rebellion, Massacre, assassination and destruction" targeting "all the white Inhabitants."[88]

Rebelliousness among those slated for enslavement in Africa and those held captive in the Americas was a factor that restrained the scope of the slave trade, thus restraining the unjust enrichment that characterized London and, ultimately, New York.

Rebelliousness among Africans has yet to disappear from North America and sheds light on why descendants of the enslaved tend to vote most heavily against the political expression of the settler class, a trend manifested most recently in November 2016.

IN SUM, THE SEVENTEENTH CENTURY is critical to comprehension of the rise of capitalism and the companion rise of London, then New York. Spain and the Netherlands weakened each other, creating an opening for England, which was able to establish a toehold in what is now Virginia in the early seventeenth century. Buoyed by the wealth brought by dispossession, merchants and nascent capitalists, particularly in New England, backed Oliver Cromwell as the monarchy was symbolically and actually beheaded in the 1640s. The end of the Thirty Years' War in 1648 allowed Europeans to concentrate more pointedly on Africa and the Americas. By 1654 the Dutch were driven from Brazil by returning Portuguese and fleeing alongside them were some from the Iberian Jewish community, who had invested heavily in sugar and slaves. They were then welcomed into Jamaica, which in 1655 had been taken from Spain by Cromwell's forces. By 1660 a royal restoration of sorts had taken place, and arguably the monarchy, playing second fiddle to the rising merchants and capitalists, was already on a glide path to the figurehead status it enjoys today. The Caribbean venture led to a sugar boom and still vaster wealth that was then used in 1664 to attack the Dutch on the mainland, with Manhattan and many of what are now the U.S. Mid-Atlantic States falling. This opened up more land to be stocked with enslaved Africans, particularly in what is now New York City. By 1672 the slave trade was systematized in the Royal African Company under the Crown. By 1683 the Ottoman Turks were halted at the gates of Vienna, providing more breathing space for Western Europeans, allowing them to turn more fully toward plundering Africa and the Americas. Then in 1688, the "Glorious Revolution" marked the deregulation of the slave trade and even more enrichment for merchants—and the dawning of an apocalypse for Africans and the indigenous.

The fierce resistance of the indigenous and the Africans later caused concessions to be granted by the colonial elite ultimately to poorer Europeans, with 1676 and Bacon's Rebellion in Virginia a turning point, creating a cross-class collaboration between and among Europeans that has yet to disappear in North America, the headquarters of settler colonialism.

The interpretation of this epochal 1676 crisis is also revealing, with some on the U.S. left initially interpreting it as a righteous revolt by the poor against the wealthy, eliding the uncomfortable reality that a central demand was a more aggressive colonial offensive to plunder the indigenous and parcel out their land to poorer settlers. Then it was interpreted as a joint uprising by poorer Africans and Europeans against the elite that was foiled by concessions to those defined as "white" to the detriment of those not so designated. I tend to agree with the scholar J. Kehaulani Kauanui, who argues that the uprising "reveals a lost chance for alliance politics between African and indigenous peoples."[89]

AS ONE CONSIDERS THE MANY CRIMES committed in the name of slavery, white supremacy, and capitalism, what might be most shocking is how these bloody felonies have been rationalized, even justified—even by some who consider themselves to be "radical." The by-product was supposedly an advancement of the productive forces or the flowering of bourgeois liberties, which even today many of African and indigenous descent in North America hardly enjoy, notably in due process of law before being executed by an officer of the state. This rationalization of crime makes it all the more difficult to overcome the odious legacy of tragic events of recent centuries. But what is similarly revealing is that those who heartily castigate and declaim the crimes of socialism, a system that led directly to the liberation of millions of Africans and "darker peoples" from the domination of the routinely praised North Atlantic powers,[90] lose all sense of proportion when they simultaneously downplay and warp what was required to build the United States and "modernism" and a supposed "democracy."

Future historians may very well conclude that an explanation for this abject hypocrisy is that too many could not see beyond the deliverance of poorer Europeans from the barbarism they endured on their home continent to a sympathy with those victimized in the process. Ultimately they could not overcome the poisonous snare of white supremacy. That is, the seeds of the fiasco of an election in November 2016 in the United States, where the less affluent of European descent, including more than half of the women of this group, found their tribune in a vulgar billionaire, has roots in the cross-class coalition that spearheaded colonial settlement in the seventeenth century at the expense of the indigenous and enslaved Africans.

In other words, it is not premature to contemplate life after capitalism in what is now the United States,[91] the disastrous result of November 2016 notwithstanding. When this monumental task is undertaken, however, never to be forgotten is that those who were victimized in the first instance—enslaved Africans and the indigenous—need to be compensated and made whole (somehow) as this elongated process unfolds.

This is a book about the events in the seventeenth century that led to the creation of what is now called the modern and advanced world. It concerns the roots of slavery, white supremacy, and the ultimate expression of the two: capitalism. These events mostly unfold on the eastern seaboard of North America, the Caribbean, Africa, and what is now Great Britain. Though the mode in these pages is decidedly historical, I am seeking to shed light on the contemporary moment, wherein it appears that these malevolent forces have received a new lease on life.

CHAPTER 1

Beginning

Though slow to the colonial banquet that was enslavement, England was not altogether unfamiliar with this phenomenon. Dublin was Europe's largest slave market during the eleventh century.[1] Scotland, for example, was filled with English slaves.[2]

This was an aspect of the larger point: at the height of its power, the Roman Empire, which once controlled England, trafficked in hundreds of thousands of slaves annually; in the previous millennium, slavery and the slave trade were rampant, a praxis in which the Vikings and Scandinavians excelled, often preying on the English and other Europeans. When the Islamic world boomed in the eighth century, there was a sharp rise in the demand for slaves.[3] During that era, more than a millennium past, one trader alone boasted of selling more than 12, 000 enslaved Africans in Persian markets.[4] Yet this slavery, as horrid as it was, did not reach the dimensions of the racial slavery that took off in the seventeenth century.

This older version of slavery was tied intimately to war, with the former being the fruit of the latter. This did not bode well for Africa, as Western Europeans developed the weapons of war.

The fifteenth century marked the onset of a newer kind of slavery: by 1441, Portuguese pirates had seized Africans for sale and by 1470

Spaniards had begun to do the same. It was in 1482 that Portugal began construction of a large fort to facilitate trade in Africans.[5] By the middle of the fifteenth century, enslaved Africans formed as much as 10 percent of Lisbon's population.[6]

The leaders of the Iberian Peninsula had a first movers' advantage in reaching the Americas and sailing to Africa, which then allowed Spain to press England, forcing London for reasons of survival, if nothing more, to seek to follow in Madrid's footsteps. Simultaneous with Columbus's voyage was the launching of the Inquisition, which, ironically, also provided an advantage in that it provided the framework for a centralizing institution, essential for the process of state building.[7]

Most notably in the 1490s, this form of hateful commerce accelerated, when Christopher Columbus and his band of cutthroats began to dispatch Tainos from the Caribbean to the slave markets of Europe. Columbus's first business venture in the Americas involved sending four boatloads of indigenes to Mediterranean slave markets. Others followed in his footsteps, including the English, French, Dutch, and Portuguese. These powers all participated in this dirty business, but infamy in this regard was held by Madrid, which was to indigenous slavery what England and the United States were to African slavery.[8]

Appropriately, Amerigo Vespucci, the man who gave his name to the continents across the Atlantic from Europe, was a slave trader, too. Columbus's voyage, as noted, had been driven by the takeover of Constantinople in 1453 and a few years later the Ottomans were seizing Aegean islands, as churches were converted to mosques and children were taken into slavery. Columbus's Genoa showed that the acts of the Turks were not that unusual since this Italian town exemplified the belief that slavery was a legitimate business and thus allowed significant investment in the odious commerce that brought young men, women, and children from the Black Sea and sold them to buyers in Muslim Spain or Egypt. Unlike Venetians, who paid their galley rowers, Genoese staffed their war galleys with the enslaved. The Genoese pioneered in enslaving Africans, though the Portuguese were also premature in this regard, and by 1452 had received a papal dispensation for it. Columbus, as a consequence, was well positioned to turn his trailblazing journey into a new zenith in slave trading, particularly since his crew consisted of leading criminal elements, who over the centuries were to be leaders in this dirty business.[9] With the arrival of the Spanish on the American mainland in the early 1500s, the commerce in Africans can be said to have increased dramatically there.[10] Between 1500 and 1550 the Portuguese took at least 1,700 slaves per year out of Africa and more than half ended up in São Tomé.[11]

Tiny Portugal, with a population today of about nine million, was enmeshed in an overstretch almost from the beginning of its thrust into overseas navigation that was to reach into the Americas, Africa, and the Asia-Pacific. Lisbon found it necessary early on to rely on laboring Africans for various tasks. An African pilot, Esteban Gomez, sailed up what became the Hudson River abutting Manhattan in 1525, while another African became the first non-indigenous resident of this valuable island.[12]

But just as Lisbon and Madrid were tightening their respective grips on vast swathes of territory abroad, the Ottoman Turks had moved into Egypt and deeper into the Balkans, causing Erasmus to announce in the first half of the sixteenth century that this was leading to an epochal clash since "the world cannot any longer bear to have two suns in the sky." The future, he predicted, would belong either to the Muslims or to the Christians because it could not belong to both.[13] When the Ottomans were blocked at Vienna in 1683, it seemed that the only sun that mattered was the one that soon was never to set on the British Empire, and then later the secessionist appendage in North America.

However, European encroachment was resisted fiercely by the Africans. Soon the Portuguese were at war in West Africa, with three hundred of these Europeans massacred in one fell swoop in 1570 alone. The Africans had gathered in the forest and watched carefully as these invaders decamped before killing them all. On another occasion they severed the invaders' heads from their bodies, leaving their bodies on the beach, then placed their skulls on wooden stakes.[14] A few years later, Portuguese again fell victim to angry West Africans, as the invaders were slaughtered once more.[15]

Since Africans often rebelled vociferously against enslavement, this caused Europeans in response to offer more inducements to those recruited to confront them, including land grants in the Americas and other enticements.

By the first decade of the sixteenth century, Granada—only recently recaptured from Islamic forces and once the center of Moorish civilization on the Iberian Peninsula—was enmeshed in a slave trade that heavily consisted of Africans. Again, this well preceded the push by Englishmen, for at this juncture few from their monarchy had visited Africa, let alone sold and traded its denizens. However, as early as 1530 there were Englishmen bringing enslaved Africans to Brazil, but, again, not in the systematic manner that was to flourish in the following century. The first English voyage to West Africa was said to be made in 1553 by Captain Thomas Windham, accompanied by a Portuguese pilot. By 1562 John Hawkins had seized Africans to sell into bondage,[16] with the settlements in Hispaniola as purchasers.[17] Allegedly, Hawkins was funded directly by Queen Elizabeth, indicative of the high-level support for slaving.[18] Reportedly, along with Windham's voyage, twenty-seven enslaved Africans wound up in England in 1553.[19] Anticipating the various forms of resistance that were to define the slave trade, on one of his voyages Hawkins was traduced by an African leader who had pledged to sell him "prisoners of war," but instead the leader deceived him by reneging on the arranged delivery. Flesh peddlers often "encountered hostile towns" during their sixteenth-century African forays.[20]

It was in the sixteenth century that Africans in Panama were convinced to pledge allegiance to Madrid in exchange for autonomy.[21] This autonomy could then be leveraged to forge separate deals with the indigenous or competing European powers. It was evident early on that implanting this rapacious colonialism would be no simple task given the rambunctiousness of Africans.

This flexibility by Madrid was an understandable response to the necessity to preserve the obvious accumulated wealth generated by the emerging antagonist that was Spain, along with a reflection of the strength of mercantile interests that was to blossom in a full-bodied capitalism. By 1555 enslaved Africans were brought to what were to be termed the British Isles themselves.[22]

Moving away from the internal conflict with Irish and Scots that had been wracking England to the external engagement that was to occupy London for decades to come brought a new set of issues. By 1584, Richard Hakluyt, an ideologist of this new engagement, compared offenses of the rival Spaniards to "Turkish cruelties," which was bracing to consider. Yet, dreamily, he contemplated a "Northwest passage" to the riches of China and the risk of encountering mere cruelties then seemed worthwhile.[23]

The success of Hawkins stimulated the avarice of his countrymen to the point that the monarch granted charters encouraging this baneful commerce in 1585 and 1588; then in 1618 a charter was granted to Sir Robert Rich in London for trade from Guinea, in West Africa, followed by another charter in 1631 and yet another in 1662, as the African Slave Trade began to take flight. The latter charter was allocated to the monarch's brother, allowing for the delivery of 3,000 enslaved Africans to the Caribbean. Then, on 27 September 1672, in a hinge moment in the history of capitalism, slavery, and white supremacy alike, the fourth and final exclusive company was chartered, the Royal African Company. From the point of view of capital, what made the "Glorious Revolution" really glorious was the banning of such exclusive charters, the seeds of which were planted in 1688. The deregulation of this trade opened it to the strenuous efforts of merchants, led to the takeoff of capitalism itself and imbricated participation in the African Slave Trade with bourgeois democratic rights against the power of the state.[24]

IN THE EARLY STAGES OF THIS PROCESS, Africans—slave and free—in the Americas proved to be indispensable allies of London as it sought to plunder Spanish colonies in the late 1500s and early 1600s. This established a transformational template that was to accelerate in the seventeenth century and became a hallmark of the entire experience of enslavement: Africans rebelling against those who seemed to be in control and aligning with a foreign invader to topple a shaky sovereign.[25] Near that same time in the sixteenth century, the English received a dose of this medicine when Portuguese traders on a now growingly beset continent successfully encouraged Africans to attack arriving mariners from London.[26] It was in 1527 that Spanish explorers were accused of inciting perhaps the earliest rebellion of enslaved Africans on the North American coast, and one of the earliest anywhere on this continent, when Africans revolted in what is now South Carolina, serving to foil European competitors.[27]

This contestation with Madrid led to London's increasing ties to Levantine and Mediterranean Muslims, meaning Turks and Moors were to be found on English soil in growing numbers in the 1500s.[28] That is, the final ouster of Islamic rule in Spain in 1492 left lingering resentments between Muslims and Catholics that Protestant London sought to exploit.

It is fair to infer that increasing competition with Spain was driving London's policies, not only in terms of diplomatic entente with Islamic forces but also in terms of seeking to barge into the colonial banquet. By the 1580s Sir Francis Drake had arrived at Roanoke on the North American mainland with hundreds of slaves in tow that he had captured in his attacks on various Spanish colonies; these included indigenous Americans and Africans alike.[29] This escapade also included a vehement attack on St. Augustine, Florida, the Spanish settlement that was to bedevil Georgia and points north in the eighteenth century. There he took away hundreds of the enslaved, dropping them off in North Carolina.[30] This barbarous episode forms the prelude to the story that will be told here about the seventeenth century and the onset of an apocalypse, whose reverberations continue to vibrate. In short, enslaved Africans arrived in North America under the English flag decades before the notionally accepted date of 1619 and, if one counts the European trade generally, decades before the 1560s when the Spanish arrived in Florida.[31]

Sir Francis's venturesome journey, like that of Hawkins years earlier, was both a way to bring Spain down a peg,[32] while leeching parasitically onto Madrid's booming wealth,[33] and feeding proliferating mercantile interests that by the end of the seventeenth century had managed to bring the monarch down a peg by way of their "Glorious Revolution." The aristocracy may have been distracted, oblivious to the rising political strength of merchants given the profits of Sir Francis's journeys, which by one account garnered an eye-watering 4,700 percent return,[34] some of which flowed into the pockets of various dukes and earls. (Admittedly, like caterpillars becoming butterflies, some aristocrats by lineage became merchants by currency.)

At this juncture, England could well be viewed as a piratical nation—or more formally, engaging in the primitive accumulation of capital—by plundering Spain of precious metals and enslaved Africans alike. This involved intensified militarism and grandiose levels of violence, which could be glorified as a defense of the Almighty. Unsurprisingly, the sails of Columbus's vessels carried the sign of the cross. But as the foundations of capitalism were established, the need for piracy, at least in the traditional sense, declined, along with religiosity.

Correspondingly, the population of a fattened England and the Low Countries almost doubled between 1500 and 1800. The English and the Dutch both had the Spanish in their crosshairs. And, ultimately, Madrid was not able to withstand the dual musket shots. The Dutch may have been the biggest loser, however, of this three-cornered conflict. After all, this sea-hugging nation was shipping three times as much by value as the English by 1650, the zenith of Holland's global influence. By that point, London's naval expenditure began to assert itself more forcefully, eventually consuming nearly a fifth of the entire national budget, which served to insure that English vessels would not endure the fate so often endured by those of Spain under assault by Sir Francis Drake and his minions.[35]

Spain, in sum, was battered by Sir Francis Drake's forces, as Madrid was compelled to consider the implications for both Cuba and Florida early on.[36] By mid-1587, Spain had failed to enter the Chesapeake,[37] a response to the real fear that Londoners were arriving in droves just north of St. Augustine. "I have been unable to learn anything further or more definite," Madrid was told, "except from certain Negroes who ran away from Francis Drake."[38] So motivated, Christopher Newport by 1592 had journeyed to the Caribbean, seizing Africans all along the way.[39] He was soon followed by James Langton, who traveled to Hispaniola where he encountered unwelcome "well armed" Africans. Undaunted, he carried off four or five slaves from an estate.[40]

Sir Francis Drake's encounter in Roanoke coincides with evidence about a rise of the number of Africans in England itself. By 1596 the Privy Council, at the request of Queen Elizabeth, issued a directive ordering the removal of all Africans from England. At the same time, there was a rise in the number of enslaved Englishmen in the Mediterranean and North Africa in the late sixteenth and early seventeenth centuries. Arguably, the increase in the number of discontented and oppressed Africans paved the way for London to enter more forcefully the lush profitability of the African Slave Trade, just as seeing more Englishmen forced into bondage—ironically— enhanced the arrival of this ugly reality.[41]

London was in a bind, however. For just as Spain had challenged English sovereignty most dramatically in 1588—and barely was turned back—there was in 1602 a sudden and enormous increase in London's Admiralty Court evidence of the coastal pirate trade, which kidnapped men, women, and children for the Moroccan slave markets. This, in turn, led to an increase in naval expenditure, which, in turn again, proved quite useful in overseas expansion.[42] According to one account, the enslavement of European Christians exceeded the number of Africans and Native Americans captured for sale by the end of the sixteenth century, with this European trade serving to inspire Europeans not toward abolition but toward utilizing this dirty commerce more profitably than the principal beneficiary at that moment—the Ottoman Turks—by yoking it to an ascending capitalism.[43] It is estimated that Algiers held 20,000 Christian captives in 1621, as corsairs from there sailed as far as Iceland, while reportedly Moroccans by 1625 had hijacked forty ships off the coast of Newfoundland.[44]

In brief, this geographic venturesome of Africans, combined with their increasing presence in the Americas, points to the reality that there was a real contestation for continental control that Europeans, least of all Englishmen, were not destined to master.

As London was moving aggressively to enslave more Africans to bolster its North American settlements, persistent complaints of "hostility" and "violence" and "great wrongs done unto them at seas" were visited upon the English at the behest of Algiers and Tunis particularly,[45] not to mention continuing Spanish irritants as Madrid sensed the import of this English incursion into new territories.[46]

Intriguingly, Charles Sumner, who was to become an embodiment of U.S. abolitionism, complained bitterly in 1853 about the so-called Barbary States, particularly Algiers, which had become a "terror to the Christian nations" as early as the sixteenth century. "Their corsairs became the scourge of Christendom," he raged, as they "pressed even to the Straits of Dover" as "unsuspecting inhabitants were swept into cruel capacity. The English government was aroused to efforts to check these atrocities," which at once led to increased naval expenditure, quite useful for the fortunes of settler colonialism, though it diverted energies to North Africa and away from the waters separating Bermuda and Virginia. "In 1620," Sumner reminded, "a fleet of eighteen ships, under the command of Sir Robert Mansel" was "dispatched against Algiers." He deplored the "deplorable inconsistency" that then led to London being responsible for enslaving Africans, but more than castigation, Sumner could have gone further to point out what Englishmen learned about enslavement from their captors that was then applied to West Africans or how warfare with North Africans prepared Englishmen to fight West Africans, etc. To his credit, he did note the irony of those being enslaved by North Africans becoming settlers in a slave society that normatively brutalized Africans and indigenes.[47]

Supposedly, piracy was introduced into Algiers in the sixteenth century by a Turkish pirate, his aid having been sought to repel the Spaniards then in possession of the surrounding vast North African land. The territory then fell to Turkish rule for scores of years. During this period, reputedly 30,000 Christian slaves were said to have been employed in constructing a harbor in Algiers. The dreaded and formidable strength of the pirates only increased in the seventeenth century. The growth of kidnapping and enslaving of Christians did not seem to make London more sensitive to bondage and probably increased naval spending as a deterrent, which was detrimental to Africa and the Americas.[48] By the early seventeenth century, it was estimated that more than 3,000 from the British Isles were engaged in involuntary servitude,[49] which is probably an underestimate.

EARLY ON, THE LABOR of the colonial settlers was probably six times more profitable than comparable labor at home, thus encouraging moving west across the Atlantic. The settlements offered a protected market for English manufactures, as well as cheap sources of raw materials that stimulated home production. This, in turn, created products that could be exchanged for enslaved Africans to be deposited in the colonies, thus completing a virtual circle—for London.[50]

It took a while for the new reality of Africans as seen through a London lens to take hold. By the late sixteenth century, those who were to be called "Negroes" were not always represented as "savages"; the recurrent descriptor after the flourishing slave trade necessitated more dehumanizing language. But the trend inaugurated by Hawkins did mean that Africans were often seen as threateningly unpredictable and potentially hostile, which was no surprise since Africans had reason to believe that Englishmen were intrigued devilishly by the possibility of their enchainment. Of course, the long-term entente with the North Africans had contributed at times to a separate assessment of those referred to as "Moors," since they often appeared in London as diplomats and ambassadors. Yet those called "blackamoore" in London were sufficiently visible in 1596 that Queen Elizabeth proclaimed there were "already to manie"—or too many—in the realm and seized the opportunity to exchange several for English hostages held in Spain and Portugal. The conflation that was "blackamoors" should not lead to the perception that no difference was drawn between, say, North Africans and those further down the coast stretching into Senegambia and the Gold Coast. The former were thought to be calculating and the latter unreasoning.[51] Spain, as the common enemy of Morocco and London, in any case, tended to drive the latter two together.[52]

There was good reason for anger at Spain in Turkey. It was not just that the Iberian Jewish community, fleeing the Inquisition, was racing into the arms of the Ottomans; it was the reality that Turkey was being swamped by specie—coin—from Spanish America, driving indigenous coins with low silver content from circulation, disrupting the economy and placing the local elite in ill humor as the regime borrowed from personal fortunes in compensation. With this crisis, the Jewish population of Turkey, many of whom were prominent in commerce, left for the Netherlands, where they again came into conflict with Madrid, which was seeking to strangle the nation in the sixteenth century.[53]

There were other factors contributing to London's venture into mass enslavement of Africans, besides emulation of the Iberians and the riches delivered by cruel exploitation. Joint-stock trading companies were generally unknown in London in the 1500s but numbered in the hundreds a century later.[54] This facilitated investment and limited liability, all useful when the time came to take the plunge into what became Virginia.

Then there was the great inflation of the sixteenth century, with the value of money being worth only half as much as a century earlier, which provided an incentive to accumulate new wealth.[55] Fluctuating ties to Russia often threatened to cut off England's lucrative cloth trade to that nation and Ottoman influx blocked London moving further south and east to Persia, providing more incentive to seek new fields of exploitation in the Americas. In any event, as England began to plunder Spain's colonies, London's population swelled from 85,000 in 1565 to 140,000 by the early seventeenth century. As a result and culmination of this trend, the East India Company was founded in 1600,[56] promising untold riches from a colonial conquest that was to serve as a model for the invasion of what became Virginia.

London's buoyancy was also a function of Russia's growth, at least when ties between the two were on the upswing. For as England was expanding, so was Russia: the latter expanding into northern Asia from 1580 to 1700; as Russia expanded, England benefited from the resultant increased trade, like a bicyclist being dragged along in the wake of the speediness of a lead competitor.[57] As matters evolved, there was a complementariness between Russia's spread east and England's spread westward to the Americas and southward to Africa, except that Russia had less competition from major powers and competition from China only intermittently.[58] "The greatest transformation of the world of the seventeenth century," says one scholar, "was the explosive expansion of Russian trade and settlement across Siberia. . . ." Thus, by 1639, Russia had reached the Pacific.[59] Boosting London not only was the ability to work out an entente with the Ottomans and the Dutch but good relations with the continent's giant—Russia—too.

As London grew corpulent from the business of a growing merchant class, the English became more ambitious in their overseas adventures.[60] In some ways the formation of the Muscovy Company in 1555 served as a model for the expansionism of the Turkish Company—later the Levant Company—in 1581 and the English East Indian Company and the commercial colonialism that beset what became Virginia a few decades later.[61] Interestingly, one of the first families of London's settler colonies, the Van Cortlandts, for whom a major park in the Bronx continues to be named, had roots in Russia. Oloff Stevense Van Cortlandt arrived as a soldier in North America in 1638. Of noble ancestry, he was lineally descended from the Dukes of Courtland in Russia, but eventually his family became tied by marriage to other grandees in what became New York State, including the Van Rensselaers, the Schuylers, the Jays, the Livingstons, and the Barclays.[62]

As Russia was expanding eastward and Western Europeans were expanding southward to Africa and westward to the Americas, gobbling land and resources as they proceeded, Japan entered two centuries of self-imposed isolation, methodically massacring missionaries seen as the first wave of an invasion, until the nation that was the major result of westward colonialism and enslavement, the United States, pried open the archipelago in 1853.[63] Word may have reached Japan that in 1565 the Spanish had occupied what they called the Philippines, and a few decades later the Dutch colonized what became Indonesia.

In sum, the stars were aligning for London's merchants, as Russia was distracted eastward and the Ottomans sought ties with England (and vice versa) to countervail Spain.

HENCE, AN ACCUMULATION OF factors propelled England into North America—Virginia, more specifically—in the early seventeenth century. The lust for wealth, the competition with Spain and the Ottoman Turks, and related factors led to this settlement project in what became Virginia. In the late sixteenth century, Sir Walter Raleigh ventured to South America, dazzling Londoners with the potentialities of all sorts, wealth not least, unveiled,[64] providing a path to reach the eminence of Spain by dint of emulation of its skill in enslaving the unwary. Sir Simon D'Ewes was among those who backed settlements in North America, particularly in order to exploit timbers and pelts and fish—and to block the so-called Papists. Doing so would prevent their antagonists from exploiting same, garnering funds by which England could be invaded again.[65]

In 1609, the English Virginia Company, which had established Jamestown in Virginia two years earlier, moved to dispatch settlers across the Atlantic with more vigor.[66] Initiating centuries of contestation between Madrid and London, Spain as early as 1611 was pondering destruction of the new settlement in Virginia.[67] Of course, the indigenous were not necessarily thrilled when invaders wandered into their bailiwick, leading to severe conflict,[68] at both ends of a colonial chain from Massachusetts to Virginia.[69]

BUT WHY WERE BERMUDA AND VIRGINIA early targets for settlement? In a sense, London was taking the path of least (European) resistance in that a good deal of the Caribbean had been gobbled up by Spain already, not to mention a good deal of the Americas generally. Despite seeking to conciliate the Ottoman Turks so as to better confront Spain, both of these European powers continued to irritate London during this era.[70] Seeking to oust the Dutch from the Malay

Peninsula produced results as dismaying as attempts to oust Madrid from the Western Hemisphere.[71] It was during the decisive year of 1619 that the Dutch East India Company captured what became Jakarta and burned it to the ground, providing resources for this European power that brought it to the top table.[72]

Indeed, a betting man in 1624 would have wagered that the winner of the century in diffusing their tongue globally would be the Dutch. They had arrived on the African coast in 1592 and established Pernambuco and New Netherland by 1624, seemingly outstripping the English.[73] As early as 1624, the Dutch were hauling tobacco from Virginia,[74] helping to inculcate in the minds of some colonists the value of Pan-Europeanism—or what became the "whiteness" project.

At the same time, Captain John Smith was complaining about Dutch and Spanish incursions into Virginia,[75] suggestive of the weakness of London's position. (Smith, who escaped Ottoman Turks by beheading his captors, knew something about a weakened position.)[76] Yet London's success was partly derived from Continental Europe being sucked into what became the Thirty Years' War, which weakened England's rivals at a propitious moment. Just as the culmination of the U.S. Civil War led to an offensive against Native American polities, this European inferno contributed in inception and conclusion to the same result. Though it may not have been realized at the time, London's colonial success was also vouchsafed when in 1628–29 Spain suffered a stinging defeat at the hands of the Dutch, one of the most profound setbacks for Madrid since they were turned back from England in 1588. Spain then was bogged down in Italy and, quite simply, had taken on too many foes.[77]

In fact, His Catholic Majesty, King Philip of Spain, spent every day of his forty-four-year reign at war—against the Dutch (1621–1648); against the French (1635–1659); and against London (1625–1630 and 1654–1659); and, generally, on the Iberian Peninsula (1640–1668), including Portugal. U.S. imperialism should take note that even the ostensibly strongest powers, which certainly Madrid was in the seventeenth century, can quickly find themselves being not-so-strong powers after being involved in seemingly ceaseless war.

The point here is that the Dutch and Spanish were denuding each other in the first few decades of the seventeenth century, which also allowed England to rise.

Also benefiting London was the reality that France continued to reel from the impact of the Edict of Nantes of 1598, which generated tremendous religious conflict between Protestants and Catholics while attempting to grant basic rights to the former.[78] At the same time, unlike Paris, London was not consistent in observing the "Freedom Principle," the notion that the enslaved became free upon arriving on French soil. This was the case especially when it mattered in the late sixteenth century, when Paris consistently ruled in favor of Africans seeking their freedom, a trend in which London wavered until 1772 with the celebrated decision of Lord Mansfield, which in turn helped to convince wary North American settlers that counterrevolution was the preferred route to escape the logic of abolitionism. Thus the internal religious conflict in France made it difficult for Paris to turn its attention fully to what was becoming its eternal foe across the Channel, which also propelled London's rise. This included anti-Jewish fervor: issued during the same year as the revocation of the Edict of Nantes in 1685, the Code Noir—or slave code—reeked with religious intolerance, enjoining colonial officials to "chase all the Jews who have established residences from our isles" and barred the practice of any non-Catholic religion by either masters or the enslaved.[79]

IN 1618 KING JAMES I GRANTED a royal charter to the Company of Merchants, who were trading in Africa, leading to the first London stronghold on the Gold Coast; the first English trading post was constructed at Kormantine that same year.[80] Enslavement of Africans took a notional leap forward when "Twenty Negars" arrived in Virginia in August 1619, inaugurating a new era in settler colonialism and slavery alike.[81] However, as we have seen—at least going back to the depredations of Sir Francis Drake—there were enslaved Africans in the precursors of the thirteen colonies that rebelled against London in 1776 well before 1619.

However, London's entrance into the ghastliness of the slave trade was not as straightforward as it appears in retrospect. As late as 1620 an English explorer in the upper waters of the Gambia River was offered bonded laborers by an African merchant. He replied that "we were a people who do not deal in such commodities, nor did we buy or sell one another, or any that had our own shapes,"[82] a defiant attitude that had disintegrated by century's end, as we have seen.

Enslavement of the indigenous is another story altogether. By 1622, it was not Spaniards but the indigenous of North America who rebelled and almost wiped out the adolescent settlement.[83] And this conflicted tension, driven by the enslavement of the indigenous, was yet another factor impelling the settlers to seek a different supply of bonded labor, one that was unfamiliar with the local landscape and less capable of rallying the neighbors of the settlers to wipe them out.

At this point, enslavement not only ensnared Africans and Native Americans but Christian Europeans as well. A census in Virginia in 1625 identified only twenty-three Africans,[84] suggesting that even with the incentive of seeking an alternative to enslavement of the indigenous, other factors would have to arise to bring on increased enslavement of Africans.[85]

Nonetheless and perhaps not coincidentally, the previous downplaying of the African Slave Trade began to retreat in the early years of the seventeenth century when the settlement in Virginia was formed. A statute in Bermuda in 1623, the first of its kind in the English-speaking world, denied the right of Africans to engage in free movement or to participate in trade and to bear arms.[86]

Limiting the mobility of Africans and denying their right to be economically independent and to defend themselves by martial means should have indicated to the settlers the innate debility of their project. Instead it was also in the early 1620s that Londoners were to be found on the River Gambia with one of them lasciviously observing that "the women amongst them are . . . excellently well bodied." These flesh peddlers should have contemplated more intensively the implications of encountering forty armed men; at least the chronicler "took special note of the blade of . . . sword[s]."[87]

Instead, by February 1627 there was the arrival of 80 settlers and 10 enslaved Africans in Barbados.[88] Revealingly, although this was an English settlement from its inception, it had a Pan-European patina, which meant that as Europeans became a distinct minority the seeds were already planted for the emergence of a "white" identity politics to confront a growing African population (a similar process unfolded on the mainland). A leader of the initial settlement was Sir William Courteen, a rich London merchant of Flemish descent, who had a wide range of interests in Amsterdam and trade contacts in what became Surinam. From the beginning, there were close ties between Dutch, French, and English in Barbados.[89]

From the outset there was a basis for moving toward a "whiteness" that transcended ethnic, then religious boundaries. From the outset, one glimpses how the mutual interest in exploiting Africans and the indigenous in the Americas not only generated "whiteness" but also fomented the lessening of religious conflict that had so devastated Europe. In the early stages of French colonialism in the Caribbean there were Catholic Irish, Dutch Calvinists, and Portuguese Jews, all with a mutual interest in enrichment at the expense of "others."[90]

However, this too was not a straightforward process. Settlers began receiving land grants on the eastern shore of Virginia in the early seventeenth century These came to include the African Anthony Johnson and his sons John and Richard who were to hold about 800 acres of land in Northampton County. He had arrived in Virginia as a slave in 1621, apparently from Angola, an indicator of London's ever closer ties to Portugal, an early colonizer in Africa. Seeking to elude being taken over by its larger Iberian neighbor, Lisbon and its relationship with England solidified. There is some doubt if so-called *durante vita* enslavement—slavery for life as a racial birthmark—existed in Virginia at that moment.[91] Yet by the end of the century it was increasingly difficult for the likes of Johnson to climb the class ladder, as intervening events—the seizure of Jamaica from Spain in 1655, the seizure of Manhattan from the Dutch in 1664, and the resultant formation of the Royal African Company in 1672—served to ossify the equivalence of African and slave, which amounted to a grand downfall for Native Americans now subject to the rapacity of land hungry settlers, with said territory then stocked by a growing cascade of enslaved Africans.

As the prospects for the likes of Johnson were falling as the seventeenth century unfolded, the prospects of Maurice Thomson, born in London in the early years of the century, were rising, and he would soon be known as England's greatest colonial merchant. Like many merchants, he bet heavily on Oliver Cromwell's revolt against monarchy, an expression of the shoots of capitalism seeking to break through the concrete of feudalism. But before that he became a major planter in Virginia, receiving a massive land grant near what is now Newport News in 1621, just as Johnson was departing a slave ship from Angola. Thomson himself was involved deeply in the pre-feudal institution that was slavery, now hitched to the star of a rising capitalism, transporting bonded Africans to the Caribbean. Straddling the major nodes of the colonialism that was to propel capitalism, he also invested heavily in the fur trade of Canada.[92]

The rise of Thomson and the decline of Johnson was a synecdoche for the contrasting fates of England and colonialism on the one hand and Africans and Native Americans on the other. As the latter was declining, the former was rising, with the two phenomena being inextricably linked.

CHAPTER 2

No Providence for Africans and the Indigenous

Between 1629 and 1645, thousands of religious dissenters, notably Puritans, migrated to the Americas to escape tyranny. But just as men, women, and children from England endured bondage in North Africa while London abjured abolitionism, the Puritans and other so-called dissenters proceeded to impose a tyranny on the indigenous, dispossessing them, enslaving them, murdering them.[1]

Although indigenes and Africans were the primary victims, in a manner that would bedevil settler colonialism for centuries to come, other settlers too were disfavored. For example, Roger Williams and his spouse arrived in New England from London on February 5, 1631, slated to reside in Massachusetts Bay, before moving to the separate colony in Plymouth, where they lived about two years. Sometime in 1633 they moved to Salem in the jurisdiction of their original point of arrival. In October 1635 the Massachusetts Bay General Court, which in this reputed "democracy" held all legislative, executive, and judicial power, sentenced Williams to banishment after he spoke out against attempts to punish religious dissension and against the brutal confiscation of the land of the indigenous. Eventually, the authorities sought to ship him back to Europe. He escaped by January 1636 into the wilderness, where he was succored only by his indigenous allies and finally settled in an area he termed "Providence." Despite a subsequent coloration of "liberalism," what became Rhode Island was also land confiscated from the indigenous, exposing the contradictions of "progressive" settler colonialism.[2]

Williams himself facilitated the enslavement of indigenes,[3] despite their rescuing him from the wrath of Massachusetts Bay. Of course, it was not as if Massachusetts Bay were sui generis. In the New Haven Colony in Connecticut, the community was centered on the church and the word of the minister was law. Dissent was not permitted. Potential informants were everywhere. Any person so bold as to question the minister risked being brought before the General Court and banished, or worse.[4]

It is still true that from the inception, settlements—to a degree—evaded the religious snarl of Europe. This was not necessarily because settlers were more enlightened. It was more because the perils of subduing Native Americans meant that the colonial elite could not be too choosy in selecting allies. Still, since the so-called Gunpowder Plot of 1605, an alleged Catholic conspiracy in predominantly Protestant England, anti-Catholicism had become almost normalized. James VI of Scotland inherited England, Wales, and Ireland and the Channel Islands from his cousin Elizabeth but was perceived as much too conciliatory toward Catholics. This conciliation did not necessarily go down well and, in light of centuries of conflict between England and Scotland depositing a reservoir of mutual hatred and suspicion, this was bound to cause problems for his rule. Conciliation toward Calvinists—or Presbyterians—was not necessarily helpful either, given their prominence in Edinburgh. Catholics were a minority in England, perhaps 5 percent of the population, but they inspired a disproportionate popular hatred and fear as they included many prominent adherents (including James's spouse and son and many of their courtiers), as well as some presumed extremists, for example, the group led by Guy Fawkes.[5] Ultimately, many of these Catholics were to flee to what became Maryland, as London did exhibit flexibility in deciding who could populate settlements. But again, it was not enlightenment that dictated this choice but the necessity to corral settlers of whatever hue to subdue the indigenous. However, lingering anti-London resentment in North America helped to fuel the 1776 revolt.

London's policy seemed to be support of exporting such presumed antagonists to the colonies, which could backfire if and when these opponents chose to ally with the Crown's antagonists abroad. Thus, by 1634, certain privileges were granted to arriving Irish and Scots in Massachusetts Bay, who would have been disfavored in London.[6] In other words, homeland bigotry had to yield in the face of subjugating the indigenous.[7]

This exportation policy carried over to disgruntled Africans who routinely were shipped from, say, the mainland to the Caribbean—or vice versa—which also allowed for allying with the Crown's antagonists in the new venue of oppression.

Thus it was in the early 1630s that a Catholic, George Calvert, the first Lord Baltimore, sought a charter from the Crown in the territory that became Maryland. Virginia protested vigorously, but to little avail[8] as the Crown in seeming anticipation of the new era of republicanism and its complement, "whiteness," did not sustain these objections.[9] It was not preordained that this request would be fulfilled for anti-Catholicism had yet to disappear from London. "We must fortify ourselves both abroad and at home," said Sir Edward Giles, since "Papists increase and grow, braving and outfacing," their "chief aim" and target being "England and in England [targeting] the King and the Prince."[10] Contrary to today's suspicion, it was not as if Englishmen became more enlightened once they crossed the Atlantic Ocean. It was more that the light of fires set by indigenous arsonists and embattled Africans helped to convince these settlers that larger racial stakes loomed that surpassed religious bigotry.

These Catholics were responding to a set of repressive laws in London that were inviting them to depart, a precursor of the rise of the violently anti-Irish Oliver Cromwell.[11] In 1633, departing from the Isle of Wight, were emigrants bound for North America. Perhaps appropriately, the sources of fear that accompanied them along the way included apprehension about Turkish pirates determined to enslave them, just as they intended to enslave those they would encounter in North America. They landed in Barbados, then Montserrat where they met a colony of Irishmen who had been banished from Virginia because of their Catholicism. Then it was on to the Chesapeake. St. Mary's County, which they helped to establish, was from its first settlement by Europeans a Catholic county.[12]

Apparently aware of the hostility that surrounded them, not only in Virginia but among Africans and the indigenes too, the early Marylanders sought to remove religion as an issue of contestation,[13] as if they were saying, "No one here but us European settlers." And yes, this ecumenical approach set the stage for an entente with the so-called Catholic powers, that is, Paris and Madrid, that led directly to the anti-London revolt of 1776. As early as 1638 Whitehall—official London—was complaining about being ignored by the region that became known as New England,[14] as thousands of miles away that part of the colonies charted a new path.

As in the case of Roger Williams, the idea of "progressive" settler colonialism was a contradiction in terms, and an utter misnomer. It did not take long for the Jesuits—the typical advance guard for the colonialism of predominantly Catholic nations such as France—to seek special privileges for themselves in Maryland, which ignited a bitter struggle.[15] It is not easy to seize land on which another people reside, oust them, then shout from the rooftops about alleged democratic principles. Thus, this Catholic refuge became one of the first mainland colonies to recognize slavery as a matter of law; as was now typical, being persecuted was no guarantee that your group would reject persecution of others. The Marylanders were no less harsh toward the Piscataways, the Chapticos, the Nangemy, the Mattawoman, and other indigenes in a manner that mimicked the harshness of their New England counterparts in their relationship to the Pequot.[16]

It was not just religious dissenters who were being shipped abroad, however. Food riots in England rose from twelve between 1600 and 1620 to thirty-six between 1621 and 1631, with fourteen more during the months stretching from 1647 to 1649. The hungry were willing to risk arriving in a war zone, which assuredly was a fair description of North America, and were willing to dispossess those who stood in the way of their sating their growingly voracious appetites.[17]

The participants in food riots then became a vast pool of potential indentured servants. This form of labor was deemed initially to be a roaring success. Between 1625 and 1650 perhaps 60,000 contract laborers set sail for the Caribbean, with Barbados being a primary destination. Rapidly this small island, which even today has only about 285,000 residents, became the most densely populated area in the world, with hellish and inhumane working conditions besides. These dissidents were at times joined by rebellious Irish, which was not ideal for producing island calmness, raising the perpetual possibility of mass mutiny.

The situation demanded an alternative, soon to be delivered by more bonded Africans. Despite their best efforts, the Dutch, busy supplying Brazil, were not in an ideal position to satisfy the unquenchable appetite for enslaved Africans. Still, the Dutch tried, and reaped the whirlwind as a result. Dutch slave ships became notorious for engendering mutinies. Out of the 1,500 slaving voyages under the Dutch flag during this period, more than three hundred were rocked by slave revolts, a very high proportion.[18]

BY 1637 THE SO-CALLED PEQUOT WAR had erupted in New England, as settlers inflicted numerous atrocities upon indigenes in order to oust them from their land.[19] Settlers had to worry that indigenes would ally with their European competitors—notably the French and Spanish—and liquidate them, which seemed to increase English ferocity. "Resist both forraigne enemies & the natives" was the watchword as early as 1629,[20] and if there were a slogan for colonial settlements and the early United States, which inherited the initial barbarity, this was it. Since many of the so-called Pilgrims spoke Dutch—they had migrated from the Isles to England's antagonistic neighbor before settling in North America—this intensified the ordinary nervousness of London, then involved in what seemed to be an endless cycle of conflict with Holland. Since the Netherlands also

opened the door to those who were Jewish fleeing Spanish inquisitorial terror, the Dutch, even more so than the North American
republicans, should be seen as pioneers in developing overarching
racial identities in order to facilitate colonialism, a process that took
the name of "whiteness" on the west bank of the Atlantic.[21] It was
also the opportunistic Dutch who pioneered in forging ties with
persecuted French Protestants—Huguenots—creating a kind of
Protestant mercantile international that was important in the rise of
both the sugar industry and capitalism itself. Intriguingly, it was precisely the Dutch who built the highest stage of white supremacy at
the southern tip of Africa, just as it was the Catholics—for example,
the French elite—and not the English Protestants who allowed their
enslaved to be baptized: many of these Africans received catechism
lessons and were married legally.[22] The Dutch also exemplified the
value of what came to be called the "military-industrial complex."
Their war with Spain, roughly from 1569 to 1648, stimulated its arms
industry, which in turn sped the pace of overseas conquest. By the
time of New Netherland's founding, the Dutch republicans were
manufacturing an estimated 14,000 muskets annually, most of them
for export, a figure that grew larger year by year. No other European
nation came close to this level of production until decades later.
Furthermore, Dutch gunsmiths were introducing technological inno-
vations to their weapons that made them even more attractive to those
who might quarrel with English colonists—the Iroquois foremost
among them. This also helped to stimulate a trade of slaves for guns
that decimated Native American groupings, opening their lands for a
massive land grab by European settlers.[23]

Consider also that there were Dutchmen resident in the critical
colony that was Barbados, as early as the 1630s.[24] Consider as well
that English tobacco growers endured a crisis of overproduction in
1636, leading to a search for alternative crops, and like manna from
heaven Dutchmen arrived in 1637 with sugarcane, technology, capital, and slaves, a process that was to be repeated again in the 1650s
after Hollanders were ousted from Brazil by the Portuguese.[25] Many
of these "Hollanders" were actually Spanish Jews who had fled to

Recife, inaugurating a "Golden Age" of sorts for them—though not for those they enslaved—before fleeing as the Portuguese made a comeback in 1654.[26] When, in August 1641, the Dutch drove the Portuguese from Luanda, Angola, and in 1642 obtained a monopoly of the external slave trade from there, this was ultimately of benefit not only to New Amsterdam but, as things evolved, became an unanticipated gift to London's settlements too.[27]

The Dutch slave trade got off to a flying start, with 25,000 Africans soon being shipped to Brazil. This was occurring as the English were just settling into the Caribbean, and given the nature of Africans as commodities, it was ineluctable that many of these bodies would wind up in the Caribbean, converting these islands into a darling of empire. The demand for labor grew as the demand for crops produced there grew concomitantly, including export crops such as tobacco, cocoa, cotton, and indigo, all thought to be optimally grown in the tropics.[28]

It was unrealistic, however, to expect a proper settler colonialism to depend for its labor supply upon a competing empire, particularly when the Netherlands and England seemed to be embroiled in what seemed to be a perpetual cycle of conflict. Sir Benjamin Rudyerd told Parliament as much in 1641, as he demanded more spending on vessels, also a necessity if England were to avoid a replay of 1588. "As we are an island," he asserted, "it concernes our very being to have [a] store of ships to defend us and also our well being by their trade to enrich us." No matter how sliced and diced, the route to prosperity was propelled by vessels. "Now let us consider the Enemy we are to encounter, the King of Spaine" in this limited instance; what made him strong is "his Mines in the West Indies,"[29] and if England were to become stronger the Crown would also need "mines" worked by slaves, procured from Africa, requiring more ships.

There was a kind of domino theory in process in the seventeenth century that was to benefit London. Though surely it was not their intention, Dutchmen were a kind of stalking horse for England, weakening Spain over the decades, then ousting the Portuguese from the northeast coast of Brazil between 1630 and 1654 and extending tolerance to Catholics and Jews, providing a model for a kind of

Pan-Europeanism that was to redound to London's benefit when it battered the Dutch into submission within the following decades, which provided a Pan-European model for republicans in North America in the following century.[30]

Those fleeing inquisitorial Madrid also helped to bolster the so-called Muslim Corsair Republic of Saleh, 1624–66, in North Africa. Historian Jonathan Israel has limned the "Jewish role" in this project, which involved a corresponding role for their comrades in Amsterdam and Rotterdam. As the Netherlands went into decline, not least because of its battering by London, English settlements were to become the beneficiaries of this enterprise, along with the pragmatic religious tolerance it subsumed, which represented a step forward toward a kind of Pan-Europeanism so useful to the border-less boundaries that capitalism was to demand. However, as this enterprise was unfolding, this North African project was able to instill fear and loathing in Englishmen and Spaniards alike. Arguably, the embrace of the fleeing Jewish community in North Africa provided an incentive for London to do the same, lest the "Corsair Republic" become stronger, to England's detriment.[31]

Throughout the 1630s, England's Guinea Company, a forerun-ner of the Royal African Company that was to ravage Africa, had been mainly concerned with the direct import of redwood, elephant's teeth, hides of all sorts, and above all, gold. But as new opportuni-ties emerged with the arrival of settlements in such sites as Bermuda, Barbados, and Providence Island, the company by the early 1640s sought to reorient toward the slave trade, perhaps the most lushly profitable business of all. This was part of a larger reorientation in that by the late 1620s most of the main London companies spearheaded by merchants had collapsed. The major spurt of colonial economic development that took place over succeeding decades was executed by a new group of traders from outside the circle of this earlier circle of merchants. This roiling, however, was to provide the seedbed of the civil wars in England that were to erupt in the early 1640s, which meant so much for the subsequent dispossession of the indigenes and the enslavement of Africans.[32]

For in a premature version of the "creative destruction" that was said to characterize capitalism,[33] the cornucopia of opportunities opened by the new realm of settler colonialism created new elites as it displaced old ones, with the latter often unwilling to leave center stage willingly.

Thus a number of the men who sided with Oliver Cromwell within a few years in his conflict with the Crown had laid the foundations for capitalism and republicanism in Massachusetts. This lengthy list included Vincent Potter, who actually fought against the Pequots in the 1630s; Hugh Peter, a Puritan and a prime mover in the founding of what became Harvard University during that same conflicted decade; Winthrop's nephew, George Downing; and Owen Rowe, a merchant with ties to Virginia and Massachusetts and Bermuda alike.[34]

By 1641 Massachusetts Bay, in large part because the authorities wanted to define the legal status of the hundreds of indigenous Pequot captives then in bondage, passed one of the first laws peculiar to the enslaved in London's colonies. Some of these captives wound up in Bermuda, the Caribbean, the Azores, Tangier, and possibly even Madagascar. "We sent them to Bermuda," boasted John Winthrop, as if that were the sole destination. Despite their subsequent preening of being a sector of settler colonialism bereft of enslaved Africans, there is actually evidence of the presence of this group as early as 1633.[35]

Because enslaved indigenes were for the most part cheaper than the price of an enslaved African—perhaps a quarter to a tenth of the cost of the latter—there was a powerful incentive to enchain them, which also brought the added bonus of ousting them from their land.[36] Of course, enraged indigenes were not ideal neighbors, which meant that mainland settlers eventually would have to settle for enslaved Africans as the least bad option.

The cycle endured by indigenes is instructive when contemplating their twin in immiseration, the African. From 1630 to 1650 the status of the indigenous under the heel of those who were to term themselves New Englanders cycled from contract workers to servants to perpetual slaves.[37] As early as 1640 colonial courts in Virginia began constructing racial identities to determine who could be enslaved and who could be enslaved for life. What was to become the "Old Dominion" was tailing after Bermuda, Barbados, and St. Kitts, as these islands continued to set the pace for settler colonialism.[38] Critically, Virginia mandated a law in 1640 "preventing Negroes from bearing arms," perhaps an indication of worry about in which direction these weapons would be pointed.[39]

Invading a territory and seeking to enslave the current residents is a guarantee for a lengthy insecurity. This is especially the case given the speed of the demographic debacle: the indigenous population fell from an estimated 144,000 before 1616 to about 30,000 by 1670.[40] Making these so-called New Englanders even more vulnerable was the fact that for London this settlement was a sideshow. More settlers defined as "white" resided in the Caribbean and the surrounding islands (about 40,000) in 1650 than in the Chesapeake (12,000) and New England settlements (23,000) combined. And the great majority of these lived in Barbados.[41]

The main event was in the Caribbean. This would not change appreciably until the mid-eighteenth century, which suggested that the Royal Navy would be more prone to be concerned about challenges to Barbados, not Boston. As early as 1627, the now eminent New Englander John Winthrop sent his son to Barbados for betterment, economic and otherwise. There the Winthrop grubstake grew accordingly, which suggested further that even New Englanders were more concerned about the security of the Caribbean, as opposed to their own backyard. Winthrop was busily selling wine in St. Christopher's, a Barbadian neighbor. Since letters from New England sailed to London via Barbados, this was indicative as to what was the main arena and what was the periphery. This lasted until the 1770s when the North American settlements were on the verge of secession. Moreover, Winthrop and his fellow New Englanders faced keen competition not only from London traders but even more from the Dutch, who seemed to be the rising power then. Undaunted, Winthrop sought to establish a foundation for New England manufacturing based on Caribbean cotton, but in an early sign of a rationale for secession, this was resisted by London. But England and New

England could agree on the necessity of increasing enslavement in the Caribbean, with those ousted from their land in North America and Africans dragged across the Atlantic becoming the chief victims of this inhumane process. New England quickly became a chief supplier of food for the Caribbean, along with horses, casks, and barrels for rum too. The latter product was traded for enslaved Africans.[42]

From 1630 to 1640 at least twenty ships are known to have sailed between New England and Barbados, Bermuda, Providence Island, St. Kitts, and Tortuga, returning with cotton, tobacco, sugar, tropical produce—and the enslaved. Again, the preeminent Winthrop family of Massachusetts Bay are a stand-in for this commercial relationship: when young Samuel Winthrop moved from Tenerife to Barbados and eventually Antigua, the Winthrops, centered in England and Massachusetts, extended their trade from Rhode Island and Connecticut to the Caribbean.[43]

It would be an error to ascribe fiendish barbarity to Western Europeans alone, even settlers. The Winthrops were rising as the Thirty Years' War in Europe was establishing a record for rapacity that continues to astonish. When Magdeburg fell in 1631, women were subjected to mass rape and 30,000 were butchered indiscriminately and the city was put to the torch. Religion—not race, the raison d'être for barbarism in the Americas—was at issue. By 1639 the city now known as Chennai was taken by the British East India Company in the face of stiff resistance.[44] Reverberations from this mass violence could not help but spread and was in turn reinforced by contemporaneous trends in the Americas and Africa.

Nevertheless, the symbiotic relationship between ferocious island slavery and New England emerged clearly in 1630–31 when Puritans from the latter established a colony on Providence Island, a process which, revealingly, involved ousting Dutch privateers, a harbinger of things to come. Though London's settlements were not necessarily a single unitary formation, it would have been unwise for those in, say, Virginia, to ignore events in the waters surrounding the southeast quadrant of North America. Hence, as the settlement in Providence Island was being organized, the laws of Virginia showed a sudden increase in the number of regulations constraining the activities of enslaved Africans.[45]

The population of the enslaved on the island exploded after 1634, allowing subsequent generations of New Englanders to look down their noses piously and hypocritically at slavery,[46] even though their economy had been buoyed by enslavement of the indigenous, while being an extension of a slave-owning Caribbean. As was London's tendency, this colony allowed for piracy, with Englishmen parasitically preying on the Spanish Empire.[47]

Dauntlessly, settlers pursued the dangerously inhumane course of slavery on Providence Island in the face of fierce resistance by the enslaved. In March 1636 it was decided that "Negroes" were "to be disposed into families and divided amongst officers and industrious planters," though, it was cautioned, "a strict watch" must be "kept to prevent plots or any danger to the island being attempted."[48] A year later the investors in Providence Island were complaining that there were "too many Negroes in the island" with a fervent plea for "directions concerning them." It was urged that "some" should be "transported to Virginia and the Somers Islands,"[49] meaning Bermuda. But this was simply exporting problems, a perilous version of musical chairs.

Providence Island did not have many options. The investors had many reasons, they announced, for "disliking so many Negroes in the island," principally because of their "mutinous conduct." Their presence was becoming unproductive since it was mandated that "whoever keeps a Negro shall maintain a servant one day in the week upon the public works."[50] "Restraint of buying Negroes" was mandated, but a central directive was one thing, compliance was quite another.[51]

It did not take long for investors to order that the "taking in of Negroes" be "excused," though it was well recognized that there was an abject "danger of too great a number." Somehow they wanted to "send 200 English to be exchanged for as many Negroes," swapping slaves for settlers or indentured servants, but it was unclear as to who would volunteer willingly to arrive in a kind of war zone. Yet the rule crafted was "to two English men in a family, one Negro may be received and no more." Barring Negroes altogether was apparently out of the question; instead, the superfluous advice was rendered that "special care ... be taken" to avoid at all costs "the Cannibal Negroes brought from New England." Instead, the recommendation was "buying Negroes from the Dutch," though placing coin in the pockets of antagonists was hardly a sound solution.[52] Besides, what was to keep the sly Dutch from smuggling their agents into the island under the guise of selling the enslaved? This may serve to illuminate why many of the vanquished Pequots wound up being enslaved on Providence Island and Africans from there wound up in New England.[53]

On 1 May 1638—in anticipation of the late nineteenth-century salutations to laborers worldwide—the enslaved of Providence Island executed the first slave rebellion in any English colony. Thereafter, frightened oppressors engaged in a fire sale of Africans, which indicated that this settlement's shelf life was to be limited. In possible response, in 1638 the first known attempt to "breed" enslaved Africans happened in Boston, as if in anticipation of twenty-first-century bioengineering, to produce slaves and become less dependent on the market.[54]

Providence Island was soon to be overrun and destroyed by Spaniards (not the Dutch), but just before that investors were revealing their dilemma. "Laid aside" were "thoughts of selling their Negroes," said the investors, though their presence would not enhance settler security when the inevitable Spanish invasion occurred. "If the number be too great to be managed," they said disconsolately, "they may be sold and sent to New England or Virginia."[55] But like many investors before and since, they held on to this asset too long and lost when marauders dispatched from His Catholic Majesty arrived.

The inherent frailty of island settlements was an inference drawn from the fate of Providence Island. Yes, mainland settlements had their own problems, but as of that moment, New England and Virginia were surviving. The destruction of this island colony, however, sent an ominous signal about the destiny of Barbados and its neighbors.

Were island settlements harder to defend than their mainland counterparts? Was it easier to deliver aid to hurricane wracked mainland
settlements, as opposed to their island counterparts? If both queries
were answered affirmatively, this was further reason for a great trek to
the mainland, which was a condition precedent for the emergence of
what became the United States of America.

THE MUTUALLY BENEFICIAL relationship between New
England and London's island colonies meant that the Crown could
afford to import more enslaved Africans. The population of the latter
in Barbados jumped from about 2,000 in the 1630s to over 20,000 by
the 1650s. The mainland also benefited from this boom, as a trickle
of migrants to Jamestown in 1607 became a stream by 1629, then a
flood by the 1640s: 100,000 were said to have arrived during the seventeenth century.[56]

The mainland was a satellite floating in the orbit of the Caribbean.
The so-named West Indies were probably far more key to New
England's prosperity than New England was to the Caribbean.[57]
This allowed more latitude for the mainlanders and more opportunity
to collaborate with the Crown's opponents, particularly in French
Hispaniola, an exercise that eventuated in a unilateral declaration of
independence in 1776 that was to be backed by Paris.

Though London's emphasis on the Caribbean made sense in the
short term, in the longer term the North American mainland held
more potential for exploitation compared to small islands. In the
latter, Africans would soon become the majority, making security
problematic at best. Yes, the mainland delivered security threats too,
but a retreat from islands across open seas was more difficult than
across land. Similarly, it was easier to build linked settlements in a
chain-like fashion in the vast mainland than across disparate islands
of varying size.[58]

Part of the problem was on the mainland during this period. A
major reason was the tyranny of the Massachusetts theocracy, which
repelled many besides Roger Williams. Instead of wandering into
the wilderness and founding a Providence, others fled to the warm

embrace of the more cultivated and congenial Caribbean, underlining the continuing importance of these settlements. Though increasingly surrounded by bonded labor on the verge of revolt, the islands seemed to be more inviting than a colder Boston.[59] Besides, opportunities and concessions were easier to obtain in the Caribbean, even though Europeans were increasingly being outnumbered by Africans, as opposed to Boston, which would not endure this dicey fate.

Meanwhile, as the migrants from the Isle of Wight indicated, Europeans on the open seas continued worrying about being taken by the Ottoman Turks and their proxies. As we have seen, this bracing experience did not tend to make these Western Europeans more sensitive to enslavement but, to the contrary, seemed to spur them along this road.[60] It was "worse than the Egyptian bondage," complained one Londoner speaking of what occurred in Morocco. "What misery can be more than for a man or woman to be bought and sold like a beast"—said with seeming indifference to what English merchants were doing in the Americas and Africa.[61] It was as if the mantra was "be an enslaver or a slave."

The settlements delivered wealth along with storminess in the form of revolts by bonded labor and the "creative destruction" delivered by the rise of new centers of capital. At the same time, London was being pressed on all sides by the Dutch and the Spaniards, as well as the French and the Ottoman Turks. (As for the French, the considerable unrest across the Channel was bound to have an impact in what became known as the British Isles.[62] And, as so often happened, rebellion in mostly Catholic France often meant corresponding revolt in mostly Catholic Ireland.)[63] This was not a prescription for steadiness, a reality that would become clear when civil war erupted and a monarch was beheaded by comrades of Oliver Cromwell, some of whom had whetted their seemingly bottomless appetite for violence in battles on the North American mainland. The violence that had become normative ignited cycles of revenge, which was not ideal when merchants sought to muster settlers for colonial occupation, though many were still smarting from religious, class, and ethnic repression and licking their wounds.[64] When the tenure of Cromwell, the Lord Protector, expired and royal restoration occurred, the clock was not turned back. Instead, the merchants and those who flexed their increasingly powerful muscles in temporarily deposing the Crown moved aggressively to weaken the Spanish (taking Jamaica) and weakening the Dutch (taking Manhattan), both of which set the stage for an increase in the arrival of enslaved Africans, who brought with them more wealth, and more storminess as well.

CHAPTER 3

The Rise of the Merchants and the Beheading of a King

liver Cromwell was "the greatest Englishman of the seventeenth century," said Theodore Roosevelt in the midst of a
fiery philippic against the Lord Protector's foe in Madrid,
words that simultaneously rationalized Washington's knockout blow
against the Spanish Empire, which had recently been administered in
Cuba and the Philippines. Roosevelt was completing what Cromwell
had begun.[1] That the embodiment of U.S. imperialism would salute an
anti-monarchist Puritan should be seen as logical. The republicanism
that Cromwell foreshadowed would erupt in 1776. The republicanism that evolved in North America found it difficult at best to corral
the Pan-Europeanism that set it in motion (witness the anti-Catholicism and anti-Semitism of early nineteenth-century New York, for
example). Likewise, Cromwell's anti-monarchical project, engaging
in bloody anti-Irish pogroms, created the template for republicans
staring down the indigenous and slave revolts in the Americas.

In short, England and the immediately surrounding territories
were rocked by internecine martial conflict between the early 1640s
(actually as early as 1639) and the late 1650s, when Cromwell passed

from the scene and the monarchy was restored about a decade after the king had been beheaded in 1649. In short, 1640 to 1660 transformed the Isles; though Cromwell died, neither Cromwellian republican nor merchant capital was subdued altogether, and this led in 1688 to their roaring comeback, when the monarch was placed on a glide path to becoming a figurehead. The emerging primacy of those captivated with the idea of captivity of Africans and Native Americans were then to rise on the curious platform of being tribunes of "enlightenment" and progress, an ideological victory so grand that even those who supposedly sought to overthrow the capitalist draper in the deceitful finery of republicanism accepted this fundamental canard.

The losing side in this titanic European conflict had a justifiable fear that they would become bonded laborers, particularly in the Caribbean, which gave them an incentive to fight with ferocity, just as it normalized what was unfolding in any case: enslaving Native Americans and Africans. By 1642 a quarter or even a third of the adult male population in the regions surrounding London were in arms at one time or another, according to one estimate. Casualties, as a result, were quite high; as a percentage of the English population, they were higher than for the British dead during the First World War. The figures for Scotland were higher, and for England, much higher still. Unremarkably, foreigners found these Europeans to be rude, aggressive, and violent.[2] Testimony from indigenes and Africans doubtlessly would have been even more denunciatory.

Another estimate claims that 10 percent of all adult males—about 140, 000 out of a population of five million—were armed.[3] Yet whatever the actual figure, the cruel reality was merciless murder in the streets and in the fields, creating a dislocation that made faraway Barbados or the deceptively named New England seem like paradise by comparison. Moreover, the relentless bloodletting also created a labor deficit in the Caribbean, swelling in importance with every passing day, thereby contributing to a growing mania for more enslaved Africans. (This would be a problem throughout the era of the slave trade. By 1642 the Dutch, still a major force in this dirty business, were accusing Africans in Africa of "criminal matters," that is, "conspiring against the sovereignty" of the Netherlands and being "rebellious or seditious" besides.)[4]

The ousting and beheading of a monarch was the most direct expression of the anti-monarchism involved, but this conflict was also an adjunct of Europe's Thirty Years' War, then lurching to a close. There were pent-up tensions brought by class displacement, as newly enriched merchants with wealth based in colonies displaced their less blessed counterparts. There was also religious cum ethnic conflict, denoted as mostly Catholic Irish versus mostly Protestant England. And much more. The ostensible religious conflict included the unavoidable point that gold and silver from the Americas were enabling Spain, and the time had come to deny Madrid this revenue and redirect it toward London. Moreover, the impending end of the Thirty Years' War indicated minimally that the long years of steady Habsburg advance had ended, creating a vacuum that London could well fill.[5]

The rise and fall of Cromwell is best seen as part of a lengthy process that began decades earlier with London's piratical attacks on the Spanish Empire, providing seed capital for England's own venture into settler colonialism in Virginia by 1607, fueled by canny investors. By the 1620s, this class was climbing the ladder of prestige and power and by the 1640s it was contributing to the republican cause. After Cromwell, these nascent capitalists made a peace of sorts with certain royals, particularly those involved in forming the Royal African Company. This was in 1672. But by 1679 these maneuvering bandits were complicit in the exclusion of the Catholic Duke of York from succession to the Crown, and by 1688 they had pulled off a "revolution," that weakened the monarchy, particularly in the commerce in Africans, which opened the door to even more wealth, as well the rationalization of empowering Parliament as against the King. Then finally, in 1776, they pulled off the ultimate coup and exhibited their novel display of patriotism by ousting London altogether from the mainland colonies south of Canada, while convincing the deluded and otherwise naive (to this very day) that this naked grab for land, slaves, and profit was somehow a great leap forward for humanity.[6]

THE PRAGMATIC CROMWELL embraced republicanism and a proto-imperialism, which made him a hero to Roosevelt, among others in North America. He not only devastated Ireland[7] but escalated the conflict with the Netherlands, a raw maneuver to control Atlantic trade routes and the related slave trade, all the while collecting taxes to propel further conquest.[8]

The environment was not conducive to peaceful progress. Europe saw only three years of complete peace during the entire seventeenth century, whereas on the southeastern flank, the Ottomans had only ten. The Chinese and Mughal empires were warring almost constantly, as resort to arms became the norm for resolving local and global problems. The two were connected, as interstate war often fed intrastate revolt by driving regimes to extract resources from their subjects more forcefully. And intrastate revolts could become interstate wars when alienated subjects summoned foreign intervention on their behalf. Not atypical was the advance of a Cossack army through Ukraine in 1648 that led to an anti-Jewish massacre of 10,000. The following year Cromwell massacred 25,000 soldiers and at least 1,000 civilians (including Catholic priests) at Drogheda in Ireland.

The 1640s possibly saw more rebellions and self-described revolutions than any comparable era in world history. The spores of republicanism were loosed in Catalonia, Naples, and England, collapsing in a matter of days, weeks, and years respectively, suggesting larger trends at play. The frenzy led Catholic gangs to round up Protestant settlers (Scots as well as English) in Ireland and either stab them to death, burn them alive in their homes, or drive them into icy waters where they perished. What is more, this murderousness was reciprocated.

From 1640 to 1660 hundreds of thousands were maimed or rendered homeless, making escape to the Americas seem like a tonic by comparison. Arising in the turmoil were "Diggers," "Levellers," "Ranters," and "Quakers," many of whom were less than enthusiastic about Cromwell. The rise of the radically egalitarian Levellers in particular was cause enough for merchants to reconcile with royalists.

Yet some trends did not collapse in a heap. Two are of monumental significance to the story here: the ongoing demise of Spain as a great power, a development that led to the loss of Jamaica in 1655, and the Protestant ascendancy in Northern Ireland, which helped to induce increased migration to the Americas.

These conflicts also had a religious pretext that Cromwell's dispossessions of the Irish and his comrades' dislodgement of Native American "heathens" did not conceal. Later Montesquieu was to claim that Islam created despotism, Catholicism created monarchy, and Protestantism created republics, but this clerical gloss was meant to conceal the reality that Protestant London was more and more in the grip of merchants who were willing to exercise any ploy, be it religious, republican, or religious republicanism, in order to gain a dominant market share.[9]

Tellingly, the displacement of Irish by Cromwell is eminently comparable and even a precedent for Virginia's dispossession of indigenes, an initiative hastened in 1676 by Nathaniel Bacon, whose revolt was a precursor of 1776.[10] Just as Cromwell pursued a virulently anti-Catholic program against the Irish at home and the Spanish abroad,[11] republicans in North America pursued a virulently anti-Negro program at home combined with hostility to abolitionist Haiti and Britain abroad.[12]

Cromwell, in sum, provided a deadly model in Ireland for his compatriots to follow in North America. In 1649 he "ordered" that Irishmen be maltreated acidulously: "Put them all to the sword." Said Cromwell, "I forbade them to spare any that were in Arms. In the Town . . . that night," he added with bloodthirst, "they put to the sword about two thousand men," with "every tenth man of the soldiers killed, and [the] rest shipped for the Barbadoes."[13]

Yet it was this policy of deportation that at times boomeranged spectacularly. Just as Cromwell counseled shipping surviving Irish to the Caribbean, Nicholas Foster was lamenting a "late horrid rebellion acted in the island of Barbados" and "their inhumane acts and actions."[14] Foster lamented that "at the time of England's troubles," meaning Cromwell's ascendancy, "we retained peace amongst us" and opted for "neutrality" on Barbados. This did not prevent some from fleeing to London and others grabbing their estates, signaling an unsteadiness that "servants" and the enslaved were eminently capable of exploiting. Those remaining on the island, complained Foster, then began to "act in a very high nature" and with "severity" and "cruelty," as they began to "prosecute all such persons" in order to "declare their approbations of the Parliaments proceeding against the King; cutting out of tongues, stigmatizing and banishing all such persons."[15]

Soon Cromwell's London replied by sending a formidable fleet to the Caribbean to keep settlements in line, which, as things evolved, was a prelude for sending a formidable fleet to seize Jamaica in 1655.[16] Cromwell's forces completed the process of helping to ensure that those allied with him would preserve power, with an edict that demanded "all . . . Servants, Negroes and other goods be restored to their right owners, except such servants as had freedome given them." This latter point was yet another distinction drawn between "Servants" and "Negroes" as the process unfolded of marking the latter as the prime labor force to be exploited.[17]

Sending Irish and other dissidents to labor in the Caribbean was unwise in any case, providing them with an incentive to ally with London foes in the neighborhood, with mischief in mind. The complaint in Barbados in 1650 was that diverse "acts of rebellion have been committed by many persons," all conducted "most trayterously by force." Some of these alleged "traitors" had "usurped a power of Government and seized the estates of many well-affected persons into their hands and banished others, and have set themselves in opposition to and distinct from the state and commonwealth," leaving no alternative but "suppression of the said rebellion in the said plantations." But this would be neither simple nor easy, given the "horrid rebellions" and the "notorious robbers and traytors" involved. Quarantine was one answer: "The Parliament," it was intoned haughtily, "doth forbid and prohibit all ships of any foreign nations whatsoever to come to or trade in traffique with any of the English plantations in

America."[18] But why should the Dutch or Spaniards or Frenchmen obey London's edicts?

This occurred to London , which also issued an ordinance directing Virginia, Bermuda, and Barbados, all harboring royalist sentiment to a greater or lesser degree, to curb export ties to "France, Spain, Holland and other forraigne parts."[19] Strikingly, while the roundheads (or Cromwellians) upheld the cause of freedom within the settlement itself, the Cavaliers (or royalists) maintained the political rights of the settlement against the Commonwealth at home.[20] Interestingly, the question of home rule versus who should rule at home was to animate the mainland colonies in the run-up to 1776.

In other words, what has been termed the Civil War in England and the surrounding territories had multiple consequences for colonial settlements and the enslavement and land dispossession that it involved. After directing violence against each other, those of the Isles directed this organized force externally, with devastating results for Africans and Native Americans.[21] Indeed, it would not be far-fetched to suggest that violence directed outward became a substitute for violence directed inward with the ultimate prize—dispossession of the indigenous of the Americas and mass enslavement of Africans—being sufficiently enormous to divert revolt in the islands off the northwestern coast of Europe.

The 1640s witnessed one of the most violent and unsettled eras in the history of Maryland, for example. In 1645 the colony was invaded by a band of privateers—legalized pirates—under the leadership of Richard Ingle, a Puritan, who with the aid of other Protestants (in what would later be termed "sleeper cells") overthrew the government of Lord Baltimore. As was typical of the times, he looted and plundered Catholics, as once again sectarian differences became a cover for capital gain. The unrest in London was the precondition for the success of this attack. The recurring cycle of what has been termed "revolution and counterrevolution" in this mostly Catholic settlement was characteristic of Maryland's political climate,[22] until 1776,

when "counterrevolution" finally triumphed in reaction to Britain's
seeming move toward abolitionism. Ultimately, a kind of civil war
in Maryland unfolded until 1657 when Cromwell helped to settle
it.[23] However, this calmness did not arrive absent much hair-pulling,
much of it ignited from Virginia.[24]

Despite the choppy waters that reached from the North Atlantic
to the Caribbean Sea, both Virginia and Barbados enjoyed unprece-
dented prosperity during the 1640s, and the planters, who often leaned
toward the royalists, did not fail to grasp the connection among political independence, free and open trade, and more profitable sales, as
opposed to preferential trade agreements that locked these settlements
into relationships designed to benefit England above all. The execution of the monarch provided the ultimate excuse, if any were needed,
for these settlements to declare their open defiance of London. Just as
religion was a pretext for gaining market share, pro-monarchism was
a pretext for something similar. By 1650, Barbados, Antigua, Virginia,
and Bermuda had risen in revolt, making transparently clear that they
would not bend a knee to the usurpers in London.[25]

Virginia not only proclaimed its allegiance to the monarchy but
also outlawed those who thought and acted otherwise. The governors
of Bermuda, Antigua, Newfoundland, and Maryland followed suit,
and in the Massachusetts Bay region, despite republican sentiment in
Boston, only Rhode Island recognized Cromwell's Commonwealth
formally. They were only mimicking Europe, since virtually no government there followed Rhode Island; Russia expelled all English
merchants, and royalist exiles murdered diplomats dispatched by
Cromwell to Spain and Holland and almost killed another in Russia.
Still, when in September 1650 some 3,000 Scottish soldiers died and
10,000 more were imprisoned at the Battle of Dunbar, the Reverend
John Cotton of Boston hailed the victory as a sign that God approved
of Cromwell, as he wrote a personal letter of congratulation to the
Lord Protector and celebrated a special day of thanksgiving. An
inspired Cromwell attacked again on the first anniversary of Dunbar,
and another 3,000 Scots fell and 10,000 more became prisoners, many
of them shipped to colonial settlements.[26]

Cromwellian London knew that Barbados, Virginia, and Bermuda needed to be reined in by the self-proclaimed commonwealth of England.[27] No goods from these outliers were to be landed in Boston or Salem since they were "in rebellion [against] the commonwealth."[28] In the meantime, London had its hands full in 1650, seeking to redeem captives seized by "Turkish, Moorish and other pirates."[29]

On the other hand, one of the Lord Protector's most important advisors was George Downing, a member of the graduating class of Harvard in 1642. On September 3, 1651, he was to be found at the pivotal Battle of Worcester, which the Lord Protector, foreseeing its consequences, called his "crowning mercy." His closeness to Cromwell was signaled in 1657 when he was appointed London's chief delegate to Holland. He was blamed for the Navigation Act of October 9, 1651, intended to boost England's shipping force, which was said to have ruined Holland and, in an example of collateral damage that was to inflame republicans in the eighteenth century, was also thought to have almost ruined North American colonies. By 1664, after Cromwell had expired, the nimble Downing was to be found alongside the Duke of York, who was to give his name to territory seized from the Dutch that year, as the two collaborated on an attack on Dutch interests in Africa, site of the growingly profitable African Slave Trade, which the Duke was to regularize soon by way of forming the Royal African Company. Though the future U.S. president, John Adams, was to call him a "scoundrel," his opportunism, leaping from anti-monarchism to collaboration with royals, was exemplary of the flexibility that allowed an emergent capitalism to combine elements of feudalism—and slavery.[30]

Indeed, fourteen of Harvard's first twenty-four graduates—this included Cromwell's spymaster, Downing—were republicans. This list included the Lord Protector's favorite preacher, Hugh Peter, and at least seven colonels in his army (including Stephen Winthrop, son of John). John Winthrop rejoiced when Cromwell ascended. Other New Englanders, including Henry Vane, who led the vanquishing of the Pequot, were part of the Cromwell cabal. They were in the vanguard, seeking to kill royalists with their prayers and sending sermons, poems, letters, and treatises of encouragement sailing across the Atlantic. This group included Anne Bradstreet of Cambridge, Massachusetts, who with the venom that had become customary in North America said of the hated royalists and Cromwellian detractors, "destroy and tread them down."[31]

Another fanatically loyal and crucial ally of Cromwell—and one of the regicides who signed the death warrant for Charles I —was his cousin, Edward Whalley. He arrived in Boston on July 27, 1660 as royal restoration was in motion.[32] Whalley hailed from a prominent family of merchants. His sister resided in New Haven, Connecticut.[33] Susanna Winthrop, a member of a founding family in New England, returned to England to aid Cromwell directly and later helped to formulate his "Western Design," that is, attacking Spain in Hispaniola.[34]

Most of London's merchant elite supported the monarchy during the civil wars, but most of those who traded with the colonial settlements supported the monarch's opponents. In return for their support, these "colonial merchants" demanded protection for their trades against royal privateers, and Cromwell complied by building sleek frigates, suitable for long voyages escorting convoys—in other words, suitable for deepening colonialism.[35]

By 1652 Cromwell had secured Barbados and forced a royalist capitulation in Virginia; simultaneously the numbers of enslaved increased, perhaps quadrupling in the settlements during the 1650s, as the republican scent for profit was unleashed. As for Ireland, colonial merchants had advanced large sums to uphold the Protestant cause there and then demanded the confiscated lands that had been offered as collateral. In August 1652 London authorized land confiscation and condemnation of priests, with the link generating more Irish defections to His Catholic Majesty in Madrid.[36] Hence, colonial merchants were essential to two major dispossessions—in North America and Ireland.

DESPITE THE APPARENT FLOW of the tides of history toward African and Native American enslavement, it was not evident in the 1640s that this trend would become so dominant. By 1646 in

Massachusetts, there was a castigation of the "sinn of man stealing," a "vile and odious" practice. There was an "order" for a "Negro interpreter" so that the man in question and others "unlawfully taken" be "sent to his native country of Ginny [Guinea]," along with a "letter with him of indignation."[37] This African "fraudulently & injuriously taken & brought from Ginny" should be "sent home" forthwith.[38] This "killing, stealing & wronging of . . . Negers" was deemed reprehensible.[39] Yes, there was concern that those arriving from the West Indies like the complainant at issue might be delivering "plague" and "disease," and there was no companion effort to halt the arrival of Portuguese ships, notorious for bearing kidnapped Africans. Still, the authorities continued to denounce the "sinn of man stealing."[40] "Send them back . . . without delay," it was announced.[41] And yes, as denunciation of Guineans was being denounced, the indigenous were being shipped halfway around the world to the Azores and Madagascar. Though shipping indigenes to foreign nations, the settlers in Connecticut ruled that it was "not lawful for any Frenchmen, Dutchmen or person of any foraigne nation . . . to trade with any Indian or Indians."[42]

Also illuminating is that in the Plymouth Colony in 1646 it was ordered that since it was expensive to imprison the indigenous and since "they are [likely] to prove more insolent," they should be "shipped out" and "exchanged for Negroes."[43] It was this trend that became hegemonic.

This was understandable to a degree, for at that time, in the context of clashes between England and the Netherlands in what was to become Indonesia, London denounced a "friendly correspondence and a mutual assistance against the common enemy, the barbarous Indians," who were being tasked by the Dutch "to attack English settlers." With indignation, London added that "this diabolical plot" meant the Dutch "supplied the Indians with arms and ammunition." Worse, "the French" were the "confederate" of the "Dutch and Indians."[44] The document containing this explosive charge was well circulated in London, as perhaps indicated by the fact that copies can be found in a number of libraries in today's United States.[45]

The "blood sucking Dutch," argued one Londoner, needed to be squashed if England's settlements were to survive.[46]

Roughly, this is precisely what occurred. Thus, the Dutch arrived in what is now Mauritius in 1598, and this archipelago seemed a natural site for colonizing by an empire that needed a port between what became its two major colonies: at the Cape of Good Hope and the Malay peninsula. These islands, considered to be part of Africa, were then occupied in 1638 but then there was the failed attempt to implant a settlement in 1664—the year Manhattan was lost to London—and, then, was abandoned by 1710 as the Netherlands crept closer to colonial decrepitude.[47] As the Dutch fell, the English rose.

Nevertheless, another apparent liberalizing measure may shed light on this solicitude shown for a solitary Guinean. In the midst of contestation between mainland royalists and Cromwellians, the local Massachusetts militia allowed Native Americans, Africans, even Scots to enlist.[48] A truer sign was to emerge in New England by 1656 when it was ruled that Africans and indigenes—and only Africans and indigenes—should no longer be trained in the use of firearms.[49] This decision came in the wake of another turning point in this story: the ouster by England of Spain from Jamaica in 1655, which opened the door for a skyrocketing of the African Slave Trade and a further downgrading of Africans.

It is useful to distinguish slave-trading interests, often merchants and pro-Cromwell, from planters who deployed small armies of enslaved workers. Planters were often royalists. The merchants often resided in New England and the planters in Virginia. Thus, what became the "Old Dominion" declared emphatically for the Crown. Neighboring and comparable Bermuda had not only acted similarly but had sent emissaries to Barbados demanding the same from colonists there. The seeds of their conflict would explode in civil war in 1861. About 210 years before this fateful year and about 125 years before 1776, a fleet was headed to these rebellious settlements determined to compel allegiance to the new commonwealth.[50]

Thus when the royalist Richard Ligon arrived in Barbados from England in the 1640s, he found that those of a similar ideological persuasion abounded. In 1646 alone, 12,000 prisoners from the depleting civil wars had been dispatched to this island. This included several thousand Irish who had been taken prisoner or simply kidnapped or, as was said then, "Barbadosed." Then there were the hundreds of Scots captured at Dunbar and Worcester in the 1650s who were sold in Massachusetts and New Hampshire. In 1650 Barbados had four Europeans for every African, a skewed ratio that would change quickly, engendering murderous conflict with the arrival of boatloads of manacled Africans. By 1660, this island barely contained 27,000 enslaved Africans and 26,000 defined as "white," and it did not require a seer to divine that something must be done to demarcate a sharp line between and among these laborers. "Racial" categories, perpetually lurking and intermittently operating since the first Africans were seized for Portugal hundreds of years earlier, soon emerged more forcefully.[51]

Evidently, it was not London alone that was using the Caribbean as a dumping ground for foes and detractors. By 1650 there were numerous Catholics from Europe, besides the English and Irish; there were also Portuguese Africans like Mathias de Sousa, whom Andrew White brought to Maryland. This ethnic and racial stew was making for a combustible brew, on the mainland and islands alike.[52]

But out of a potential disaster London was able to transform Barbados into a cash cow. By 1649 sugar had virtually eliminated all other crops as a form of payment, becoming a kind of currency. This was a direct outgrowth of a war that began in Pernambuco in 1645, as the Portuguese ousted the Dutch from their sinecure and sent fleeing northward those with knowledge of how to make sugar from the blood of Africans. (However, as the following chapter suggests, there is evidence to suggest that sugar had been introduced into Barbados years before this.)

"There is no doubt," says the historian Stuart B. Schwartz, "that Sephardic refugees from Dutch Brazil who had experience in the sugar trade, as well as in direct contacts before 1650, had an impact on the sugar economy of the island."[53] London, which had helped Holland escape the suffocating grasp of Spain in the late sixteenth century, then benefited as competing powers ganged up on this now retreating empire. But the problematic fate of the Dutch was dwarfed by what befell Africans, for with the advent of the rigorous and brutalizing project of sugar production, more of the enslaved were needed.

Scholar Russell Menard has suggested that what occurred in the Caribbean was a "sugar boom," rather than a "sugar revolution."[54] Yet this attempt to downgrade the import of what occurred in Barbados then Jamaica, only serves to indicate its far-reaching impact. For sugar was not only used to sweeten tea and coffee, but was for years seen as a marker of sophistication and refinement, ideal for a rising capitalism that exploited such a trend with merciless dedication.

Almost 100,000 from the Jewish community in Spain fled for Portugal in 1492; they found no satisfaction there, however, even after converting to Catholicism. They kept moving, with many winding up on the Brazilian frontier. The family connections they maintained, which often encompassed certain branches of trade, seemed to be designed with the new era of colonialism in mind. The mostly Protestant Dutch welcomed them to Amsterdam just as they welcomed them to Recife, where the Dutch ruled from roughly 1630 to 1654. But then with the Dutch ousted, these sought-after refugees were then welcomed by Protestant London and Barbados.[55] And then they were welcomed to Jamaica—post 1655: by 1713 Jamaica was producing more sugar than Barbados and had become London's wealthiest and most important colony.[56]

Whether denoted as boom or revolution, sugar became a de facto currency, which was the experience of Heinrich von Uchteritz, a German mercenary captured at the Battle of Worcester and dispatched to Barbados. Questioned by Cromwell himself before his forced departure, he was in a group of 1,300 others: "Each of us was sold for eight hundred pounds of sugar" he recalled, as they were bought by a "Christian, born in England who had one hundred Christians, one hundred Negroes and one hundred Indians" on his sprawling estate, all of whom were "slaves." But already there were distinctions, as the "Christians" or Europeans were clothed while the others, "the Negroes and Indians" tended to "go about completely naked except for a cloth tied around the privates."[57] Soon the Europeans were to be clothed in the protective cloak of "whiteness," while the Africans and indigenes were to be devoid not only clothes but rights, demarcated as permanent outsiders, notably in North America.

As sugar took hold in the Caribbean, the fortunes of Africans declined as their numbers rose. Africans remained a minority in Barbados into the 1650s, but by the early 1670s Africans outnumbered Europeans by a ratio of three to two and by three to one by the early eighteenth century.[58] But as their numbers rose, the probability of felonious revolt rose accordingly, which was to drive many settlers to the mainland, setting in motion a pro-slavery revolt in 1776.

As the numbers of Africans surged, Richard Ligon was not the only one who fretted that they might "commit some horrid massacre upon the Christians, thereby to enfranchise themselves and become Masters of the land."[59] It was this fear that rested near the core of slave-based colonialism; that is, that the bountiful crops produced required large numbers of Africans and the idea might occur, as it did in Hispaniola in 1791, that they should simply seize power.[60] This fear haunted slave owners, including those in North America who were so concerned about this prospect that it factored into their fateful decision to oust London altogether.[61] In Barbados, Ligon noticed that as a direct result of this miasma of fear, the Africans were "not allowed to touch or handle any weapons."[62]

Ironically, the decline of the Dutch brought a mixed bag of results for Africans. Obviously, the decline of a serial slave trader is not to be lamented. However, as the Dutch were removed, it made it more difficult for the enslaved to escape from New Netherlands or the Dutch settlements in North America to another jurisdiction, for example, Connecticut, as occurred in 1646, or from Maryland to New Netherland, as also occurred. In short, arbitrage opportunities were reduced as the Dutch faded from the scene.[63] Still, when in 1654 the retreating Dutch of New Netherland ousted Swedes from Delaware and then sold them into slavery, knowledgeable Africans may have thought, "better them than me."[64] Again, more enslavers meant more enslaved Africans but, paradoxically, this could create opportunity for indigenes and Africans to play one European power against another. Before the Dutch were ousted by the Portuguese from Brazil, Spain in 1629 had sent a fleet of twenty-four ships and fifteen frigates to this giant nation for the same purpose. Spain intended to oust the English from St. Kitts, too; their successful raid on Tortuga in the 1630s was designed to liquidate the settlement. Such ambitious plans left plenty of opportunity for Africans and indigenes to maneuver.[65] And this profound trend was to continue in the eighteenth century and thereafter.

AS SUGAR DROVE COLONIALISM and along with it the arrival of more Africans to the Caribbean, opportunities were opened for bonded labor to ally with one group of Europeans against another. It was in 1652 that policymakers in Barbados passed a statute "against the stealing of Negroes from off this island," perpetrated by "divers[e] wicked persons" who were not above "promising them freedom in another country."[66] As colonizers escalated the African Slave Trade, they stumbled. Between 1650 and 1710, an average of 40 percent of the Africans imported to Barbados came from the Gold Coast, totaling about 136,000. Many of them were of Akan origin, which facilitated rebellion, given their commonalities. Only Jamaica had a higher total in the British Caribbean. Thereafter, colonizers sought to make aggregates of enslaved Africans more heterogeneous, complicating their bonding for purposes of revolt.[67]

Room to maneuver was the byword for the Caribbean, especially as the population grew and changed in coloration. Barbados was not unique. Between 1650 and 1660, 50,251 souls from England, Ireland, and elsewhere in Europe arrived in the Chesapeake and the Caribbean. During the same period, 40,726 Africans arrived, mostly in the Caribbean. Though these Europeans outnumbered Africans in the colonial labor supply during the course of the Cromwell era, that is, 1640 to 1660, Africans came to outnumber Europeans much earlier in Barbados than in the Chesapeake Bay region, where this demographic imbalance did not arrive until the 1690s, with multiple consequences for the construction of racial identities, particularly whiteness.[68]

Keep in mind, however, that the comparison above may be misleading because by the mid-seventeenth century the northern English colonies had more slaves than those in the Chesapeake. This ratio was to change in coming decades, enhancing the domination of merchants in New England, just as planters in Virginia came to dominate, harboring a latent conflict that was to explode in yet another civil war two centuries later.[69] Yet about eight decades before that war of rebellion, there was another against London that united merchant and planter alike, both of whom knew that more wealth would accrue if they cut loose from British rule. As early as 1652 in Massachusetts, for example, in seeming anticipation of this secession, Massachusetts had begun to mint its own coinage with no mention of England included.[70]

As was to occur so frequently in the emergent United States when opponents of the status quo were deemed to be mere pawns of presumed foreign foes, the "premature" republicans in London in 1642 charged hotly that the "King, seduced by wicked counsel, doth intend to levy warre against his Parliament; and . . . the jewels of the Crown which by the Law of the Land ought not to alienate . . . are either pawned or sold in Amsterdam."[71] This was the foe that England would have to dislodge, it was thought, if the nation were to advance.

Somehow, in the midst of the turmoil of civil war, London found the time to escalate involvement in the African Slave Trade. In a sense, this domestic conflict was derivative of the larger conflict, which was the effort to dislodge competing powers from the Americas and the source of the labor supply: Africa. This effort involved the enhanced hegemony of merchants, which would arrive full force in 1688, which was the predicate to London itself being ousted from its African perch in 1776. There were a reported nineteen English ships buying the enslaved at El Mina in West Africa between 1645 and 1647 and eighty-four between 1652 and 1657. This led inexorably to more Anglo-Dutch conflict, as a beleaguered Africa and the riches it produced became a magnet for European war.[72]

Hence by 1647 Jan van Delwell, the Dutch Director General at El Mina Castle in what is now Ghana, detected more ships and yachts of other European nations infesting nearby waters, including stalwart competitors such as England, France, Denmark, and Sweden. They too were seeking to enslave Africans to toil in their present and would-be colonies. This increased competition allowed for arbitrage by counter-parties—meaning Africans—as they quickly cut a deal with the Dutch to attack what seemed to be the weakest link, the Swedes, and promptly expelled the bumptious interlopers. Another group of Africans injected themselves in the intense rivalry between the Dutch and the Portuguese and supported first one, then the other, seeking to weaken both.[73]

It was also in the 1640s that an English settlement in Madagascar would generate countless numbers of enslaved Africans suitable for island and mainland colonies alike.[74] London merchant Richard Boothby upon arrival was mesmerized by the sight of this massive island, asking why not found a settlement here. He was taken by the "comeliness of the Natives though naked, yet personable" who were "only black or rather tauney [tawny]"; importantly, "their weapons" were "not dangerous or of great annoyance." If not a source for slaves, Madagascar could become a watering hole between London and the riches of India and Persia.[75] As slave-based colonialism evolved, Madagascar was to play a major role.[76] Euphemistically, by 1650 plantations were being plotted there, worked by "Negro servants."[77]

But it was not just Africa that was being dragged into a vortex of conflict by rising European powers. By 1652 the Dutch had established an outpost at the southern tip of Africa, a refreshing station en route to the riches of the Malay Peninsula, from which laborers were enchained and brought to what became Cape Town. Some of these bonded laborers were Chinese.[78]

By helping the Netherlands to escape the grasp of Spain, London had helped to create this budding superpower, which it now proceeded to diminish. Between 1652 and 1674 there were to be no fewer than three Anglo-Dutch wars, with control of colonialism and the slave trade at the throbbing heart of the disputes.[79] Floating on a sea of filthy lucre flowing from enslavement and dispossession, London was now poised to deal a staggering blow against Spain by seizing Jamaica in 1655. At once, this provided land for Europeans, often alienated and dispossessed in London itself and Barbados alike, who could now deploy the technology of producing sugar with the compelled labor of Africans. This, in turn, provided a boost for the seizing of Manhattan in 1664, hastening a circle absent of virtue that meant more enslaved Africans and more wealth. But it also meant more Africans in Jamaica who began to revolt, chasing settlers to the mainland, and engaging in the same dirty work until they had accumulated the strength and wealth to oust London in 1776.

CHAPTER 4

Jamaica Seized from Spain: Slavery and the Slave Trade Expand

As we have seen, the overall environment was conducive to tempestuous change during the two decades stretching from 1640 to 1660. The demographic debacle in Europe—mass slaughter in the Thirty Years' War, along with the depopulation engendered by the civil wars in England and the surrounding territories—unwound as colonial settlements were demanding more labor: this led colonizers to Africa's doorstep and also facilitated the enslavement of Native Americans.

Climatic adversity and political crisis during this era reduced France to a shadow of its former self. Similarly, though the Isles were not to experience anything as severe as the "El Niño Autumn" it endured in 1621, which, among other catastrophes, ruined the harvest and pushed islanders to move westward, this climatic event was still being felt as Cromwell was rising. The so-called Little Ice Age of 1641 may have tripled the number of Protestant deaths in the Isles, placing the country in a mood inimical to compromise. The subsequent famine in Scotland did not help matters. Neither did the freezing over of the entire Chesapeake Bay in 1641–42 facilitate civility; the same could be said during the winter of 1657–58 when the Delaware River was frozen.

As this was occurring in the 1640s, Catholics, who had owned about 60 percent, and Protestants 40 percent, of Ireland's cultivable land, saw this ratio reverse in the 1650s: by then Protestants owned 80 percent and the Catholics only 20 percent. This tended to benefit colonial merchants, bulging their purses and making it possible for them to enslave more Africans and seize more indigenous land.

The freedom of worship guaranteed by the Lord Protector seemed to be a cynical ruse to many Catholics, allowing them to pray but not own land. Such a turnabout, guaranteeing civil rights while ignoring economic rights, was a fixture of the emergent capitalism that republicanism was to deliver.

For a good deal of the seventeenth century, England could easily have passed as a failed state. Persecution of minorities was cruelly innovative. Widespread enclosures drove the poor off the land. Prices rose and wages fell in real terms. Harvest after harvest failed. Plague cut a prodigious swathe through the population, along with famine. Children as numerous as the proverbial "lice of Egypt" were forced to move westward across the ocean, at times unbeknownst to their parents, who were left to wallow in grief. Even as things began to improve in the aftermath of the ouster of Spain from Jamaica in 1655, Puritans continued hanging Quakers in the prize settlement that was Boston.[1]

The chronic upheaval generated profound movements of population. Virginia had only 1,200 settlers in 1624, and after the uproar of several decades, by 1650 only 15,000 settlers were there. Not until the 1680s when their number had reached 60,000 did the population become sufficiently viable to overwhelm consistently the growing African population and their indigenous allies. However, during the pivotal 1650s the population of colonial settlements quadrupled from around 50,000 to 200,000. In 1647 in Barbados yellow fever eliminated one in seven Europeans, and decimated other Caribbean islands similarly, along with the Yucatan. Africans seemed to have immunity, which only enhanced their attractiveness as a labor force, underscoring a trend already in motion. Two million were deported from Africa to the Americas in the seventeenth century. Before 1641, ships from Spain and Portugal accounted for 97 percent of the total but after that, England, France, and the Dutch Republic intervened. Revealingly, of the 160,000 Africans arriving in the hemisphere in the 1680s, over 141,000 came to the Caribbean.[2]

In Virginia, soon to be the trophy mainland settlement, in 1649 the African population was about 300, but by 1699 there were 6,000, most of whom arrived after 1660. That year marks a crucial transition in settler attitudes toward enslavement of Africans. As the African population grew and the handcuffs around their wrists tightened, settlers perceived them as more dangerous, leading inexorably to their being defined as a people without rights. This rising population increased the possibility of runaways (that is, capital loss), revolt, and even miscegenation.[3] Runaway Africans who for "a long time cannot be found" were targeted in Virginia in 1662, while "English servants" that chose to "run away in company of any Negro" were to be punished severely too, providing them with an incentive to observe demarcated racial lines.[4] Statutes adjusted accordingly to this new reality, which was to persist and get worse in the run-up to 1776 and the disintegration of 1861.

HELPING TO GENERATE THE DRAMATIC rise in enslaved African labor was the takeover by London of Jamaica in 1655, as the sugar boom sounded and dispossessed Europeans were seeking newer horizons, given the displacement of war in the British Isles. The seizure of Jamaica not only inflicted a mighty blow on the already teetering Spanish Empire, reeling from its disastrous encounter with Holland, but was a shot of pure adrenalin for London, not only in terms of the sugar boom but providing an idea of the riches to be garnered by plundering rivals. This contributed to the building of more naval vessels, for example, which had knock-on effects ricocheting throughout the economy. Carla Gardina Pestana has argued that the taking of Jamaica marks the "first time the state became directly involved in the business of expansion," as opposed to investors playing this important role.[5] The royal restoration a few years later could not arrest this powerful trend unleashing, that is, what became state monopoly capitalism with the state acting in the first instance on behalf of the ever more greedy investors.

The ground had been prepared for this successful invasion in that, according to one listing, in 1633 a significant number of the principal planters and settlers in Jamaica already carried non-Spanish names.[6] However, Jamaica revealed strains in the model of colonialism based on enslavement of Africans—strains that were to explode in Hispaniola by 1791. That is, Spanish leaders, just as Lord Dunmore in 1775 and Abraham Lincoln in 1863 did, found it necessary to free the enslaved in order to foil England's invasion, though as in 1775 this stratagem proved unavailing. Similarly, London felt that it could prevail with the aid of disgruntled Africans languishing under Madrid's misrule.[7] In other words, in making their calculations, European combatants had to take account of Africans, who could tip the balance against either, or as happened in 1791, against all of the colonizers.

Whatever the case, even before 1655, London was eyeing Jamaica ravenously and repeatedly sought to seize the island.[8] As ever, Cromwell's indictment against Madrid, designed to whip up hysteria for an invasion, charged Spaniards with "enslaving, hanging, drowning and cruelly torturing to Death our Countrymen."[9] This misbehavior, said one Londoner, justified "conquest," which "is free to all people, no Law of Nations can prohibit the power of the Sword, 'tis only God that sets its bounds and limits."[10]

Unquestionably, London laid down its typical barrage of propaganda as the time approached for invasion and even afterward. "No country exceeds" Spain, it was announced tremulously, "in a barbarous treatment of slaves or in the cruel methods by which they put them to death," as they were "condemned to flames." So moved, an energized London was considering seizing Jamaica as early as 1635. Part of the problem for invaders was that uncooperative Africans were continually switching sides, seeming to entice invaders, then cutting a deal with the Spanish colonizers to block them, or aiding the English to attack Spaniards, then weakening both, a pattern that continued in the eighteenth century after the takeover.[11]

Slipping into Jamaica in 1643 was James Martin along with

comrades from Barbados and St. Kitts as part of a raiding party. He was a Cornishman from Plymouth. The raiders envisioned Jamaica, according to Martin's amanuensis, as a "veritable promised land for in those small islands. . . . The most fertile parts had already been divided among a relatively small number of wealthy planters." They noticed that the Spaniards "distrusted" the Portuguese among them, their ostensible compatriots, on the "suspicion that some of them were Jews," which encouraged the idea of a takeover. They "were also visited by a few Negroes," who "professed to be overjoyed when told that [Martin et al.] would soon be returning to take possession of the island," but these invaders knew enough to be suspicious of the Negroes' intentions. Martin, who had studied the Spanish language at Oxford because of his interest in the "immortal Cervantes," was informed that in Jamaica all indigenes had been slaughtered and the Spaniards were "too poor to buy large numbers of African slaves," which meant persistent economic decline. At the same time, a weakened Madrid tried to keep non-Spaniards far distant from this island. Martin estimated that upon his touching ashore, there were "700 Spaniards" there, "75 foreigners—mostly Portuguese," and "more than 700 free Negroes, slaves and Indians or nearly 1,500 in all," ratios that did not reassure.

Martin was still there on May 9, 1655. That is when he detected the arrival of his compatriot invaders. Spaniards were "fleeing" in all directions, as the "38 ships" from the Isles "struck terror" in their hearts. There were almost 16,000 invaders, arriving from Hispaniola, which they had failed to seize "with the loss of a thousand men"; at least "one regiment had been put to flight by a few Negro hunters." The Jamaican Africans were terrified by the arrival of the invaders because of the propaganda spread by Madrid's men. These Africans formed brigades—or palenques. One was led by one Juan Lubolo, who became a "thorn in the flesh of the English," who "greatly feared the Negroes and had done their best to come to terms with them but without success." Some Englishmen taken prisoner wanted to return home but were afraid of what Cromwell "would mete out to them. . . . Many who deserted were Irish Catholics."

Then there was De Serras, who was "not a full blooded African," but was a leader of the insurgents; "His great grandfather had been a Spaniard" and he was a "Christian" and a "free man," but "little by little" he "encouraged his followers to hate and distrust all white men," pushing an insurgency against London and Madrid alike, in anticipation of what was to occur in Hispaniola in 1791. As late as 1658 Spaniards were trying to retake the island and found that Lubolo was not only sympathetic to London but deemed himself to be "one of their leaders." "The disaffection of Lubolo," said Martin, "would be fatal to the Spaniards. He knew all their hiding places and all their plans," making it "obvious that their days in the island were numbered." Generally, "owing to the disaffection of the Negroes it was no long possible to maintain a footing in the island."

De Serras was less taken with the invaders and claimed that he was the new governor of the island. In the flux brought by regime change, the Africans preyed upon travelers and isolated homesteads. With each successful raid, they became more daring and formidable, particularly after they obtained and mastered firearms. This tendency magnified as the enslaved fled to join De Serras and Lubolo, who set the tone for the fabled Maroons—Africans who escaped the jurisdiction of colonizers—who almost drove settlers from the island in coming decades. These were Mandingo and Koromantyns with well-earned reputations for militancy. Martin also encountered Jews, overjoyed by the Spanish ouster. Said one, Benjamin Lopez, of Portuguese Jewish extraction, who was forcibly "converted" but now would tell Englishmen about his true origins: "The English tax us unfairly," he conceded, "but they do not persecute us for our religion."[12]

Some Spaniards under the leadership of Cristobal Arnoldo de Ysassi fled to the mountains and freed many of the enslaved Africans who, having escaped during the fighting, formed bands of Maroons, who were to bedevil the new colonizer for decades to come.[13] Belatedly and unsuccessfully, the Spaniards made desperate pleas to one group of Africans to stand alongside Madrid's men.[14]

Captain Julian de Castilla of Spain met an African on the battlefield whom he thought was pro-London. This clever Angolan was literate, he found, and was one of a number in this category. This wily African, it was said, diligently sought to learn of the whereabouts of "the rich people" based on "information furnished by certain fugitive Negroes."[15]

London begged to differ, charging that in Jamaica the Spaniards, "after they had fired their first volley of small shot," would then send "out of the wood (being assisted by Negroes and Molattoes)" a contingent with malignant aims.[16] The "English army took possession of Jamaica on May 10," it was announced happily and "the people"— meaning the invaders—"found upon the place" about "1,400," many of whom "having fled to the hills, except some Negroes and Portuguese who have submitted to the English."[17]

Martin's experience exposed the weakness of Madrid's debilitated empire, with its archaic anti-Semitism, which was converting subjects into enemies. The Africans, as the precursors of the Maroons indicated, were not ebullient about the presence of dominant Europeans of any type, a point the new rulers dispatched by London would soon discover.

But the overriding point is that Europeans from tiny islands like Barbados envisioned an amplitude of riches in Jamaica in 1655, driven by sugar and slaves. That is, these Europeans—or "whites" as they were to be termed—could climb the class ladder with sugar stalks and Africans as the rungs. The opening of Jamaica in 1655 marked an era when merchants ascended, with their minions gaining a real— or imagined—stake in the expansion of slavery and its complement: racism. (Hypothetically, political repression and the magnificent wealth flowing after the subjugation of Jamaica was used to buy a kind of class peace unleashed by the rise of the "Levellers" and other poverty-stricken, though militant, elements.)[18]

Ultimately, the new Jamaican rulers overdid it, bringing in so many Africans that the entire colonial project was in jeopardy by dint of revolt. But then a "Great Trek" from the Caribbean to the mainland helped to extend the shelf life of slavery, especially after enslavers revolted against London in 1776.[19]

Even after taking Jamaica and consolidating their unsteady rule,

London continued to blast their Spanish predecessors because of their cruelty, which, it was thought, soured the Africans against colonialism. "It is not an easy matter," lamented Henry Barham in 1722, "to overcome so numerous a people as we see by the difficulty we have at the time to overcome our rebellious Negroes that keep upon the Eastern Mountains which are but a handful to those the Spanish had to deal with." Seemingly regretting the takeover, he termed it an "accident," as if the Spaniards had handed them a poisoned chalice intentionally, then "retired to Cuba, leaving their mallotoes and Negroes in the woods to harass the enemy and to keep possession of the island til they returned." The elated Africans, he recounted, proceeded to "cut the throat of the Governor" left by the Spaniards "and chose one of their own comrades to command them," referring to Juan Lubolo. They and others "kept in the mountains and lived by robbing and hunting" in coming years, though, he alleged, "the greatest part of them made their escape to Cuba in canoes."[20] This conqueror's remorse needs to be juxtaposed with the companion idea that taking Jamaica would also serve as a springboard for supplying more enslaved Africans to Cuba too, making London the heavyweight champion in this filthily lucrative commerce.[21]

This was also a turnabout of sorts since the Cromwell crony Thomas Gage had advised that Spaniards in Jamaica were so despised that they could be easily defeated since the Africans would ally with the invaders.[22]

The Londoner Richard Blome was outraged, though one would have suspected that he would have celebrated the murder of Spain's governor. Yet, he fumed, "instead of giving [Africans] fitting correction, they were constrained to court them for their assistance" as they headed for the hills and Cuba.[23] One remedy was to broaden the base for colonialism by recruiting settlers—not just from Boston and Jamestown—but from Europe more broadly: that is, moving toward a synthetic "whiteness," that would receive its fullest deployment in the broader expanse of North America.[24] In sum, Jamaica was like a dress rehearsal for the main production that was to sweep from the Atlantic to Pacific oceans in coming decades.

Slave-based settler colonialism was an inherently unstable process, as the bonded labor force had little incentive to ally with their masters when foreigners invaded, providing the latter with incentive to overthrow the status quo. The Dutch were convinced that the Africans would act as a fifth column on their behalf: the Dutch may have heard that an African in Chile named himself "King of Guinea" and demanded vengeance against the settlers, which could have succeeded with Dutch aid.[25] Thus, when Dutch forces invaded neighboring Peru in the 1620s, they brought along a chest full of manumission letters to hand out to the enslaved, along with weapons. Another contingent descended upon Pisco, where they sought to foment a slave revolt. As early as 1627, there was a fear in Virginia that there would be a replay of this stratagem by the Dutch. In the early stage of Dutch colonization in the Americas, race relations were not always informed by racial hierarchy, providing an advantage over competitors not likeminded. Anti-Cromwell loyalists in Barbados were confident that the Dutch would back them, just as those who joined Bacon's Rebellion in Virginia in 1676—yet another landmark on the road to white supremacy and capitalism in North America— thought likewise: the French settlers who revolted in Martinique thought the same way in 1665. This meant that squashing colonial competitors was seen as important by London in seeking to prevent slave revolts.[26] Since Caribbean islands were then seen as the embodiment of grand wealth, this argued further for building a grand navy, useful in squashing European rivals and revolts of the enslaved alike.

Throughout the 1640s the indigenous of the mainland, especially the Lenape and Minquas-Susquehannock of what is now called the Delaware Valley, had played the Dutch off against the Swedes, until the latter were driven out.[27] The Dutch were not unique in this regard, and settlers perpetually had to account for the prospect of confronting shrewd Africans and indigenes backed by European rivals. U.S. Founding Father George Mason reminded his fellow rebels that Cromwell sent instructions to arm the enslaved in order to smash royalist rebellion in the seventeenth century—and this could happen again in the wake of 1776.[28]

CROMWELL'S AMBITIOUS CARIBBEAN plan, denoted as the "Western Design," intended taking Hispaniola. More than this, the overall "design" was to reorganize the imperial economy around slave trading, slave labor, and state-sponsored piracy; more than 1,000 of Cromwell's forces died in just twenty days of campaigning, many in chaotic ambushes staged by freed slaves who may have heard what might befall them if republicans and merchants prevailed.[29] The Lord Protector seems to have been unduly influenced by colonial merchants like John Cotton of Massachusetts, who begged him to seize Hispaniola, and Thomas Gage, who argued passionately that existing settlements, in New England for example, could supply sufficient settlers. These merchants, still dizzy from accrued gains from the conquering of Ireland, Barbados, and Virginia, now offered to fund the ill-conceived Western Design.[30]

After this failure, the Lord Protector sent one of his closer comrades, Robert Sedgwick, a pioneer colonizer in New England and Nova Scotia, to the Caribbean. He was the son of an ardent Puritan and had crossed the Atlantic in 1635. His initial mission was to drive the Dutch out of New Netherland but that did not pan out. Cromwell's policy of pacifying Africans and indigenes perhaps was not taken seriously by intended beneficiaries, who may have been aware of the larger designs of Cromwellians, which included massive dispossession and increased enslavement. Arriving in Jamaica, Sedgwick quickly ascertained that Africans were not greeting him with sweets and candies but with bullets and other murderous projectiles. These antagonists, he contended, "must either be destroyed or brought in upon some terms or other, or else they will be a great discouragement to the settling of a people here." Both Sedgwick and Cromwell subscribed to the notion that older colonies should provide settlers for newer ones. This gave New England and Virginia a stake in Jamaica's success, just as "Gone to Texas" became a mantra after 1836 when U.S. nationals migrated to this province recently seceded from Mexico on anti-abolition grounds and 1845 when it joined the United States after proving unable to stand up to abolitionist Britain and Haiti. Resettling also allowed for the recycling of undesirables,

cutthroats, and desperados into territories where their savagery paid
bountiful dividends.

The Lord Protector once considered becoming a New Englander
himself, suggesting his closeness to this settlement. Soon Port Royal,
Jamaica, had become a pirate's lair, with the new settlers replaying the
older script of parasitically draining Spaniards and others, becoming
in the process one of the most notorious piratical societies in world
history. The town was replete with Englishmen, New Englanders,
Bermudians, Barbadians, merchants and planters, sailors and pros-
titutes, with rowdy debauchery becoming its signature. By the late
1650s, Spain thought it could make a revanchist return on the backs
of disgruntled Africans, already disappointed by the misdeeds of the
latest colonizer.[31] Validating the perception of fearful overreactions by
republicans in Jamaica was a Cromwell comrade sending to the island
vicious mastiffs used in bear baiting.[32] These fearsome canines could
just as easily be used to overawe Africans.

One eyewitness in 1655 opined that the Africans in Jamaica "dispatched" a number of Spaniards. A satisfied Cromwellian fleet sailed
on to Cuba, then Florida, as if it were eyeing coming acquisitions.[33]
From London, Thomas Gage began to swoon now that Jamaica had
placed his nation even closer to the prize that was the mainland,
auguring a further deathblow to Spanish colonialism.[34]

AFRICANS MAY NOT HAVE BEEN receptive to Spanish or
English colonizers, but as the case of Benjamin Lopez exemplified,
the Iberian Jewish community was of a different mind. Reportedly,
Jewish migrants from Flanders had Cromwell's ear and had in any
case invested in London and offered to finance his Caribbean venture
in payback against the creators of the Inquisition. This community
felt they fared better under Protestant than Catholic rule.[35]

Thus Dutch mercantile interests had sought to attract and employ
Sephardic Jewish merchants in their effort to control Brazil and
undermine the Iberians simultaneously. In April of 1655, the Lord
Protector issued a pass to Abraham de Mercado, leader of a congre-
gation in Recife (with roots in Amsterdam), and his family to travel

to Barbados from Brazil, weeks before the unraveling of Spanish rule in Jamaica. Even before then, Sephardic merchants from Hamburg and Gluckstadt, during the years of the blockade of Amsterdam, had traded tobacco from Barbados and had shipped supplies from Europe to the colony in the 1640s. It is likely that a substantial influx of this Jewish community arrived in Barbados even before the 1654 Dutch loss of Recife. In order to circumvent London's Navigation Act of 1651, meant to circumscribe Dutch shipping, the Sephardic community in England became crucial to the Barbados-Amsterdam trade. It is likely that their brethren traded alongside the Dutch in Barbados. As the island transitioned from tobacco to sugar, these investors proved to be instrumental in this process.

Benjamin Bueno de Mesquita left Recife in 1654, headed to Martinique on a Dutch vessel that was captured by the Spanish, but by 1655 he managed to make it to Jamaica, bringing his skill as a merchant, and where he was granted legal residency. His son, Joseph Bueno, departed for Manhattan where he purchased a site on the Bowery in 1682: their travels—and travails—illustrate the facileness of seeking to detach the mainland from a larger narrative about colonialism.

In any event, the Dutch were essential in the introduction of cotton and sugar into Barbados when tobacco began to wane. Again, illustrating the ineffable ties between the Caribbean and the mainland, the island's share of the tobacco market was being squeezed relentlessly by Virginia, as cotton was also declining as a profit center, making sugar's rise even more necessary. Just as the disruption of the sugar market at the beginning of the nineteenth century, given the Haitian Revolution, meant a boost for Cuba, the disruption in Brazil meant a boost for Caribbean sugar, to London's benefit. Barbados brought another reputed benefit in that, since it was an island and thus, unlike Brazil and Surinam, there were fewer opportunities for the enslaved to escape.[36] (Apparently, colonizers had not contemplated swimming skills or the ability to procure vessels or the vulnerability of small islands to internal revolt and foreign invasion as means of escape.)

At the same time, all tobacco producers were placed in a bind when the Ottoman Sultan, in the early seventeenth century, forbade the growing and consumption of tobacco, which had been delivered by English traders—a reaction to some Turks spending night and day smoking in coffeehouses. The weed was so popular that the ban had to be reiterated. By the 1650s, a man in Turkey was beheaded after being caught smoking tobacco. Thus it became difficult for investors to plan effectively for this populous market in the face of such bans.[37] This restriction was more damaging to the Chesapeake, which was tobacco territory, than the islands, which were growing rapidly as the province of sugar.

Though the introduction of sugar is routinely ascribed to those fleeing Brazil to Barbados in 1654, it is possible that this commodity arrived on the island as early as 1637, thanks to a Dutch sea captain. Even the Dutch were dependent upon the Portuguese in this context, since as early as 1620, Brazil, Lisbon, and Oporto were the major centers of the sugar trade. Then Amsterdam became the major refining center in the middle of the century, a position it held until the 1660s, when it began to retreat in the face of hammering by London and her sugar islands alike. By the end of the century, London was the king of sugar, which was a propellant flinging the English and their allies into global preeminence. Though the Jewish presence in Barbados is generally marked from 1654, there is evidence that they were present at the time of the first settlement in 1628.[38]

The year 1654 was perilous for enslaving colonizers. It was during that pivotal year that Caribs in St. Vincent launched a pan-regional assault that could have driven the French from the immediate region. Fighting alongside the indigenes were African Maroons, setting an example that would soon be emulated in Jamaica. Like those Africans who were to propel the sugar boom in Barbados and Jamaica, these fighters also may have been "exported capital" from Brazil. Fleeing for their lives were Europeans, who learned via hard experience that exploitation could arrive with a heavy price tag. Soon these Maroons were joined by their counterparts in Martinique under the fabled leadership of Francisque Fabulé, an African Spartacus of Herculean proportions. He forced the colonizers there to capitulate embarrassingly in 1665 and even joined Paris forces in fighting off the invading

English before being routed by 1671, though paving the way for victorious Africans in Hispaniola by 1791. In fact, the impact of the Maroon heritage on this island may have been the most significant of all.[39]

Thus, by 1655, the Jewish community in South America reached a fork in the road when the Dutch began to flee Recife, along with their Jewish allies. Some wound up in Jamaica and were helpful during the invasion and were repaid afterward. Just before the invasion, Rabbi Menashe Ben Israel, who had ties to both the Dutch and the Portuguese, met with the Lord Protector and walked away with a pledge that London would aid resettlement of the cleric's co-religionists in Jamaica, including some from Amsterdam. By 1720, this grateful community was an estimated 18 percent of the island's population, though special taxes were levied against them for the defense of Jamaica from foreign invasion and Maroons alike. As early as 1700, this community bore the bulk of taxes levied in Jamaica, receiving at times triple the normal level of taxes. Undeterred, they built family networks with their co-religionists in Carolina, then Georgia, trading meat in particular. On the mainland, the Jewish community of Jamaica developed close ties to North American traders, including slave traders—for example, Aaron Lopez and Jacob Rodrigues Rivera of Newport, Rhode Island, and Daniel Gomez of what became New York.

Despite their involvement in slavery and slave trading, this community was accused by their merchant Christian competitors of underhanded dealings with Africans, including selling them guns and ammunition and trafficking in stolen goods. The rebellion of the Maroons, which was to last for decades and almost toppled the London regime, was also thought to be aided by Madrid.[40]

Intriguingly, the Jewish community had fled the anti-Semitic society of the Iberian Peninsula for another society with anti-Semitism that was Jamaica, where they helped in the transition from societies with slaves to slave societies and societies with racism to racist societies. In this, they mirrored the Puritans who fled persecution in London, only to foist this plague upon Native Americans and Africans.

Though the retreat from an anti-Jewish society to a society with anti-Semitic tendencies has been ascribed to Enlightenment attitudes, there was something less elevated at play. Another factor leading to greater acceptance on the part of the European Christian population of the Caribbean to their Jewish counterparts was racial solidarity. For those increasingly described as "Barbadian whites" were acutely conscious of their status as the dominant minority in the Caribbean, particularly as the number of furious Africans grew exponentially. Europeans now routinely referred to as "whites" were a majority at the inception of colonialism but then steadily declined in Barbados to 40 percent, then to 30 percent, then far less. This, says one analyst, led to "psychoses" as a result of being a "minority in a slave society," despite "futile attempts to increase the white population." This desperate search, contrary to the views of Enlightenment scholars with their heads in the clouds, led to a lessening of anti-Semitism and more acceptance of non-English Europeans, a process driven by nervousness about the looming and intimidating presence of Africans and their indigenous comrades.[41] Correspondingly, there was no "enlightenment" for Africans since the sugar boom of the 1650s led to growth of their enslaved numbers in the Caribbean.[42]

The scholar Yda Schreuder argues that the Dutch authorities in Brazil had ordered in 1644—as a debt-fighting measure—that slaves "could only be sold for cash" and this, he says, "engaged the Jewish merchants in Brazil who, as a middleman, bought slaves at generally reduced prices in cash, since many planters had no cash on hand." Their networks in West Africa, which had begun as early as the fourteenth century when bigotry drove them from the Iberian Peninsula, gave them a further advantage, which was then brought to the Caribbean after they were expelled from Brazil.[43]

As suggested, the Iberian Jewish community was not alone in joining the gold rush opened by the seizure of Jamaica. New Englanders were probably first in line and this was not by chance. Jamaica was seized by May 10, and by September 26, London's instructions encouraged "the people of New England to remove to Jamaica in convenient numbers."[44]

As Cromwell rose, so did John Winthrop. In 1645, "one of our Shipps [*sic*]" he said, that had gone to the Canary Islands with "pipe staves" returned and, in a complex trade with Barbados and Cape Verde, the staves had become wine, sugar, salt, and tobacco—and profits.[45] Ten years later, New Englanders were flocking to Jamaica, as the mainland's then firmly established role as a satellite of the Caribbean, and a recipient of its trends, not only continued but accelerated. This stream of would-be Jamaicans included Tobias Payne, who had ties to Massachusetts but was frequently in and out of both Jamaica and Barbados.[46]

The New Englander John Cotton apparently influenced Cromwell to take Jamaica; when Spanish prisoners were deported to Cotton's vicinity it was apparent that his compatriots would benefit.[47] William Penn, who gave his name to a mainland state, was the son of the admiral who conquered Jamaica.[48]

The arrival of Spanish Catholics in Cotton's neighborhood seemed to do little to arrest anti-Catholic sentiment,[49] which Cromwell had helped generate in his plundering of Ireland. Coincidentally, just as Japan benefited in 1950 when the United States and its allies chose to invade the Korean Peninsula,[50] when London's army of 10,000 arrived in Barbados in preparation for a 1655 invasion of Jamaica, the troops were fed almost entirely with supplies regularly brought from New England for that purpose, which bolstered Boston.[51] The mainland elite was aware that gobbling territory could lead to enslaving more Africans to produce more profits, a formula applied with a vengeance after ousting London in 1776.

It would take more dedicated and implemented threats from Africans and indigenes and their foreign allies before this pandemic of abusing Africans and indigenes for malodorous profit was to retreat. With Jamaica becoming part of the nascent British Empire, indentured labor began to fade and enslavement of Africans rose accordingly.

The teleological conceit that detaches the Caribbean from the mainland, à la 1776, is not useful in understanding what was going on in the mid-seventeenth century.[52] By 1656 the authorities in

Massachusetts were discussing intently "transplanting of persons to Jamaica."[53] By then, racial lines in Boston were being demarcated more sharply, for at the time of the Jamaica debate the edict was enunciated that no Africans or indigenes were to be allowed to join the militia. However, this time, and unlike previously, Scots maintained their access to this important right.[54] Though it had been thought that the Pequot had been routed and dispersed to the four corners of the planet, even as Cromwell was rising, the settlers found that they "grew to an excess of violence and outrage."[55]

Still, it was with good reason that Cromwellians were gloating in 1656, boasting, albeit a tad prematurely, about "the conquest of Scotland" and "the reducing of Ireland," that is, its subjugation; and then there was the "reducing" of royalists in the "Carybe [Caribbean] islands."[56]

The slave traders responsible for dumping Africans in Jamaica and Barbados often had ties to Boston and the emerging city of Baltimore. For various reasons—oversupply driven by dreams of what Jamaica might deliver, for example—the price of this valuable commodity was dropping, which was an encouragement to manacle even more. During the second half of the seventeenth century, slave prices were substantially lower than in the late fifteenth and early sixteenth centuries. In a related trend, the 1640s and Cromwell's ascension marked a sharp increase in the sale of English—and Dutch—ships then arriving aplenty in West Africa with more textiles to trade, fueling Manchester and Bristol.[57]

But it was not just England that was beginning to boom. George Lambertson was one of the ten richest men in New Haven during this conflicted era. He was truly an Atlantic entrepreneur, like so many of his counterparts, dabbling in West African trade and gold and elephants' teeth—a derivative of the trade in Africans that drove settler colonialism in the Americas. The depredations created much wealth for him at home.[58]

Ominously for Africans, in 1662 the restored monarch in London concluded a pact with Tunis concerning the bondage of Europeans. Included was the telling phrase that if North Africans seized any ship, "any Englishman serving for wages . . . are to be made slaves, but if merchants or passengers, they are to enjoy their liberty and goods free and entire." Class privilege was to be the signal trend of the onrushing era, and it was being sanctified even as class degradation of West Africans was similarly skyrocketing. That this provision was confirmed and renewed in 1675 suggests that this also gave added leverage for merchants and aristocrats (and at times aristocratic merchants) to negotiate on behalf of those "serving for wages," hence solidifying their developing alliance grounded in "whiteness."[59]

By 1683, with the Ottoman Turks halted at the gates of Vienna, the "threat" began a steady decline, which freed merchants and their grateful workers by wage to focus more on enchaining West Africans. However, this "threat" continued to reverberate since London tended to conflate Muslims and Native Americans, to the detriment of the latter. These were the two major non-Christian peoples (Africans set to one side) that those from England and its closest neighbors interacted with most widely.[60]

Perhaps not coincidentally, it was also in 1662, as the pact with Tunis was inked, that the Company of Royal Adventurers of England, the local masters of the African Slave Trade, solicited further investment in anticipation of a profit boom. The investors included merchants, royals, and politicians, with these roles sometimes combined in one person. Investment was also opened to the public at large, supposedly giving ordinary subjects a chance to hitch a ride aboard a gravy train that was to accumulate eye-popping profits of 1,700 percent return on investment, while feeding ancillary industries such as shipbuilding, insurance companies, and banking, with the lush profits provided by sugar, then feeding tea and coffee production, being the end reward. All, it was said, were "very sensible," given "how necessary it is that the English plantations in America should have a competent and a constant supply" of enslaved Africans.[61]

It was also in 1662 that the Virginia authorities ossified the status of enslaved Africans by defining slavery based on the condition of the mother, guaranteeing enslavement for the progeny of these women.[62]

The worsening of the conditions of Africans in North America could be marked from this juncture.

This ironic juxtaposition, seeking to reduce bondage of European Christians and hastening that of West Africans, was linked quite cruelly. The grateful former could then be invited to become the overseers of the furious latter on Caribbean and mainland settlements, which was a recipe for continuous brutality and volatility.

Days before the Royal Adventurers made their stock offering, the King issued a proclamation "for the encouraging of Planters in His Majesties Island of Jamaica in the West Indies." Generously, the proclamation stated that "thirty acres of improveable lands shall be granted and allotted to every such person, male or female, being twelve years old or upwards." If history was any guide, New Englanders would be heading to the Caribbean sooner rather than later to grab a grubstake—though few might be teenagers or "female." Like a carrot dangling in front of the burro as the beast pulled the cart along, this luminous prospect of becoming a landowner could be enough for the deprived to continue support of colonialism and enslavement, even if its luxuriant abundance was never quite delivered.

Of course, it was not just mainlanders who were hastening to the new El Dorado that was Jamaica. Just before its taking, Cromwell's forces were involved in a "great and terrible fight" that was quite "bloody" in Barbados. "The reducing of the Wild Scots," it was lamented, would "prove a work of great difficulty."[63] Pent-up tensions could now be released by shipping the wildest of them all to Jamaica, as this sizable island emerged as a safety valve, where opponents could be dumped and compelled to subdue unruly Africans and Maroons. From 1660 to 1667, 10,000 mainly landless freemen and small farmers left Barbados; and from 1668 to 1672, 5,000 more; and from 1678 to 1682, 2,000 more. They were not only heading to Jamaica but also to South Carolina, which was a de facto neo-colony of Barbados. Some moved to Pennsylvania, as Quakers were prominent in both places. Some wound up in Rhode Island, since during this era the two sites were exceedingly close and there had been a constant flow from island to mainland and vice versa. Naturally, Barbados's trade with its partner in enslavement, Virginia, was considerable, and some islanders moved there, too. However, in a sense, what made this flux possible was the seizure of Jamaica, which caused a reshuffling of the deck, an opportunity for more gain derived from slavery that then sent ripples from the Caribbean to the mainland.[64]

The problem for colonizers was that it was not as if the bonded laborers were cooperating with the changes. Civil wars and repression had produced a bountiful labor supply for the Caribbean but such a policy had an upper limit, as London ran the risk of depriving the homeland of labor in order to build the settlements. Enchaining Africans, despite their demonstrated ability to rebel, seemed to be the "least bad" option. But every year the African population was increasing as the European was diminishing, increasing fear and instability alike. Intensified repression of Africans, along with sharpening "racial" difference was a response, along with Europeans beginning to flee to the mainland, bringing with them their well-developed hostility to enslaved Africans.

Moreover, of the thousands who invaded Jamaica, about 5,000 died early on, and though some 230,000 Europeans came to Barbados, Jamaica, and the Leeward Islands during the seventeenth century, their combined population rose only from 34,000 in the 1650s to 40,000 in the 1690s. The civil wars which riveted London and its environs led to the premature death of perhaps 500,000 there, adding to a looming demographic debacle in the Caribbean, as the African population surged.[65]

The mainland, the ostensible source of many Caribbean settlers, was hardly in a position to comply, and not just because of the ongoing threat of being overrun by indigenes, Africans, or both. It was after the taking of Jamaica that Cromwell had to intervene to "forbid any force or violence" as mostly Protestant Virginia continued to squabble with heavily Catholic Maryland.[66] Many Irishmen were involved in the invasion of Jamaica and stood to profit as a result, but Spain's appeal and Cromwell's inveterate anti-Catholicism stood as a formidable barrier to converting Irishmen into tame Caribbean settlers.[67] One way to make up for the shortfall was the acceleration of the convenient category that was "whiteness," which was ongoing in any event, that is, inviting more Dutch and other Europeans to swear allegiance to London.

Something had to be done, since the Africans were not necessarily complying with the doomsday that awaited so many of them. Thus the same year that Jamaica was taken the authorities in Barbados found it necessary to craft "an act for the prevention of firing of sugarcanes." "Forty lashes upon his naked back" and being "branded on the forehead with a hot iron with the letter R" was the prescribed remedy.[68] A few years later the authorities decided to impose penalties for those who "shall lay violent hands upon his or her Master, Mistress or Overseer or any person put over them in authority to govern them." Included were detailed provisions to punish and restrain runaway slaves.[69] However, settlers did not have many choices. In early 1661 a settler sought a "permit to export a crazy Negro to Virginia," who was "sometimes not in his right mind." Of course, those who chose not to cooperate with enslavement could be thought to be crazy, but this semantic confusion did not dilute the imbroglio.[70]

The taking of Jamaica reflected London's rising strength and Madrid's decline. The coup also benefited mainland settlers in terms of opportunity for all classes among this group, be it migration or trade, including the commerce in Africans. However, even when inviting other Europeans to join the project—as happened at the inception of Barbados in 1628—it remained true that there were simply not enough people in the Pan-European community willing to venture into the war zone that was the Americas. This created pressure for a broader base for the colonial project, boosting republicanism, anti-monarchism (as signaled by Cromwell), the emerging category of "whiteness," the concomitant devaluing of Africans and indigenes and, not least, the process of launching capitalism.

CHAPTER 5

The Dutch Ousted from the Mainland:
Slavery and the Slave Trade Expand

The taking of Jamaica was transformative for the fortunes of settler colonialism and disastrous for Africans and indigenes alike. It took place as the sugar boom was launched, enriching colonizers as it doomed Africans to deadly toil. It provided a model for mainlanders, which they pursued vigorously well into the nineteenth century, ousting indigenes from the land while stocking it with enslaved Africans in order to generate immense wealth. This nasty enrichment contributed to a hastening of formation of racial lines of demarcation encapsulated in the militarized identity politics that was "whiteness." It provided a foundation for the takeoff of capitalism. And it motivated London to deliver a knockout blow to the Dutch, driving them from Manhattan in 1664, and eventually from the lucrative trade in enslaved Africans, which provided a model for their brethren in 1776 when Britain was knocked out by rebels, and then limped toward abolitionism. Just as the English fattened the Dutch for slaughter—in the guise of aiding their battle against Madrid—London in retrospect seized land from North American indigenes that was then used to bolster revolting republicans in 1776, who then began to surpass the British Empire in succeeding decades.

After decades of savage struggle among colonizers, London was emerging triumphant. London was more flexible than Madrid in accepting a Jewish community and more accepting than Paris in embracing fleeing Huguenots. But more than that, by being ferocious in enslaving Africans and seizing the land of the indigenous of North America, it accumulated capital that guaranteed its rise to unparalleled heights in science, which was parlayed into further attainments. Jamaica was essential to this bloody scramble.[1]

For our purposes, consider that the enslaved population of Barbados rose from an estimated 12,800 to 50,000 between 1661 and 1700, while Jamaica's rose from an estimated 500 to 42,000 during this same period.[2] Barbadians had for decades been a prime customer of Dutch slave traders: from 1638 to about 1665, most of the Africans shipped to what was rapidly becoming London's richest colony were borne on Dutch ships. Yet now, with the opportunity opened for enslavement by Manhattan and Jamaica, most of the Africans to be delivered there and Barbados and the Leeward Islands were coming on English ships at the rate of thousands per year. Gobbling a rising share in the remunerative market in slaves allowed London to leapfrog and secure a foothold in the slave trade to French settlements in Martinique and Guadeloupe, meaning more taxes accrued, more buttressing of the Royal Navy—and even more Africans dragged from the continent. Then, with disturbances increasing along Africa's coastlines due to the transition to English supremacy in the slave trade, Spanish colonies were forced to look to traders from Liverpool and Bristol to supply them too, as the Dutch sailed off into the sunset.[3]

However, the Dutch outpost at the southern tip of Africa remained an essential link in the enslaving chain. In 1664 an English slaver sailing from Madagascar to Barbados stopped at Cape Town to negotiate with fellow Europeans about other potential sites to buy human flesh. A few years later, showing they had not abandoned the field altogether, the Dutch temporarily ousted the English from nearby St. Helena Island, then seized a slave ship en route from Mozambique and Madagascar to Barbados, demonstrating that it would be shortsighted to altogether ignore that small European nation.[4]

The Dutch did not surrender market share willingly. But they were swimming against a high tide. Yes, they picked on an even smaller Portugal and ousted this overweening nation from its stronghold in Angola,[5] a prime site for enslaving, which complemented the companion seizure of Recife, Brazil. But when Portugal made a swift comeback in both,[6] this should have been a giveaway that competing in the high-stakes game of colonialism and enslavement may not have been the Dutch strong suit.

Nonetheless, English slave traders in Africa complained bitterly that these unscrupulous competitors "have set natives upon us" and "shot at our flag," with little long-term awareness of the downstream racial effects. Hopping mad, this only encouraged London and the increasingly important class of merchants and traders to be even more inclined to wage war against the Dutch. Many in this class were swimming in success in light of the restoration of the monarchy in 1660, after Cromwell died. They were or at least pretended to be solidly Anglican Royalist and thus were willing to display their belligerent colors.[7]

The Africans were similarly bellicose, if not more so, which added to the overall combustibility. Those arriving in the area stretching from Boston to New Haven, then Manhattan, were sometimes multilingual, giving them an ability to dicker with Dutch and English alike to the detriment of both. At times they had ties to the Persian Gulf and Madagascar, making them more cosmopolitan and sophisticated than their often unlettered, monolingual captors. It was during this time that Massachusetts passed a law specifically targeting arson, as Africans were well aware of the destructive impact of fire.[8]

With the loss of New Netherland[9] and the complementary assault absorbed by the Dutch in West Africa, London attained a kind of vertical integration, creating a supply chain that reached from Africa to the Caribbean, producing commodities then sold in Europe and elsewhere.[10] The wealth—of some—in London rose accordingly, along with the ire of the enslaved. Eventually this was to impel settlers, notably in Barbados, to repair to Carolina, serving to ignite events that were to culminate in secession in 1776.

Correspondingly, there were an estimated 300 Africans in Maryland in 1650, 758 in 1660, and 1,190 in 1670 (about 9 percent of the population), with the trend line continuing upward in succeeding decades. By 1670, Virginia's African population had soared to 2,000. Most, if not all, had arrived to these two future states not directly from Africa but from the Caribbean, underscoring the unavoidable links between the mainland and the islands. Nevertheless, the status of Africans had yet to be frozen, and like Anthony Johnson, the Angolan who became a landowner in this region, some had managed to escape perpetual servitude. However, as London felt the need to downplay indentured servitude, as the hunger for profit gripped the imagination, and as competitors like Spain and the Netherlands were knocked down like tenpins, the equivalence of "African" and "slave" began to ossify.[11] That is, the foundation for capitalism was laid as racial slavery was hardened.

After Cromwell expired, his ambitious "Western Design"[12] was only partially fulfilled, at a high cost in fatalities and with Ireland bleeding and prostrate. His complicated legacy included bruised feelings in Ireland, which was to vex London's foreign and domestic policies for years to come. Even as he was departing the scene, certain Londoners were braying about the "subjection of all traytors" because of the "massacre of the Protestant English" in Ireland.[13] (Just as at the inception of the United States, the lineal descendant of London, a towering problem was created by the idea that difficulties for the Republic meant opportunities for the enslaved and indigenes, difficulty for England would mean opportunity for Ireland.)

By then, the "inhumane and barbarous sufferings of the people called Quakers in the City of Bristol" was at issue,[14] which had the colonial benefit of forcing some from this group to migrate to Barbados and the mainland, shoring up besieged settlements.

Cromwell's cutthroat record had created antagonists as it was precipitating the wealth of empowered merchants. By 1660 there had been a royal restoration of the monarch, Charles II. In 1640 in Lisbon, then a city of 175,000, about forty noblemen with about 100 followers were able to engineer a coup. Two decades later, George

Monck entered London, a city of perhaps 250,000 inhabitants, with fewer than 6,000 soldiers. Exhausted after a 350-mile march in winter from the Scottish border, they were able to set in motion a termination of the republican experiment—perhaps forever.[15]

Royalists had learned their lesson and, in some ways, their pushing for, and engaging in, the rocketing realm of slave trading and territorial aggrandizement kept merchants as a discrete class occupied, so busy counting their pounds they could find little time for regime change. Besides, some royalists had lost prestige during the Cromwell era, and new vistas in the Americas helped them to regain lost ground—at times, literally—and reduce their dependence on Parliament, viewed as a Cromwellian holdover.[16]

Regicides continued to hole up in New England, particularly New Haven, escaping potential wrath from royalists and helping to solidify a separate North American identity that blossomed in 1776.[17]

After 1655, London's rule in Jamaica was not consolidated fully. After the seizure of Jamaica, the Lord Protector considered moving New Englanders around as if they were pieces on a chessboard, a kind of high-handedness that helped as well to fuel a distinct identity by 1776. They should "people Ireland," it was thought at first, after that nation had been depopulated through massacre and dispersal. Or maybe their "bettering" would involve residing in Jamaica: It did not seem to matter if settlers had sunk roots in Boston, when a high-handed London requested—or demanded—they move to a boisterous Jamaica.[18]

Emoluments and enticements of various sorts continued to be offered—land in the first instance. However, putative settlers were also told bluntly that they would be expected to "serve in arms upon any insurrection, mutiny or foreign invasion," which was a sign of the unpredictability of this latest acquisition.[19]

By mid-1660 the Royal Navy was instructed that in Jamaica Spaniards had been "beaten off, not one left in the island, and no enemy but thirty or forty Negroes who were in rebellion with the Spaniards."[20] Shortly thereafter, as the situation was apparently calming, the Earl of Marlborough was again mulling over proposals designed to "encourage all willing to transplant themselves to Jamaica," which meant "hasten the settlement of New England affairs, from whence [a] good store of men may be expected." Jamaica should become "the staple for the sale of blacks," and the "Negroes to be delivered to the island" should become a regional center for distribution. To facilitate the arrival of settlers, "religious toleration" was "to be granted to all who desire it," and to curb complicating miscegenation, London should "send over women for planters' wives." The former, in particular, was to receive plaudits from students of the Enlightenment who confused a measure designed to gain an adequate racial supply with intentional avant-garde thinking.[21]

From 1660 to 1688 there was over a 1,000-ton increase in the capacity of the Royal Navy, with the average size of ships growing by 40 percent.[22] These vessels received a workout in the Atlantic, helping to ensure that Africans would continue to be enslaved and Native Americans dispossessed.

From the taking of Jamaica to 1700, the value of imports from the Caribbean and North America, primarily sugar and tobacco, roughly doubled,[23] which whetted the appetite for the methods that had delivered this wealth: dispossession and enslavement. By mid-1659 instructions were dispatched to the "Guinea Coast" with a request "to procure tenn Negroes [,] men and women, such as are lusty and of the younger sort,"[24] a non-gendered demand thereafter was "procure 12 Lusty young Negroes."[25] But London was still annoyed by the presence of competitors: the "troublesome . . . seas" in the region were "infested with Spanish men-of-war,"[26] while "Danes" and "Dutch" continued to lurk, too.[27] Methodically, as the Dutch were being driven from the field, more attention was turned to the older antagonist that was Spain.[28]

Continued hand-wringing about African intentions were refracted in the blinding light brought by a "fire at Cape Coast" that generated substantial losses.[29] As arson took hold as a major tool of slave resistance, similar fires broke out continually in Barbados.[30] Soon an uprising flared in Gambia: "31 or 32 of the English were slain," it was reported balefully, "and about 40 Negroes and the rest ran away," as the would-be slaves "rebelled and possessed themselves" of territory theretofore claimed by London.[31]

With the taking of Jamaica, and the companion desire to chain more Africans, came ever fiercer resistance and a devolving dislike of the prospective human property in what amounted to a deathly spiral downward. One conflict, occurring as Gambia was being bloodied, involved "intolerable pain" inflicted upon the potential captor "in a barbarous manner," said an Englishman; the Africans "cut off pieces of his flesh from his buttocks, thighs, arms and shoulders," while "during this time," the tables were turned and the hunter became "a slave." Still, the writer was seemingly undeterred by this ghastly episode, speaking dreamily of future conquests at the Cape, Madagascar, even Persia and South Asia, all linked to London via the potent Royal Navy.

Meanwhile, across the Atlantic in Barbados in the 1660s ambivalence grew about the rising number of Africans, while the Irish, derided by the Negroes as "white" slaves, were in ill humor (perhaps incentives could be granted them to improve their mood). Many Europeans who were capable of doing so were fleeing to the mainland, providing added reason to bring benefits to those remaining. "There are many thousands of slaves that speak English," it was added worriedly by officialdom and "if there are many leading men slaves in a Plantation, they may be easily wrought upon to betray it, especially on the promise of a freedom" by potential invaders. A true "whiteness" had yet to assert itself forcefully as it was added, "the Jews, not having like liberty as in the Dutch and French islands, have been very treacherous."[32] Thus there were persistent calls and petitions for more aid to slave trading as the importance of this commerce was seen as bolstering shipbuilding, export of goods, import of goods, and the economy as a whole.[33]

William Blathwayt, from a Protestant merchant clan in England, served as an administrator in the settlements; promoting the slave trade was one of his specialties. As if it were a model statute, he filed away a bill from Barbados from 1661 calling for the "better ordering and governing of Negroes." Stated starkly was the notion that "if any Negro either man or woman shall offer any violence to any Christian"—not "white" person, a designation soon to come—"by striking or the like, such Negro shall for his or her first offence" be "severely whipped." If it persists, "his nose" was to be "slit and be burned in some part of his face." Planters, he lamented, "have much suffered by the running away of their Negroes" and more unsparing measures had to be imposed.[34]

Ill-humored Europeans continued to be shipped to Barbados, and placing them among conspiring Africans was hardly a prescription for stability. Ultimately, Europeans began moving en masse to South Carolina in the context of phasing out indentured labor and seeking to assuage these landless men, notably after Bacon's Rebellion in 1676. But before then there was gnashing of teeth about the "lives" of European laborers becoming "as cheap as those Negroes." Planters tended to "look upon them"—meaning poorer Europeans—"as their goods [and] horses" and "rack them only to make their time out of them and cherish them to perform their work." Surely revaluing these workers' lives upward through a heavy dose of "whiteness" could allay this looming problem. Already, Thomas Burton, a comrade of Cromwell and the ineffectual son Richard who sought to replace him, knew that those who "is the Cavalier" or royalist "today, may be the Roundhead a year hence." So, why not leave wretched Christian status behind and "today" assume privileged racial status? "Two or three thousand Protestants were sent to the Barbadoes against their consent," Burton said in 1659[35] and something must be done—soon.

AFTER THE TAKING OF JAMAICA, which delivered a felt need to escalate enslavement, settlers descended upon Africa with steely determination. Charles II was restored to the throne in 1660 and realized that joining the surging merchants made more sense than seeking to defeat them, as the Company of Royal Adventurers (CRA) was given the sole right to trade in Africa from Gibraltar to the Cape of Good Hope. By 1664 Englishmen were attacking slave forts of European competitors in West Africa, as the Dutch were ousted from their foothold along the Gold Coast.[36] In 1637 the Dutch expelled the

Portuguese from near El Mina, and Lisbon's power in the vicinity began to disintegrate, and now the Netherlands was victimized.[37]

Since the fifteenth century, European merchants had sought the source of the famous gold of Guinea, from which the English coin of the same name was minted, an adjunct of the hunt for African bodies that dwarfed previous efforts. In 1662, the Company of Royal Adventurers, the chief slave traders, descended with force on Africa: they would be supplanted by London's Royal African Company a decade later, whose position was then eroded by deregulation of this ugly commerce in 1688, a major and historic victory for the merchants, whose bet in favor of Cromwell decades earlier had finally paid off spectacularly.[38]

The prelude to these transformative events occurred in the midst of a seemingly ceaseless series of Anglo-Dutch wars, which included not only attacking at the source of labor supply in Africa but looting numerous Negroes from Dutch slave owners on the mainland, notably the Delaware Valley, as a prelude to the assault on Manhattan.[39] These conflicts also exposed the dangerous reliance of European colonizers upon Africans, even considering the wealth brought by their enslavement. The French and their Dutch allies armed the enslaved with torches to devastate the plantations of the English in the island of Saint-Christophe.[40] Ultimately, the Africans of Hispaniola would emulate this trend in 1791 with disastrous consequences for enslavers.

SIX YEARS AFTER THE TAKEOVER, Jamaica was reeling with complaints about the indentured who "lay violent hands upon their masters" and would have their terms extended "two years." There was a related problem reflected in discussions at the highest level, that is, "intelligence" doled out to the "prejudice of this island" by way of labor visiting arriving vessels.[41] Do not "entertain any bought servant or slave . . . above one night" in a "house or plantation" was the admonition.[42] "Many great mischiefs," it was warned, arise from "wandering of servants and slaves on Sundays and Saturdays in the afternoon and other days." European labor may have had an advantage in that there were "great complaints made of servants running away from their masters and mistresses and the same are received and concealed by others,"[43] but concealing Africans was a mite more difficult. This was no minor matter since the administration was still battling "subjects of the King of Spain" and was worrying revenge would "awaken," meaning more "fortifications," meaning more taxes, meaning more aggrieved laborers seeking allies.[44]

By early 1662 it was announced that a fearsome group of Maroons had "voluntarily submitted to the English Government" and that "all the Free Negroes shall be in the same state and freedom as the English enjoy, and for every head being eighteen years old receive thirty acres of improvable land" that would include "their heirs for ever." The trade-off was that since the regime had purportedly "changed from a military to a civil form" that their leader's "commission as Governor of the Negroes" was to be "terminated" and instead he would be denoted as "Colonel of the Black Regiment." The Maroons' autonomy would include the ability to "determine all ordinary matters amongst the Negroes but all cases of great consequences and also of life and death shall be decided by the English." These rambunctious Africans were ordered to "bring up their children to the English Tongue"—which would carry the added benefit of allowing the regime to monitor conversations more easily. Accept this deal, said the regime with misplaced effrontery, or be "proceeded against as outlaws and traitors." The Maroons picked up the cast-down gauntlet and tossed it at the governor.[45] A chastened regime then decided to send a delegation to confer with the "Negroes," along with an "interpreter," suggesting that the demand concerning the "English Tongue" had not taken hold.[46] Apparently the meeting did not go well, since months later "several parties were sent out against the Rebellious Negroes."[47] That did not squash the insurgents, either, for now the "Negroes" had "begun to rob and kill," as "this island [was] put in a posture of War."

Throughout the 1660s the island was aflame. "Of late," there was a murder by "Negroes," not to mention "mutinies and insurrections or other mischiefs" too numerous to note. The remedy? "Such Negro or Negroes offending [are] to be sold or sent off this island,"[48] that is, export the problem to the mainland or Antigua or Barbados. The same day in October 1663, "several Servants and Slaves" had "made their escapes and run away." The remedy? "Every night chain and fasten their boats."[49]

It was not just diehard Spaniards and local "Servants and Slaves" who were bedeviling the Jamaican elite. "Certain runaway Blacks from Barbados" had been "arriving on the north side of this island" and then "committed divers[e] insolences on the planters," including "felonies and burglaries." A posse should be assembled forthwith and "in case of resistance" the message was explicit: "Slay and kill the said slaves," and if taken alive they should belong to the apprehenders "and their heirs for ever, to be sold and transported to foreign parts."[50] As the system of labor exploitation continued to evolve, slavery for life would become the destiny of too many Africans in the region— including the mainland, where many of these rebels wound up.

Memories had not faded in Jamaica of how during the 1655 invasion Africans had helped to overthrow Spanish rule. Now London's delegates seemed to be the target. Shortly after the island was taken, Cromwell was informed that "one or two Negroes make 500 Englishmen fling down their arms and run away," which was not reassuring to settlers. Pirates were hired to hunt down Africans, but these men were notoriously unprincipled and could easily turn on their paymasters if offered a larger paycheck. When hundreds arrived from New England as settlers, it was unclear if they were aware of the danger zone they had entered.[51]

The example of Maroons running free in the hills was not helpful in convincing enslaved Africans—or servants for that matter—to obey their oppressors. Months after the taking of Manhattan, which led to a new era of English and then U.S. supremacy, a harried official Jamaica was still battling "Rebellious Negroes" who tended to "beguile many Hunters and commit many murders" in ways "so contemptible and base." The "perfidious villainies," these "sneaking and treacherous rogues" who perpetrated same, were running wild. A reward was offered for their apprehension with potential captors being able to "have and enjoy to their uses, all the women and children and all the plunder they can find" in their "Palenque," or stockade, "for their pleasure.[52] Cruising in Jamaica's waters were "French and Dutch buccaneers" who would be more than willing to accept this reward— or, for that matter, ally with the rebels and wound the regime; since there was also fretting about "English . . . buccaneers,"[53] a premonition of the following century when mainlanders would advance their novel interpretation of patriotism in 1776 was already manifesting.

Little did London know that the revolt of the Maroons, which started with the conquest, would continue for more than half a century, conservatively speaking. As rumors spread that the rebels were receiving arms and ammunition not only from the Spaniards but from their erstwhile opponents, the Jewish community in Jamaica, the prospect materialized that London would suffer the fate that had befallen Madrid.[54]

RETROSPECTIVELY, THE TAKING of New Netherland was of world historic significance. It delivered a staggering blow to Dutch pretensions, as this small nation was ultimately compelled to seek an entente with its larger neighbor. It gave London control of a major site for the arrival of enslaved Africans, expanding mainland capacity and wealth. In the long term, this future metropolis of New York City became the lodestar of capital infusion that catapulted England, then the inheritor—the United States—into the vanguard of capitalism itself. More than this, New Netherland included large swathes of what became New Jersey, New York State, Delaware, and Connecticut, with outposts extending into Rhode Island.[55] This opened vast opportunities for existing nearby settlements including Massachusetts, Barbados, and Jamaica, providing a safety valve whereby indentured and poorer Europeans could be deployed. It also meant the deployment of more enslaved Africans, with all the wealth they routinely delivered. It also led to a sharper demarcation of racial boundaries.

Coming slowly into view, like a film dissolve, not a snapshot, was an identity politics of "whiteness" that has persisted stubbornly into the twenty-first century.

Challenges remained for London, however, a reality that became evident a few years after losing Manhattan, when the Dutch launched a devastating attack on Virginia, as charges flew that they were simultaneously selling arms to indigenes for a similar purpose.[56] Still, the Royal Navy softened the Dutch with repetitive blows of their own, for example, when in 1663 a Dutch slave ship headed from Angola to Curaçao was attacked, in an assault joined by the Portuguese.[57] This conflict continued in 1664.[58]

Instability was the watchword in this sector of North America. Over a span of decades during the seventeenth century, no fewer than ten different colonial regimes asserted their authority in North America, just south of Manhattan.[59] Loss came with a steep price. For example, there were reports that after the conquest of New Netherland in 1664, the victors sold some of the defeated into slavery in the Caribbean.[60]

The Dutch and the English were like two ships passing in the night. The Netherlands had advanced notoriously by welcoming dissident Protestants such as Puritans, as well as members of the Iberian Jewish community. But in 1654 a boatload of the latter group, fleeing Recife, were turned away in New Netherland by Peter Stuyvesant, who thought that acceptance would create a precedent to be employed on behalf of "Lutherans and Papists."[61] (Some apparently did arrive shortly thereafter.)[62] London did not have a reputation for being as tolerant,[63] but, ironically, began to open its doors wide in the Caribbean to those abandoning Recife, and, with even more irony, Stuyvesant himself arrived in Barbados in 1655.[64] Indicative of the perceived value of the Pan-Caribbean basin, London for a while was considering taking Surinam,[65] not New Netherland.

Relations between the English and Scots were still complicated. Hence, many of the latter were moving to New Amsterdam as early as 1660, which was generating complaints but may have caused those complained against to seek succor from London, bringing English and Scots together.[66]

The Netherlands may have been dazed by the losses it had suffered, shrinking their capacious global ambitions. Between the beginning of the seventeenth century and the Treaty of Breda in 1667, which concluded yet another Anglo-Dutch war and marked a milestone in diplomacy, only one year (1610) saw peace between the leading European states, with Holland often in the middle of the fray, bleeding profusely.[67]

The Netherlands' retreat from the mountaintop was not sure-footed. After they surrendered Recife, the Dutch sought to compensate by converting New Amsterdam into a major slave port. By 1660 this North American settlement had the largest population of urban slaves on the continent, which would soon prove to be a useful complement to Jamaica and Barbados.[68] A catalyst for the taking of this colony by London was the contemporaneous bludgeoning of Dutch interests in the fountainhead of the all-important labor supply: West Africa. Like dominoes falling, Jamaica meant battering competitors in Africa, which provided incentive to take Manhattan.[69]

Weakening Dutch rule and helping to make a London capture possible was indigenous rebelliousness. Indigenes did not accept the thesis propounded by future "radicals" in North America that their ouster from their land was a step forward for humanity. Coastal indigenes, including the Narragansett people, whom London feared, found the Dutch colony of New Netherland more to their liking than, say, Massachusetts Bay. In 1653 it was feared that this ethnic group, allied with the Niantic people, were planning a joint attack with the Dutch against their mutual antagonist: London's settlements.[70] This obstreperousness was rising,[71] as the Cromwell coalition was moving upward, too, providing a hint that New Netherland could soon undergo more than a name change. Just as London was vanquishing Spain in Jamaica in 1655, indigenes seemed to be on the verge of doing the same in what is now Yonkers, New York.[72]

Between 1649 and 1655 this recalcitrance reached a zenith. The clash was to leave not a single settler immediately west of the Hudson River. Peter Stuyvesant, the final Dutch director-general of the colony, sought to provide every farmhouse with guards to protect against arson, but this relatively tiny nation hardly had the troops to do so, particularly when the Malay Peninsula and even Surinam, which the Netherlands preferred to New Netherland, had yet to be wholly subdued. A false dawn was the settlement of what became Bergen

County, New Jersey, in November 1660, but this area too came under assault by unfriendly indigenes.[73]

The Dutch experience—and loss—of New Netherland illustrated the overreach that was inevitable when small nations sought to gorge on large overseas territories. One of the reasons for the importation of enslaved African labor was because Dutch farm servants were difficult to recruit and those who came often departed for the rosier opportunities brought by the fur trade. For the funds spent on hiring one European laborer to work approximately forty days, an African—at times—could be purchased for life.[74] With the arrival of Africans, the problem was that shipboard insurrections and conspiring with indigenes and other European powers happened en route, as well as arson and throats slit in the middle of the night, poisoning, and murder. Eventually, post-1776, the republicans would demonstrate that rather than relying upon a small reservoir of an ethnicity, the base of support for settler colonialism should be shifted to "race," allowing for dipping into a vast pool of emigrants stretching from the Atlantic to the Ural Mountains.

This provided a substantial population of Europeans, which by 2017 totaled about 250 million, larger than the populations of Germany, Britain, France, and a number of other Continental nations combined, dwarfing the population of Russia. The migration of settlers from diverse European nations not only denuded potential rivals of hard workers but provided influence for the North Americans in the departed homelands. This accumulation of the grateful were delighted to escape the barbarity and poverty of their homelands, not least because they were then accorded certain rights and privileges that post-1776 meant that too many were mute in the face of the further dispossession of indigenes and the further escalation of the slave trade.

With the takeover, Manhattan and its environs quickly developed one of the largest populations of enslaved Africans in North America, which created wealth and insecurity alike.[75] Between the takeover and 1698, the African population of what was to become New York City doubled,[76] and their oppression might have risen at a higher multiple.

Despite the departure of Stuyvesant, there was a perception that the role of the Jewish community declined with the takeover. This was possible, but the articulator of this sentiment, historian Jonathan Israel, also contends that the Jewish community in London imported a significant portion of England's sugar from the Caribbean—on the rise since the taking of Jamaica and bound to increase after 1664.[77] Linda Briggs Biemer says the role of women of all categories declined too after 1664.[78]

Yet there is little dispute that the role of Africans increased in what had been New Netherland post-1664, along with their misery. There may be a connection between this and the catastrophic events that unwound in London during this time. For it was then that the metropolis was beset by a catastrophic plague that decimated the population, enhancing further the value of enslaved labor.[79]

As Africans were wrenched, London sought, at least temporarily, to tamp down tensions with European rivals. Like a conductor revving up the woodwinds as the percussion was lightened, London in the 1660s negotiated a calming "Treaty of Peace, Commerce and Alliance" with Spain,[80] which would amount to a temporary respite before reloading. Still, it was a display of diplomatic deftness that helped to propel the British Isles to the forefront, insofar as it tended to checkmate Madrid's relationship with what one Londoner called "The House of Austria."[81] Keener observers might have deduced that détente with Madrid would remain problematic as long as Protestant-Catholic strain persisted.[82] Nevertheless, there had been a Pan-European tendency as well, which the settlement of Barbados in 1628 exemplified, and this was a precursor of the emerging identity that was "whiteness." It acted as a solvent that tended to blur sectarian difference in pursuit of the larger goal of ransacking the Americas, then Africa, then Asia.

Thus this "Treaty of Peace" was followed quickly by a similar pact with Paris, which sought, among other things, to curb contestation in the Caribbean over Antigua, Montserrat, and St. Kitts. These contestations had allowed "slaves and servants" to manipulate one power against another, but now these purported miscreants could

be "return[ed] to their masters if not sold" when caught after perpetrating sedition.[83] A now battered Netherlands was forced to accept
an imposed peace; again the key provision of the treaty ordered that
"rebels and fugitives [were] not to be received" and nor were they to
be armed or transported; instead, they should be "banished."[84]

Most definitely this stilted verbiage meant labor's strength would be
curbed, as the process of enslavement went into overdrive. However,
astute leaders of labor familiar with even recent history could bank on
painful quarrels once again flashing between and among the European
powers as they jousted for control of the rich bounty of slaves, territory,
and the wealth they produced. Nonetheless, astute leaders of enslaved
labor may have noticed the ongoing trend of phasing out indentured
European labor, which effectively converted some past erstwhile allies
into future foes. For there was a gnawing realization in London that
continuing reliance on indentures could ultimately denude the domestic labor supply, and since so many of these workers were disgruntled
Irish in any case, sending them to the Caribbean was akin to sending
allies of His Catholic Majesty to Jamaica and Barbados.

However, new territories—Jamaica and New Netherland—
required new labor. Competing to join in the enslaving feast were
not only those authorized by the Company of Royal Adventurers, but
also a long line of merchants, yearning and straining to join the gory
bacchanal, and who in coming years were to lobby vigorously for the
deregulation of this odious commerce, which became central to their
indictment against the monarchy that culminated in the Glorious
Revolution of 1688. This unleashed a chain of events that eventuated
in the revolt of 1776. The intermediate stop on this sanguinary road
was the formation of the Royal African Company in 1672, a short-
lived attempt by the Crown to monopolize this hateful business. But
the merchants, emboldened by their triumphs in recent decades and
hardly chastened by royalist restoration in 1660, came roaring back.
And just as they had ousted the Crown altogether with Cromwell,
they did so again in 1776 and ousted London from leadership of the
even more lucrative trade in Africans in the process. The merchants
had created a dynamic that a mere restoration could not resist.

The early Stuart royals had not been aggressive in the realm of overseas expansion,[85] but the restored monarch in 1660 continued Cromwell's turnabout of this lassitude, which pleased merchant powerbrokers and, perhaps, diverted them permanently from yet another beheading of a king.[86]

CHAPTER 6

More Enslaved Africans Arrive in the Caribbean—Along with More Revolts

L ondon was now masticating and digesting New Netherland and Jamaica, but that seemed only to whet the colonial and enslaving appetite for more conquests. Just as New Englanders began to flock to Jamaica, Barbadian settlers began to flock to what became South Carolina, where in an absence of mind they were to create a daunting Black Majority. However, with Spain still ensconced in Florida and Cuba, London then had to try to control the intervening territory that became Georgia, particularly when Africans from what became the Palmetto State began to find succor in St. Augustine.[1] South Carolina was a "colony's colony." Ultimately, the successor regime in what became Washington then had to try to control Florida, then Cuba,[2] because of the enchanting call of slavery.

This influence of Barbados upon the fortunes of Carolina is also reflected in one of the founders of this mainland project, Anthony Ashley Cooper, the first Earl of Shaftesbury, was not only a major investor in slave trading enterprises but was also sufficiently nimble— or unprincipled—to cycle among monarchism in London and its antipode in Cromwell, while developing a fortune grounded in the most horrendous slavery in Barbados.[3] Sadly, this often morally blind "pragmatism," doing "what works," principle set aside, so evident in today's United States, has deep roots.

In brief, the apparently unquenchable thirst for the seemingly limitless land of indigenes and the free labor of Africa was creating a human rights fiasco. In North America racial privilege and the militarized identity politics that was "whiteness" was forming the sinews of the emerging system that was capitalism.

These new acquisitions came at an opportune moment for Charles II, given the debts that had piled up in recent decades, given wars, including civil wars, military buildup, and the like. In fact, debt helped to impel these conquests.[4] Similarly, the eighteenth-century writer John Oldmixon argued that the civil wars "put discoveries out of men's heads" as the "bold had other work cut out for them and hear no more of adventure" until later.[5] Richard Blome thought that the taking of Jamaica was particularly important in this context. Not only was it convenient for undermining "Madrid's Pearl" of the Antilles, Cuba, but since Virginia was "subject to gusts of wind" it made it problematic for "ships laden with good and passengers" to reach key locales—"They could not ply to any of the outward [Caribbean] islands." "Now Jamaica being so far forward," he insisted in 1672, "is a convenient harbor for all vessels thus distressed and did some few years save three Virginia ships full of passengers and good."[6]

By 1667, as the ink was barely dry on pacts intending to relax relations with European rivals, freelance merchants were hungering to elbow aside the Company of Royal Adventurers and descend upon Africa with renewed fervor. Unctuously, they claimed that "His Majesties Plantations" were "brought to the perfection" that supposedly obtained and "principally subsist[ed] by the labour of Negro Servants and a plentiful supply of them." Previously, it was said, there "had always been a freedom of trade for all His Majesties Subjects for Negroes on the whole coast of Guine[a]," but now the CRA had interrupted their succulent reverie and "totally obstructed the former free Trade" in Africans. Worse, these organized freebooters were simultaneously supplying "the Spanish Plantations with

Negroes," leaving London in the lurch. Madrid's settlements produced the "same commodities" as London's, leaving the latter "either ill supplied" or hamstrung by "excessive prices" of Africans "or not at all supplied." This meant His Majesty's plantations were "much decayed," and "unless a timely remedy" arrived, these sites would be "brought to inevitable destruction."

That was not all. Enslaved Africans had to be borne by ships, and the sugar they produced in the colonies traveled by sea, too. The settlements had to be defended by warships, meaning a shipbuilding industry at home, which meant wage workers with money to spend, boosting the entire economy. "Shoes, stockings, serges . . . beef, butter," the list was endless, items that served to provide "employment and bread for many thousands of families," and the colonies sent "sugars, cotton, ginger, indigo, tobacco" to the homeland . All rested on the "constant supply of Negroes . . . without which the said colonies must inevitably be reduced to ruin . . . and destruction."[7]

As was their wont, merchants unleashed a steady fire of propaganda, portraying their unhindered entry into the slave trade as a matter of the nation's life and death. "Formerly there hath always been a freedom of Trade for all His Majesties Subjects for Negroes," it was announced ingratiatingly in 1667. And, as a consequence, "said plantations have been plentifully supplied with Negroes." But now the aptly named Company of Royal Adventurers had "totally obstructed the former Free Trade of all Adventurers" and not just those duly authorized.[8] The Adventurers were harming the interest of colonies, it was said, by not delivering enough Africans to the settlements.[9] "Free Trade" in Africans was the parliamentary appeal that was to undergird the stunningly hypocritical cries for liberty that led directly to 1776.

What to do? Unleash the animal spirits of these merchants on Africa and then await eagerly the magic of the marketplace.

As they read the fine print, the remit of the Company of Royal Adventurers only extended to the Cape and the same held true—operationally, it was thought—for the successor, the Royal African Company (RAC). So merchants from New Amsterdam, now renamed after the Duke of York, simply sailed to Madagascar, the island that had been eyed covetously for years, and formed a bond with European pirates stationed there.[10]

As the need for bonded labor rose, the slave trade was reorganized by way of the Royal African Company in 1672. Like the Reich that it anticipated, its charter spoke overoptimistically of a "term of 1,000 years."[11] It was only the Crown, it was thought, that could devise the firepower needed to subjugate Africa, including construction of forts alone the Atlantic coastline.[12]

Initially, John Jeffreys, heavily invested in Virginia tobacco and thus a major customer, welcomed the formation of what was by far the largest Crown-backed enterprise in the Atlantic.[13] But this attempt to bridge the interests between the Crown and colonial planters and merchants, with royals at the controls, did not reflect adequately the true balance of forces. Thus, as early as 1674 Whitehall was forbidding any but the RAC from enchaining Africans, but this edict contradicted what came to be called "free enterprise" and "market forces" and thus had to retreat, which it did.[14]

But as of 1672 the controlling interest that the Duke of York took in the Royal African Company ensured that the city that took his name would be a major colonial market for buying and selling Africans.[15] Responding to an outcry against taxes that would consume the mainland for centuries to come, property taxes on the enslaved were eliminated and tariffs on incoming enslaved Africans favored continental Africans over inter-colonial (Caribbean) importation: as early as the 1670s, merchants from the renamed New York began challenging the RAC's monopoly. This created ripples spreading outward from Manhattan, as the Phillips family of New York also had substantial interests in Barbados and Madagascar. A family that was a founder of the Republic, the Jays, were also heavily invested in the slave trade. There emerged a Jamaica-New York pirate axis that extended to Madagascar, as piracy became central to the colonial enterprise, and central to the republicanism that emerged post-1776.[16]

By 1670, proving that the apple does not fall far from the tree, South Carolina, the devil spawn of Barbados, enacted a "Fundamental Constitution" declaring that "every freeman of [this province] shall have absolute power and authority over his Negro slaves, or what Opinion or Religion so ever."[17] This mainland province was, as noted previously, a "colony's colony," as Barbadian settlers expanded to the mainland, pulled by dreams of increased wealth and pushed by the fear of being victimized by rebellious Africans. [18]

It was not smooth cruising for London, however. The Dutch had not been sufficiently humbled by being ousted from Recife, West Africa, and New Netherland. There was yet another Anglo-Dutch war erupting in 1672, which delivered devastating raids in the Caribbean; it would coincide roughly with the incipiency of the profoundly transformative Bacon's Rebellion (see chapter 7) in Virginia and King Philip's war in New England. Though this war was an intra-Protestant conflict, the obtaining environment almost had to mean that anti-Catholicism would receive no surcease, either. This was the prism through which attendant slave revolts were viewed, where the hand of Spain, the Irish, and the French was often espied. After all, Irish revolts—to which Africans could not be indifferent—accompanied the French invasions of Antigua and Montserrat in the 1660s.[19]

THEN THERE WAS JAMAICA. Enslaved Africans were more disorderly there than anywhere else in London's settlements. Deporting leaders to the mainland, a frequent ploy, only led to more disruptiveness there. Revolts on this sugar island were more frequent in the last third of the seventeenth century than at any time in the island's history. Between 1673 and 1694 Jamaica experienced at least six major revolts of the enslaved, followed by eruptions in 1702 and 1704. The first two of this cycle occurred on the north side of the island, beginning in 1673, where Maroons were known to be active, and the next occurred on a large plantation near the appropriately named Spanish Town. The most serious revolt occurred in 1685–86, involving scores of Africans on the north side. The enraged Africans burned and rampaged for months before heavy fire subdued them. Understandably, the settler population, and the indentured group too, began to decline, which only elevated the crisis, with many making the great trek to the mainland. In 1662 the total population was 4,207: 3,653 Europeans and 554 Africans. By 1673—indicative of the manic energy of slave traders—the African population had grown to 7,768, loosely equal to the number of Europeans. But then the proportions began to shift dramatically in favor of Africans, adding to their zesty brio. Imports of Africans jumped from 14, 383 in the 1670s to 33,458 in the 1680s. Arriving as well in Jamaican ports were uncontrollable displays of fury and dynamism. There was a similar trend on the mainland: the decline of indentured labor and the ascendancy of enslaved labor, and with that came less blurring of racial lines.[20]

Anguished cries from settlers were the hallmark of Jamaica. As in other settlements, there was an attempt, by 1661, to restrain a "servant" that "shall lay violent hands on his or her master or mistress or overseer."[21] By 1663 there were measures adopted concerning the "enormities done and committed . . . by Negroes" and "for the prevention of all mutinies and insurrections or other mischiefs."[22] That same year an act to make sure that boats were sufficiently chained and fastened so that they could not become vessels for absconding was passed.[23] By 1664, "certain runaway Blacks from Barbadoes" had arrived aiming to commit "insolences on the planters," including "felonies" and "murther [murder]" and "burglaries." What if Africans resisted capture? "Slay" or "kill the said slaves" was the reply.[24]

"Carmahaly Negroes," thought to be tied to Maroons, "are still in this island," it was announced tremblingly in 1665 "and have again begun to rob and kill," and thus the "island" should "be put in a posture of war."[25] By 1670 they were called the "Vermahaly Negroes," and this lack of clarity was a reflection of an uninspiring attempt to corral them. They were killing and plundering, per usual. "Many more Negroes have run away from their masters," it was reported anxiously. "The number of Indians, Mulattoes and Negroes to whom the oath of allegiance is never tendered, much exceeds that of those who call themselves Christian and daily increases."[26]

"Divers[e] murders, robberies and other outrages" were among the complaints in 1670,[27] with revanchist Spaniards with "designs to invade us" as a dismaying complement.[28] One of the temporary peaces with Madrid led to a demand to "release" all Spanish prisoners, but this could only contribute to the chaos and already had led to an "abundance of suits and disputes" about "freeing Indians, Negroes and Mulattoes."[29]

Adding to the confusion were mainland arrivals with questionable claims. This included a Virginia man who demanded "4,000 acres" from a settler in the "parish of St. Elisabeth" that would include "all the Negroes and appurtenances thereto," but this could contribute to intra-settler disputatiousness complicating the unity that was necessary to confront the Maroons and Spaniards alike.[30] This was the southwest of the island.

By 1670 "the outlying Negroes commonly called Carmahaly Negroes" were again accused of perpetrating "divers[e] Murders, Robberies and other outrages." Settlers were advised to keep a pistol nearby as a direct result.[31]

It was the north side, said the authorities in 1672, that was "not well settled" and "found to be a certain retreat for all runaway servants and slaves," with unforeseeable consequences for regional colonialism.[32] There was a "design" of the "Spaniards" to "invade us," said the authorities in late 1671.[33] Months later, there was a "horrid murther [murder]" by "certain of the Negroes who after the fact [fled to] the woods."[34] Again in 1672 there was "danger of being suddenly identified," leading to the cry: "fortify Port Royal."[35]

In 1673, it was repeated that there was rising anxiety about "designs" of the "Dutch and Spaniards" to "attack and invade this island," and the adverse appropriation of 1655 where Africans proved to be unwed to the wishes of His Catholic Majesty had yet to be forgotten. There was a "danger," and the authorities were unsure when it would be over.[36]

By 1675 a frightful rebellion of the enslaved in Barbados caused nervousness about spillover effects in Jamaica. None of the accused on the smaller island should be transported to Jamaica, it was advised, but smugglers for decades to come were to defy the most adroit regulations.[37]

A "late rebellion" in November 1675 produced taut unease.[38] "We have had lately several insurrections and rebellions of our Negroes to

the great disturbance of the peace and planting," it was said tremulously in December 1675. The remedy? Assign "one white servant for
every ten Negroes" laboring.[39] Thus the pressure from Africans led to
a profoundly material alteration of indentured status to a kind of overseer that was accompanied by referring to these poorer Europeans in
racial terms. In the companion settlement that was Virginia, between
1670 and 1680 a growing number of indentured servants were manag-
ing to acquire land and move up the class (and racial) ladder.[40]

Pessimism reigned as the colonial elite could not untie the
Gordian knot of bringing in more Africans to produce immense
wealth while preventing them from rebelling and taking power—
which finally occurred in 1791 in what became Haiti. The governor of
Antigua remarked during this fraught seventeenth-century moment
that his island, like others, was beset by "great supplies of Negroes
and no whites." (Note the term "white" that was rapidly supplanting Christian to describe Europeans.) Thus, "if once the blacks get
ahead they will make the colony theirs," and "that will be the end of
it."[41] However, profit-making did not seem to allow an exit, for in
nearby Nevis the worry was that the island was "not half planted for
want of Negroes."[42] And then there were the lurking French ready
to pounce.

The organizing of the RAC at a time when there was concern about
massive slave revolts exposed the frailty of the colonial project. By
1672, its year of origin, the RAC was moving aggressively into Angola:
"The slaves are sent to all His Majesty's American Plantations"—
islands and mainland both—"which cannot subsist without them."[43]
One scholar has suggested that the destruction of Angola and the construction of Brazil were two sides of the same coin.[44] The only problem
with this apt characterization is that it is too limited, for London's settlements too were heavily dependent upon the destruction of Angola,
providing Luanda today with a sound rationale for a dedicated program of reparations from the coffers of her past tormentors.

In the companion settlement of Jamaica, even before the turning
point in 1676, the route was taken of pitting the interests of "Christian
indented servants or hired freemen" against those of "Negroes," in

order to "secure the island from danger." Sir William Morrice was told that "everyone that has six Negroes should keep one Christian servant and one hired freeman and so on" available for suppressive tactics. This would also address the pressing problem of servant and free-man abandonment of the island, since there were "not 300 Christians upon the whole island who would not be glad to be gone upon easy terms," and compromising security further as a result. "The dangers of settlements being so far distant from the other" also required urgent expediency. In portentous words it was concluded that "the settle-ment of Jamaica will never be in a better condition without a speedy supply from England of Christian planters, not merchants, as well as servants and bringing up Negro children in the Christian religion."[45] The Christian religion could instruct in the duty to submit to the master—and God—but raised knotty questions about whether pur-ported coreligionists should be in bondage. Privileging planters over merchants made sense, but it was the latter who benefited from the tailwinds of history.

In 1670, an account accurately reported that "nothing can now hinder the future thriving of [Jamaica] but want of inhabitants and slaves" (note the distinction between the two). Purportedly, there were then 8,200 residents, 2,500 of whom were enslaved.[46]

Hence, with disquiet sloping upward, a "bill for the encourage-ment and speedier settling" of Jamaica was demanded. However, a European would have to be awfully ignorant or terribly desperate to heed this call.[47] The elite had not fully considered this call, for what was to prevent a Spaniard or Dutchman or Frenchman from appear-ing to be a loyal settler, then covertly spreading sedition? It would be a "felony without benefit of clergy," warned the authorities flintily, "for any person to serve under any foreign power."[48]

Planters were desperate, scrambling for remedies without the aid of think tanks and relaxed contemplation. As New England and Virginia were to be rocked by revolt in 1676, the authorities pleaded not to "sell or deliver any arms, powder, bullets or other ammunition unto any Negro slave unless he brings a ticket from his Master"[49]—a reasonable pro-slavery measure that adept forgery could defeat.

But the integration of Jamaica with the region was a hindrance to tranquility as well. As a 1676 rebellion in New England was being quelled, the nerves of the Jamaican elite were frazzled when "several Indian inhabitants" from there were "imported to this island," with their enslavement as the prospect, presenting a "great hazard and danger" on top of what was already being confronted.[50]

Foreigners continued to be an irritant, as when in 1677 a captain arrived from Cartagena with "near two hundred Negroes aboard... belonging to the subjects of the States General of the Provinces." Apparently these slaves were taken "piratically" from "subjects" of Holland, a "very foul piracy" indeed. But who was to say? A ship innocently arriving in conspicuously rebellious Jamaica with hundreds of Africans aboard? Understandably, the authorities were suspicious. If nothing else, it was an indicator of the tumultuous neighborhood in which they resided.[51]

Finally, Sir Henry Morgan—a Jamaican leader of affluent Welsh origins and, appropriately, a leading pirate[52]—knew a thing or two about raiding settlements, and averred that "considering the strength and position of our neighbors" and the corresponding "safety and defence" of Jamaica, that the "tenth Negro of all the Negroes in this island be employed to work at the fortifications" near the pirates' nest known as Port Royal. "A third part of all the Negroes, men and women, Indians and mulattoes and free Negroes" should be tasked to "do work every day" to "fortify Port Morant."[53] The record does not reveal if Sir Henry considered the impact of compelling these groups to labor when they were similarly the target of foreign invaders, nor does it seem that the authorities considered the implications of exempting Europeans, in the march toward a synthetic "whiteness," a stubbornly persistent identity politics that was similarly unfolding on the mainland.

Sir Henry was well aware of the martial ability of Africans. When he and his fellow brigands sacked Panama City in the 1670s, about 80 percent of the population was comprised of free and enslaved Africans who did not greet him with hosannas of praise; the same held true for neighboring Cartagena. During this century the free African population of Havana, a perpetual target of Sir Henry and his predecessors, was growing faster than other sectors. As early as the 1500s, Africans in Panama had pledged allegiance to Madrid in exchange for autonomy. It was apparent that more innovative remedies would have to be devised to overcome what was becoming an all too real Black Scare.[54] The nightmare scenario for settlers was avoiding precisely what befell them in Hispaniola in 1791: that is, an uprising where they were liquidated or forced to migrate and the Africans seized power. The problem was that settlers were so drunk on the incomparable riches delivered by the African Slave Trade that they found it hard to avoid the deliverance of more gravediggers determined to prepare their indecent burial, in the Caribbean most notably. The great trek to the mainland was one method of avoiding this dire destiny, along with providing more benefits—"combat pay"—to poorer settlers. This approach "worked" in fueling the revolt against London in 1776 and constructing a state founded on solemn principles of white supremacy, often disguised in deceptive "non-racial" words.

It should also not be lost that colonial enslavement was heavily dependent on the ministrations of pirates. Not only was there Sir Henry, there was also Charles-François d'Angennes, Marquis de Maintenon, by 1680 the largest sugar magnate in Martinique—and a notorious freebooter. Saint-Pierre, a regional capital of the French Caribbean, contained some 2,000 corsairs among a population of a few thousand.[55] At its root, capitalism not only meant slavery and white supremacy but also the ethos of the gangster.

A SIMILAR PROCESS WAS UNFOLDING in Barbados. Difficulty remained in integrating the recently arrived Iberian Jewish community. As early as the 1660s, they were accused of bribing ship captains to effectuate the release of their coreligionists being transported from nearby Spanish colonies under the orders of the Inquisition and this, it was believed, was complicating relations further with Madrid. As in Jamaica, Jews were limited in purchasing slaves in considerable numbers until 1786, which was hampering capital formation and hindering the forging of a synthetic "whiteness" besides. They were suspected routinely of treasonous behavior, and before 1675 courts were reluctant to accept their testimony. This bar too fell in the 1780s as the waves of republicanism and "whiteness" from the mainland spread to the region. Both the vestry and the Assembly, two major centers of power, conspired against them, nonetheless. Napthall Hart was a Jewish man who had migrated from Newport to Barbados, but most of the traffic in that regard was moving in the opposite direction. Christian merchants coveted his overseas contacts still, despite his commitment to the island, and their jealousy extended to resentment of the role of Jewish merchants as chief dealers in coin.

Yet this discrimination did not negate the fact that Jews were firmly in the middle and upper stratum of society, moving from anti-Semitic Iberian societies to societies with anti-Semitism under the flag of the rising power in London. This distinction—based on the absence of an organized Inquisition as in Madrid—did not prevent the repetitive accusation that they encouraged slaves to steal and then acted as middlemen in fencing, or that they negotiated with these forced laborers at Sunday markets for the sale of smuggled goods while the Christian settlers reposed in church. Ominously for London, this persecution and their exclusion from certain areas of legitimate trade tended to facilitate the development of some shared interests between persecuted Jews and enslaved Africans.[56]

This bigotry was not limited to Barbados. In Jamaica in 1671, in the context of concern about a Spanish invasion, a strange "petition of divers merchants against the Jews" was drawn up, with discussion of whether they should be "expelled" since a number were "without patents or naturalization." Competitors were eyeing their wealth invidiously, since they possessed "great stocks"; yet they were "not numerous enough to supplant us, or is it to their interest to betray us,"[57] perhaps by reigniting their old alliance with the Dutch.

As in Jamaica, there was reason why Barbadian settlers were so apprehensive. Laws had to be passed for the "good governing of servants," that is, to punish those who chose to "lay violent hands upon his or her Master, Mistress or Overseer" or steal from same. There was an attempt to limit arrival of vessels, which could only harm commerce,[58] and to ban the "selling of brandy and rum" to "Servants and Negroes" who traded alcohol for "stolen goods."[59]

By 1667, officials in Barbados were in a familiar posture: moaning about the growing number of Africans. They were not "above 6,400" in 1643 but in "1666 above 50,000." Indentured Irish were "derided by the Negroes as white slaves." Perhaps upgrading the status of Irish would foil the Negroes' psychological warfare? Settlers were busily fleeing to the mainland in fear. "There are many thousands of slaves that speak English," it was warned, "and if there are many leading men slaves in a Plantation, they may be easily wrought upon to betray it, especially on the promise of freedom." Then there were "the Jews who not having like liberty as in the Dutch and French islands, have been very treacherous." Perhaps an upgrade would work here, too?[60]

By 1670 there was debate over "an act to prevent spiriting people off this island," while "promising . . . great quantities of land,"[61] an unrealistic remedy on this small island, now in a losing competition with Jamaica and particularly the mainland. As the proportion of Europeans shrank, anxiety grew. When a bill was passed "concerning persons intended to depart this island" in 1672,[62] it was apparent that the island was losing the battle for a valuable presence: those who would be defined as "white." A reminder of this danger came when in 1671 "an act for the prevention of firing of Sugar Canes,"[63] a repetitive problem, was passed. Policymakers might have recalled that even innocent "firing of Sugar Cane" could be a mask for arson, in light of the firestorm that wracked the island in 1668.[64]

The Barbadian elite had to agonize over the decline of the settler population. By 1673 it was found that the "militia consists of two regiments," and "the utmost number of white men capable of military service" was "so small." Besides, of those many were "infirm by age, sickness and personal defects" including those of the "mental" variety. Then there were the unreliable Quakers, resulting in the compulsion to "arm" Africans, meaning the cure was worse than the illness.[65]

However, despite this dearth of Europeans, suspicion of what were called "Hebrews" was common.[66] As if there were not enough problems, there was also an attempt to restrain Quakers suspected of "bringing Negroes to their Meetings," which meant the "safety of this island may be much hazarded." Any Africans found in violation would be "forfeited."[67] That measure apparently did not work since in 1678 a strengthened bill was legislated, which gave incentives to informers to squeal on Quakers who consorted with Africans. Then, as if bars against the Jewish and Quaker communities were insufficient to halt the emergence of a synthetic "whiteness," the assembly sought measures against "Popish Recusants." [68]

This was a shortsighted, even suicidal, policy, which should have been evident in 1676. For it was in that decisive year when a revolt by the indigenes rocked New England and rebellious Europeans sought to overthrow the Virginia regime that Africans in Barbados took matters into their own hands. There was a "Grand Conspiracy," said one Londoner with fury, targeting settlers. The result: captured Africans were "burned alive, beheaded and otherwise executed for their horrid crimes" perpetrated by the "Cormantee or Gold Coast Negroes."[69] One Londoner was staggered by the "bloody tragedy intended against His Majesties subjects," this "by the Heathen, the Negroes." Their plot was "miraculously discovered eight days before the intended Murder should have been acted," that is, "the Negroes belonging to each of several plantation[s], should in the dead time of the night [rise] on the sound of the alarm" and "kill their Master and Mistresses with their Overseers."[70]

"I am sure the fewer white servants any planter has," said John Wilmore a few years after Bacon's rebellion had been vanquished, "the more it would be for his profit." Instead, he insisted, because of "some disturbances by the Blacks and the Government finding it might be of dangerous consequence, therefore made an Act for the future," ordering that "every plantation should have one white servant to every ten Blacks, being intended only for the security of the island," meaning Jamaica, though the surveillance and monitoring role of poorer Europeans was not limited to this unstable colony. The job requirement of Europeans going forward was to "keep them in awe," meaning Africans.[71]

The shedding of buckets of blood and militaristic monitoring, however, was a short-term fix for a long-term problem.

THE 1670S WERE AN INFLECTION point for London's settlements. The formation of the Royal African Company, as freelance traders remained undeterred by its presumed monopoly on slave trading, meant investors in Africans could envision black ink for some time to come. However, this meant more slave revolts, too. This would lead more settlers to flee to the mainland but that would only set in motion changes leading to 1776. Diminishing the number of indentured laborers from Europe was another approach, but that only led back to further reliance on enslaved labor in no mood to compromise. Poorer Europeans could secure more land grants on the mainland than in small Barbados or rebellious Jamaica. Port Royal would then feel compelled to stop supporting piracy, as this outlaw practice was creating too many problems for already tense relations with Spanish Cuba and Hispaniola, plus bringing parties to town that Africans could leverage. So these bandits simply sailed to the mainland, bringing their misbegotten gains and fungible skills to Newport and Charleston, which promptly welcomed them.[72] This was not an abrupt change for pirates, whose mobility meant that they were not strangers on the mainland in any case.[73] Ultimately, there were more opportunities on the land, particularly land taken from indigenes to dole out to poorer Europeans giving them a stake in the system of colonialism.

In 1676–77 a number of members from the Sephardic Jewish community of Barbados continued a trek that had stretched from the Iberian Peninsula to Amsterdam to Recife, and moved on to Newport, Rhode Island.[74] They were not alone in seeking opportunity on the mainland. Samuel Carpenter, the most energetic merchant in early Pennsylvania, was a Quaker merchant in Barbados in 1673. This bachelor slave-owner then invested in milling and lumbering and speculated in land in New Jersey.[75] One of the comrades of William Penn was Ralph Fretwell, a Barbadian sugar planter and Quaker who owned 166 of the enslaved and was mulling a move to the mainland as well, despite his wealth.[76]

Fretwell may have known that many of Philadelphia's earliest residents had formerly been settlers in Barbados and had made a smart long-term investment as a result. Though not itself primarily a slave plantation colony, this future metropolis economy nevertheless depended heavily on the wealth generated by slaves, precisely because of Barbados's central role. The now fabled William Penn did not outlaw slavery in his colony, and thus, rather quickly, 11 percent of its population was enslaved, as he and his comrades borrowed heavily from the slave code of Barbados for guidance. The Quakers, in sum—reputation aside—were complicit in the brutalization that inhered in slavery.[77]

Fretwell may have recognized that contraband trade was growing between New England and the French Lesser Antilles at that moment, which nicely complemented a growing commerce between Jamaica and merchants and planters in French Saint-Domingue[78]—soon to be one of the richest colonies ever—before the Haitian Revolution upset things. As South Carolina—a "colony of a colony," the latter being Barbados—took off in the 1670s, the scale of selling indigenes into slavery leapt into the ionosphere. In the next few decades, more indigenes were exported from the region than Africans imported to the southeast quadrant of the continent. These profits lined the already bulging purses of merchants and planters, while clearing more land in a form of ethnic cleansing.[79] Uncooperative Africans who balked at being enchained served to militarize settlers even more.[80] Settlers on the mainland may have heard about the massacring endured by their counterparts in Tobago,[81] as irruptions exploded in New England, Virginia, and Barbados. That the Dutch enemy was the major target was hardly consoling, for victories against settlers anywhere were victories for indigenes everywhere, especially in London's settlements.

The mainland's productive forces were advancing while those of the Caribbean had a foreseeable upper limit, though for seven more decades London would see the latter as more valuable. It took longer than that for London to realize that a 1776 was on the horizon.

A century earlier, tantalizingly enough, London had what has been described as a limited number of disciplined provinces, including the "Cromwellian garrison government of Jamaica," which then provided the militarization and centralization that swept the mainland after this crucial year. Jamaica field-tested initiatives that were then applied in the city named after the Duke of York on the mainland. But then the colonial chain was buffeted at both ends—New England and Virginia—and disrupted the existing model of colonial rule, necessitating change.[82]

A precise century—1676 to 1776—marked the rise of the British Empire and the resultant hegemony of the United States of America.

CHAPTER 7

The Spirit of 1676: The Identity Politics of "Whiteness" and Prelude to Colonial Secession

The fatuous idea that the routing of the Pequots in the 1630s indicated smooth sailing for the settlers in what they called New England became even more foolish when war erupted once more in the mid-1670s.[1] As ever, settlers were upset when evidence emerged that the French and the Dutch were selling "guns, powder, shot," and trading and the like "with Indians to our great prejudice and strengthening and animating the Indians against us." The authorities demanded that no boats be sold to indigenes, perhaps hampering their escape from enslavement and routing. Though the settlers had arrived in North America purportedly to enjoy religious liberty, indigenous religious liberty was curtailed, that is, "worship to their false Gods or to the Devil" was forbidden. Catholics too were restrained: "no Jesuit or spiritual or ecclesiastical person" was allowed to alight or any "ordained by the authority of the Pope" were allowed to "come within this jurisdiction." They were to be barred initially, and if they came a "second time" they "shall be put to Death." The death penalty for poisoning provided a foretaste of their real fears, while "firing and burning" was illuminatingly reproved.[2]

News then reached London of the "bloody Indian war from March till August 1676." Highlighted was the allegation that if victims were "women, they first forced them to satisfie their filthy lusts and then murthered them."[3] Londoners focused not on the fact that their compatriots had invaded a foreign land and began to oust and enslave, giving rise to a fierce reaction but instead stressed "New England's present sufferings under their cruel neighboring Indians."[4] The prominent Bostonian Increase Mather laid down a steady drumfire of propaganda against the indigenous, tracing their purported perfidy from "the year 1614 to the year 1675."[5]

After European rule had been fastened firmly upon New England, it was conceded that indigenous "captive women and children were sold into slavery," that is, "more than five hundred" were "sold into slavery from Plymouth alone" in what was termed "King Philip's war."[6] Rationalizing this crime against humanity, the Plymouth elite, it was argued, averred that "the Sachem of Pascanacutt" was working with the "French against the English in New England."[7] Still, even after it appeared that an indigenous revolt had been quelled, one settler was still sweating about what a resident termed "many secret attempts . . . by evil minded persons to fire the town of Boston, tending to the destruction" of that rapidly growing urban center.[8]

It turns out that this deportation policy may have exported revolt. The "heathen prince" who perpetrated these "notorious and execrable murders and outrages" and sought to "totally destroy, extirpate & expel settlers" was to see his comrades sold into slavery, seemingly in Jamaica, which was akin to pouring boiling oil on a raging fire.[9] Thus the "heathen malefactor, men, women and children" were "sentenced & condemned for perpetual servitude,"[10] where they could then plot alongside ungovernable Africans. Jamaica also seemed to invite disaster when it accepted enslaved indigenes from Florida.[11]

Though nowadays there is a kind of silo and stovepipe approach, separating scrutiny of New England from examination of the Caribbean, this was not the case in 1676 in London. A pamphleteer saw parallels about what was unfolding in Barbados at the time of the

indigenous rebellion due north. "Our fellow subjects," it was concluded, be it north or south, "tasted of the same cup."[12]

Both of these settlements had a problem, though in the longer run
the more capacious mainland had more potential to purchase the allegiance of poor Europeans by fighting more indigenes—swept aside
for the most part earlier in the Caribbean—taking their land, then
redistributing it.

As matters evolved, that approach was taken with the third revolt
faced by London, what has been called "Bacon's Rebellion," an
assault on the colonial regime itself. (This revolt also underscores
the asininity of assuming that under settler colonialism, a revolt from
below targeting an elite is ipso facto righteous: as in this episode,
what may be at issue is the subaltern raging against the presumed
elite's lassitude in dispossessing the designated racial "other.")[13]

In August 1676 the declaration by Nathaniel Bacon and his co-
conspirators assailed the governor "for having protected, favored
and emboldened the Indians against His [Majesty's] most loyal
subjects."[14] Bacon's band had been in a standoff with indigenes over
the stealing of their land; there had been bloodshed and the thieves,
unhappy with the perceived lack of support provided by the regime,
rebelled.[15] Bacon, the right-wing populist demagogue, established a
template that still resonates in the successor regime, the United States.
Of course, he issued a "Declaration in the Name of the People" charging that the governor had "protected, favoured and [em]boldened
the Indians against His Majesties loyall subjects," while those who
opposed him were the actual "trayters."[16] Inevitably, he was able to
mobilize hundreds for his ill-fated venture.[17]

In contrast, the regime charged Bacon and the "five hundred persons" who joined him with being "warlike" and immersed in "treason
and rebellion"—make that "high treason." A "three hundred pounds
sterling" reward was offered for information leading to his capture
and conviction.[18]

Governor William Berkeley fled Jamestown for Accomac, where,
said a subsequent analyst, he found the "last refuge of the loyal cause

of Virginia," which included "the best, wealthiest and most influential in the Colony." Ironically, one of his supporters there included Daniel Jenifer, a Catholic, wed to Annie Toft, the "wealthiest and prettiest woman then living in the eastern shore of Virginia."[19]

Bacon, it was said after the dust had cleared in 1677, "descended of an Ancient and Honourable family," though as so often has been the case on this continent, he was able to rally numerous poorer Europeans across class lines. He was well traveled, having arrived in Virginia three years earlier and becoming part of the potent Privy Council. But when indigenes attacked his landholding, he was outraged, not only at them but what he thought was the pusillanimous response of the governor. So he chose to launch his own war. One critic charged that this "very hard drinker . . . died by imbibing or taking in too much brandy," but it was more likely that he was actually drunk with dreams of power.[20] The well-born young planter was, according to a twentieth-century commentator, "more interested in fighting Indians than reform." This was a close call, in that half of his band fought indigenes and the other half fought the regime, torching Jamestown: the colony's capital was torched.[21] It was reported as "strange news from Virginia," but as the continent evolved, it was not so strange at all.

Bacon may have been defeated militarily, but he won politically, not unlike his successors: the so-called Confederate States of America in 1865. Thousands of indigenes fled, opening more land; hundreds were sent into servitude in Bermuda.[22] This occurred despite a treaty between "Virginia & the Pamunkey Indians," involving "articles of peace" directing that these indigenes "shall not be sold as slaves."[23] This was one of many pacts between settlers and indigenes that would be ignored and violated.

The rebels wanted more land of the indigenous and demanded that London shed more blood and treasure to attain this goal. In response, London inched toward satisfying rebel demands, but that was insufficient to sate voracious appetites, which led directly to 1776. Still, after this uprising more and more planters began to see indentured servants, the presumed beneficiary of the revolt, with their fixed terms and asserted rights, as a liability and to see enslaved Africans as the future. In some ways, what transpired was that Virginia was further racialized, with Africans and indigenes being the prime victims, while poorer Europeans were satisfied at the latter's expense,[24] not least through the ongoing identity politics of constructing "whiteness." Ironically, and as so often happened in centuries to come, some terribly misguided Africans aligned with the settlers led by Bacon against the indigenes, when history suggests their interests would have been better served by executing a diametrically opposite strategy of alignment with Native Americans.

The settler elites were in a bind. Indigenes were rebelling to the north and Africans to the south. Concessions to the latter, particularly in Virginia, seemed to be beyond consideration, though seizing the land of the indigenes may have been the highest priority. In that context, winning over other Europeans was, minimally, the "least bad" option and provided the fewest complications. Six years after Bacon revolted, the authorities in Bacon's settlement were in a familiar position: "I have bad news," it was reported. "The peace of the Colony" was "endangered by unruly and tumultuous persons" and "lest the infection should spread further, orders have been issued to the commanders of the militia in each county to . . . be in continual motion, by which vigilance we have some hope that the growth of insurrection may be prevented."[25]

It was also in 1682 that policymakers in Jamestown recognized that a statute passed mere months earlier had not "had its intended effect"; thus "the better preventing" of "such insurrections by Negroes or slaves" was formulated. However, to attain this desperately desired goal, there would have to be more concessions to Europeans of various classes.[26] As this trend became manifest, there was both a huge leap in the number of enslaved and a concomitant increase in statutes seeking to shape and regulate their behavior.[27] This was accompanied by a growth in wealth, which then paved the way for a unilateral declaration of independence in 1776.

In the late seventeenth century the grandee of Virginia, William Byrd, amassed almost thirty thousand acres—at the expense of indigenes. He switched entirely to deploying enslaved African labor in the 1680s in the aftermath of Bacon's revolt. Slapping taxes on this troublesome property not only raised revenue for internal improvements but also was designed to restrain the possibility of a slave rebellion. As the number of enslaved Africans rose, the number of European servants declined. From 1680 to 1720, the slave population of the Chesapeake increased at a rate twice that of the European population, tending to jeopardize the life expectancy of the latter. It was in the 1690s that the term "white" began to replace "Christian" and free," with this trend continuing through the twenty-first century. As shall be seen, the "Glorious Revolution" of 1688 also meant the imminent decline of the Royal African Company under the thumb of the monarch, the continuing rise of merchants, and a spectacular increase in the number of enslaved Africans, along with the resultant wealth and secessionist urges.[28]

Byrd encountered difficulties with enslaved Africans and he was not singular. In the fall of 1687 there was the "discovery of a Negro Plot" in the "Northern Neck" of the colony that included the "d[e]-stroying and killing" of settlers, with the "design" of "carrying it through [to] the whole Colony." In jujitsu-like fashion, Africans had begun plotting as funerals unwound: then they met in "great numbers" to plot "their Evil . . . [and] wicked purposes."[29]

There was an implicit—if not explicit—racial bias in the colonial project from its inception, the oppression of poorer Europeans notwithstanding. When Africans, indigenes, and poorer Europeans began to rebel simultaneously, simple survival meant concessions to one of these groups. In this context, scuttling the aspirations of Africans and indigenes versus assuaging poorer Europeans seemed to be the only viable options given the momentum of settler colonialism, which in any case meant more settlers, presumably European.

For as those at the summit of Virginia society were worrying about the "growth of insurrection," in neighboring Carolina settlers were warned to be on guard against "the Negro Slaves," whose "labour" was of "plenty" benefit but "whose service doubles . . . [in]security," meaning settlers' security, particularly if a "foreigner should attempt to invade them," which in the seventeenth century was a constant threat. This observer had noticed that "several families have transported themselves from the ports of Barbados" northward, but it was unclear if this great trek would save them.[30] Yet, despite the clear and present danger presented by being in close proximity to a disproportionate number of angry Africans, the chief executive in Jamaica continued to call for "ordering us supplies of Negroes at reasonable rates."[31] At least for a while the authorities continued to ship disgruntled Europeans to the Caribbean, whose presence could prove to be unsettling. Just before "ordering" more "supplies of Negroes," complaints emerged about "great abuses in the spiriting away of children" to the Caribbean to toil and be exploited. This was a "very sad story," it was said, though—tellingly—those victimized were denoted as "whites," supplanting the identity of "Christian."[32] Complaints continued to roll in to Whitehall about the "frequent abuses" of involving a "sort of people called spirits, in seducing many of His Majesties Subjects to go on Shipboard [where] they have been seized and carried by force to His Majesties Plantations in America." This rough handling of poorer Europeans in crossing the Atlantic could sour them tremendously. But upon arriving and facing the distinct possibility of uprisings spearheaded by Africans and indigenes that did not make careful distinctions between and among Europeans, a racial solidarity could be forged: the elite had devised a race-based despotism driving these recent arrivals into the arms of these same elites, particularly after the poorer settlers were granted certain concessions.[33]

The unsuitability of religion as the primary politics of identity was exposed when advocates for Africans and indigenes in the Caribbean began "suing for their admission into the Church" and clamoring in what was considered a "persuasive" manner for "the instructing and baptizing of the Negroes and Indians for our plantations."[34] It was easier to convert Africans into Christians than to somehow make them "white."

But this process was not uncomplicated. Subsequently, London sought to form an exclusively "white" settlement—that is,

Georgia—which would evade the issue of furious Africans, but this did not work very well, not only because of smuggling of slaves but also because it only reintroduced the nettlesome matter of class contradictions among poorer and wealthier Europeans. Nonetheless, this project pushed out indigenes over time which was a goal of settlers, irrespective of the source of labor.

It is important to recognize that the aftermath of Bacon's Rebellion, which brought less reliance on indentured labor, more taking of indigenous land, and more enslaved African labor, was not a radical departure from past praxis—it represented a deepening of past praxis. With the taking of Jamaica in 1655 and the coming of the sugar boom, there had been a concerted effort to dragoon more Africans and relieve the burden on small Barbados by attracting Europeans from there to this bigger island. The establishment of South Carolina in 1670 also deepened this pattern, particularly in the ouster and enslavement of indigenes, which had been a typical practice by settlers for some decades. And yes, soon after arriving in Carolina these erstwhile Barbadians were busily ratifying "an act to prevent runaways."[35]

Such practices established a cross-class alliance between and among European settlers, who bonded on the basis of "racial identity politics"—that is, "whiteness" and "white supremacy"—and the looting of all those not so endowed. This practice extended to 1776 and its aftermath, and arguably had its latest expression, at least in terms of underlying premise and intent, in the United States in November 2016. Post-1676, it was evident that settlements, and the new nation that succeeded them, were being constructed as a "white man's country," effectively the first apartheid state, a formidable hurdle that even progressive Euro-Americans have found difficult to overcome.

OTHER TRENDS WERE UNWINDING simultaneously that were favorable to colonial settlement. With the halting of the Ottoman Turks at the gates of Vienna,[36] Western Europeans could worry less about being overrun and thus could direct more resources to settler colonialism. Moreover, with the precipitous decline of their Muslim foe, they could worry less about their nationals being seized and sold into slavery and, consequently, could expend more time and effort in seizing and enslaving Africans in the Americas. With the erosion of Ottoman influence, the importance of maintaining a salient religious identity declined in importance, facilitating the companion rise of "race"—or "whiteness"—as an identity, which undergirded settler colonialism based on dispossession of indigenes and enslavement of Africans.

This epochal setback for the Ottomans occurred in 1683 but was still being celebrated well after the fact, indicative of its importance. A Londoner, indicating the Pan-Christian importance of this defeat, hailed the "prevalence of the Christian arms against the infidels" who "for many years have deluged the once flourishing part of Europe with blood," as if the victory was not the Habsburgs' alone.[37]

Even before 1683 there were signals that the Ottomans were in decline. From a certain perspective, when the sultan created the office of the "Chief Black Eunuch" during this tumultuous era, this elevation of an African was an ironic sign of weakness and impotence. In the late sixteenth century, they had challenged Portugal in Mozambique—and flopped. Persia had tied down the Ottomans for the first few decades of the seventeenth century, meaning that well before 1683 the Western Europeans had been freed up to devastate Africa and the Americas with little worry about being attacked from the rear. Even before 1683, the Ottomans had been diverted by a Tatar-Cossack alliance, which weakened this sprawling empire further and, objectively, strengthened those to their west. Their youth levy, the recruiting of Christian men to be Janissaries, had all but ceased by the middle of the seventeenth century, freeing more of this faith to join the free-for-all in Africa and the Americas. In the two decades before 1683, the Ottoman-Habsburg frontier was quiet, reassuring those to the west.

The 1683 setback was thus a culmination of ongoing trends, made all the more powerful by the exclamation point formed in Vienna. This ignominious defeat was of great psychological importance for the Habsburgs and the whole of Europe. The tide of Ottoman conquest seemed to be receding, and it was not until 1917 with the Bolshevik Revolution that such an existential threat manifested, albeit this time on more systemic and ideological—as opposed to religious—grounds. By 1686 the Ottomans' grip on Buda was loosened. Then in 1688, as London was undergoing the transformative "Glorious Revolution," the Ottomans were losing Belgrade, signaling an era of declension that extended at least until the early eighteenth century. As this empire declined and a competitor in London rose, France began to replace England as the Ottomans' dominant trading partner. Egypt was the largest province of the Ottoman Empire and, from its strategic location on the main trade routes, the richest. But by the end of the eighteenth century, this rule was in dire jeopardy and by then the once proud Ottomans were en route to becoming a virtual protectorate of London. The Treaty of Karlowitz in 1699 marked the beginning of the end for the Ottoman Empire, though it was able to hang on to a semblance of power until the end of the First World War. But for our purposes here, the lessening of pressure on Western Europe—London particularly—meant that 1699 was also a defeat for Africa and the Americas.[38]

Also a defeat for Africa and the Americas was the negotiation of a 1675 pact between London and the Ottomans, which was reaffirmed in 1809 and not terminated until 1924, an indicator of its potency. There were special provisions on what was to occur if "Corsairs of Tunisia and Barbary . . . plundered and pillaged" traveling English subjects and, indeed, "molest" them. Provisions included what to do "if any Englishman should turn Turk"; the broad expanse of this accord included Alexandria. Strikingly, the exceedingly important pact was titled the "Final Treaty of Capitulations."[39] The Lord Protector had sent his forces into the Mediterranean decades earlier to chastise corsairs, but even with this "capitulation," the emergent mainland republic would still be dogged by these marauders into the nineteenth century.[40]

Just as in the twentieth century certain Englishmen chose to ally with Moscow, Londoners "turning Turk" had been a persistent problem in the seventeenth century. Expediting the redemption of English slaves held by the Algerians and Tunisians, an emotionally wracking matter, drove London's negotiators.[41] It was New England's Cotton Mather who moaned that this form of captivity perpetrated by the "hellish Moors"—presumably setting to the side what was befalling indigenes and Africans in his backyard—was "the most horrible . . . in the world."[42] With pressure eased on London from due south and the east, the Crown could more easily plunder and pillage Africa and the Americas.

In any case, redemption of the enslaved English was big business. Again, the enslavement of the English did not tend to lead to abolitionism, at least in the short term. Interestingly, London's man in Constantinople, Paul Rycaut, who was involved in seeking to rescue these bonded compatriots, was also an investor in the African Slave Trade.[43]

THE ENSLAVING OF LONDONERS in the Mediterranean, which was ongoing in the late seventeenth century, gave England more direct experience in both the brutality and profitability of bondage, with the latter factor materializing as dominant in shaping the ongoing assault on Africa.

By 1666 Emmanuel D'Aranda was telling Londoners about the dastardly "Turks" and "how the Christian slaves are beaten at Algiers." He spoke eloquently of runaways, resistance, and cruelty in a way that mirrored what Englishmen were then inflicting on the enslaved Africans in the settlements.[44]

By 1677, as slave ships began heading toward West Africa more systematically, London sought accord with the "Duan of the Noble City of Tunis." There was mutual agreement that there would be "no seizure of any ships of either party at sea or in port"; ordinary seamen taken by Tunis were "to be made slaves" but not "merchants or passengers"— a raw class distinction. Slaves escaping Tunis by jumping aboard departing ships were to be treated as indifferently as seamen.[45] That a similar treaty with Tunis was negotiated a few years earlier[46] suggested that memories were short, filing systems inadequate, or words were insufficient to undermine a deep-seated practice.

In 1675 London once more was accusing Tunis and Algiers of conspiring to "rob" her subjects, and it was demanded that "all such English as have been taken and made slaves . . . shall be immediately set free."[47] In 1676, as settlements were on fire in New England, Virginia, and Barbados alike, it was Tripoli's turn to agree that London's shipwrecks were not to be made a North African prize, "nor the men made slaves." There was a concession, however: "all slaves to be secured" when London's vessels arrived, but "if they escape[d]," they were not to be returned, reducing the viability of trade relations between the two, insofar as it encouraged a bonded labor force to engineer capital flight.[48] By 1682 it was Algiers' turn to agree to a new wrinkle in such bilateral pacts, that is, London was "not obliged to redeem . . . subjects now in slavery," with no distinction drawn between merchants and ordinary seamen.[49]

Algiers, more than other North African sites, seemed to be a preoccupation of Londoners, including the diarist Samuel Pepys. Just as the African Slave Trade received a new birth of freedom with the royal restoration, he had gone to a local tavern "to drink" and there he bumped into "many sea commanders" in whose company "we spent till four o'clock telling stories of Algiers and the manner of the life of the slaves there."[50] Contrary to inked pacts, a cross-class coalition had emerged led by Thomas Betton, who had a controlling interest in an "ironmongers company" and who left "in trust an enormous sum . . . for the redemption of Christian slaves in Barbary."[51]

But again, mere words were not sufficient to erode lucrative practice. New Englanders too fell victim to African enslavement,[52] which could bond them closer to London. Or, alternatively, it could give rise to secession on the premise that London was not capable of protecting them, given this burgeoning empire's necessity to compromise with the Ottomans in order to outflank European rivals.

But it was not just New Englanders who were victimized. London-based Thomas Phelps was also captured, then managed to escape "after a most miserable slavery." Properly abased, he conceded that after experiencing a "most miserable slavery . . . now I know what liberty is," an admission that did not seem to impress his fellow Londoners, who continued enslaving Africans. It was an "Algerine" ship with "Turkish colours. . . . Aboard her was an ancient Moor who had been a slave in England and spoke good English." His "Negro taskmasters . . . gave us severe chastisement for our mistakes and lapses," he admitted woundingly. This did not push him toward abolition, though he confessed, "I have been several times in the West Indies and have seen and heard of divers inhumanities and cruelties practiced there" comparable to what he endured and saw in North Africa. There were "eight hundred Christians of all nations, two hundred and sixty whereof are English," languishing on the Barbary Coast.[53]

Similarly, New Englanders being enslaved by Africans seemed to do little to sour these settlers on enslavement; to the contrary, it seemed to ignite an opposing reaction. This hypocrisy caught the attention of U.S. Senator Charles Sumner many years later, when he railed against this "inconsistency" among Euro-Americans: "using their best endeavors for the freedom of their white people" but busily enslaving others. He declaimed, "Every word of reprobation which they fastened upon the piratical slaveholding Algerians" somehow "return[ed] in eternal judgment against themselves."[54]

Tunis haunted the dreams of many an English subject. John Ogilby noticed "black and white slaves of both sexes" there in 1670. "The people of Tunis," he told Londoners, are "Moors, Jews and slaves of several nations, taken by their pyrates in the Mediterranean."[55]

Temporarily, London was able to gain a foothold in Tangier in the 1660s and from there press both Spain and the Ottomans. This led to a 1666 accord with the "Prince of West Barbary."[56] However, when London's bastion in North Africa crumbled, the Crown's essential weakness was revealed.

Once again, London sought to disarm Madrid diplomatically by signing a "treaty for the composing of differences" and "restraining of depredations and establishing of peace in America." But one did not have to be a cynic to be utterly dismissive of these noble words.[57]

Complicating such a strategy was the behavior of North Africans influenced by Turkey. For in sailing southward to Africa, Europeans ran the risk of becoming what they intended for others: slaves.[58] This is what befell the English merchant identified simply as "Mr. T. S.," taken prisoner in Algiers and then carted inland. There he encountered a "trader in slaves" who declaimed, "Who will buy a Christian?" The humbled merchant correctly found this to be a "grievous change of fortune, in so short a time as a year to be reduced from that honourable Estate, in which my Father left me, to the lowest Misery, to a slave, to be sold as a beast, in a strange country, where I had no friends." That is, he endured the fate suffered by too many Africans, though this commonality did not seem to reduce the sceptered isles' fondness for enslaving others. "T. S." was bought by a Spanish woman. But he thought he had a trump card: "The Moors . . . and the Arabs do hate the Turks," he reported.[59]

When Europeans had to worry less about becoming slaves when sailing to Africa, they were freed to sail southward and enslave even more Africans. The Christian disunity—Protestant versus Christian—was not helpful in barring Africans' enslavement of Europeans and, instead, allowed them to manipulate the two sects to their detriment, not least in the 1670s.[60] The elongated era of discovery[61] and exploration provided rich opportunities to snatch and enslave Europeans in any case. On the other hand, it allowed European travelers to exacerbate tensions between and among Moslems—Turks and Persians, Sunnis and Shias—that kept them decidedly off balance.[62]

In the 1670s, as London was battling indigenes in New England, settlers in Virginia, and enslaved Africans in Barbados, they were also fighting in North Africa. The King's men "utterly destroyed them all," it was reported boastfully: "Turks and Moors slain" was the result, "to the great astonishment of the Turks." Sir John Narbrough, Admiral of the Fleet in the Mediterranean, asserted, "I fired about one hundred shot into the city of Tripoli."[63]

London was also encountering friendly Moslems in South Asia, and when seeking to compete with the Dutch in what was called the "East Indies"—or today's Indonesia—something similar occurred. Complicating this expansion was what had been irksome at the same time in West Africa; that is, the idea that merchants were too fixated on their own business to see the big picture, which required a strong hand of the state—in this case, the Crown. "England may be said to be rich or strong, as our strength or riches bears a proportion with our neighbors," particularly the "French, Dutch," Spanish et al. "And consequently whatever weakens or depopulates them, enriches and strengthens England,"[64] a lodestar that argued for a bolstering of London's long-term policy, stretching back to the sixteenth century, of an entente with the Ottomans, which was designed to weaken Madrid. But how could this occur if so many Londoners were determined to fight the Ottomans? An executive committee of the ruling class was required—that is, the firm hand of the state—to administer in the long-term interests of that ruling class. Weakening an absolutist monarch and settling intra-class disputes via the mechanism of republicanism was the remedy pursued in 1688—and then with more determination in North America in 1776.

That was not all. While grappling with fellow "Christians" on the one hand, London also found it necessary to ally with them on the other hand, an alliance that could and probably did facilitate the emergence of a synthetic "whiteness." During this era an agreement was made directing that "no subjects" of London "shall be bought or sold or made slaves" with the proviso that if any of the King's vessels arrived in Algiers, "public proclamation shall be immediately made to secure the Christian Captives, and if after that any Christians whatsoever make their escape on Board any of the said ships of war, they shall not be required back again."[65] Though returning of fugitive enslaved Africans was to be an animating issue post-1776, no such requirement was demanded for European Christians post-1676.[66]

But weakening the Dutch most notably was not easy because of the perception that this power was more forthcoming to the increasingly important Iberian Jewish community, which had found refuge in Rotterdam and Amsterdam. After arriving in London's various settlements, there was an upgrade for these migrants over Inquisitorial Spain—an anti-Semitic society—but Barbados and Jamaica particularly were societies that harbored anti-Semitism, which was not helpful either in constructing "whiteness," forestalling slave revolts, or barring foreign invasion. There was also a perception in London that the Ottomans had embraced this oft-persecuted Jewish community to England's detriment. At issue was the enslavement of London's subjects in Algiers, "upwards of 1500" was the claim in 1680. There they endured a "poor supply of bread and water for their food" along with "hundreds of blows on their bare feet." Then there was the "frequent forcing of Men and Boys by their execrable Sodomy, also their inhumane abuses" then "forced [on] the bodies of women and girls, frequently attempting sodomy on them also."

But more shocking in these allegations was the purported responsible party in Algiers. The "promoters of all the inhumane usage of Christians are principally the Jews" was the inflammatory charge. "The owners thereof are for a great part Jews," who were "the constant buyers of . . . the English captives" and the "chief instigators of the Turks and Moors." It was the "Jews who [e]nhance the price of Christian souls by buying them" and "then exacting sums for their redemption." They were the ones who "stir up the Turks and Moors so to beat and abuse poor captives." Worse, it was said, "the Jews in Algiers have too great correspondency with and countenance from the Jews here in England and that by their means it is that they in Algiers have always lists of all our English ships, especially of the fleets coming from any of His Majesties Plantations abroad."[67]

Whether this be deemed just another bigoted screed in a London that countenanced anti-Semitism or a symptom of a larger problem, the ultimate direction was clear. Facing real antagonists in New England, Virginia, and Barbados, London could hardly confront another in North Africa and, assuredly, if anti-Semitism were decreased by dint of forging a synthetic "whiteness," colonialism itself would be strengthened so that real antagonists—particularly in New England and Barbados—could be better fought. There was an implicit admission that the Ottomans were doing a better job of appealing to the Jewish community, as had been the case for the Dutch for some time. In any event, this condemnation of the Jewish community for their alleged role in North Africa was not solitary.[68]

This condemnation was a reflection of a wider bigotry that made the oft-stated distinction between an anti-Semitic society and a society with anti-Semitism not as meaningful as it appeared at first glance. Thus, like the mainland, Barbados was not opposed to settling those from the Jewish community, not least because of a concern about "whiteness" and overawing an African majority. Yet from 1680 to 1780 a blatantly unfair taxation was levied on the Jewish community, draining their wealth and perhaps making some not as grateful to England as might have been imagined.[69] It was hardly consolation and likely helped to galvanize anti-Semitism that as of 1678 policymakers in Barbados were mulling over "an act for preventing dangers which may happen from 'Popish Recusants.'"[70]

Across the Caribbean Sea in Port Royal, Jamaica, a haven for pirates, there was a growing Jewish population, an outgrowth of the ouster of Iberians from Recife in 1654. Even before the Cromwell takeover of the island in 1655, those fleeing the Inquisition had flocked to Jamaica, with a Jewish community 1,500 strong as early as 1611. By 1680, Boston had a population of about 6,000, while that of Port Royal was 7,500 and that included about a hundred Jewish families.[71]

In retrospect, to the extent that the Iberian Jewish community wound up in North Africa—tales of captivity aside—this was a wise maneuver, in that it gave them a window into neighboring Spain, which, as the citadel of anti-Semitism, had to be watched carefully. Besides, the Ottomans, undeterred by their setback in Vienna, had made overtures to what became Germany, which also had jurisdiction over a sizable Jewish community.[72]

DURING THIS ENTIRE ERA, London was squabbling with the usual competitors, especially the Dutch, about who would become the leader in enslaving Africans. As early as 1672, most of the enslaved in Virginia had arrived directly from Africa and were never seasoned in the Caribbean.[73] This coincided with the organizing of the Royal African Company, which marked a heightened aggressiveness by those in Liverpool and Bristol whose lifework was enslaving Africans. But suggestive of how the merchants were ascending even as the Crown-dominated RAC was organized, as early as 1679 privately owned vessels already were becoming more prominent in the odious commerce.[74]

Thus by 1670 Dutch traders in West Africa were carping per usual: "Blacks often quarreled with us," they grumbled, "They are constantly troublesome." Still, it was conceded, "every year we buy there 2,500 to 3,000 sometimes more slaves. . . . The Negroes who are bought in that area are bad and stubborn and often kill themselves."[75]

A few years after Bacon's revolt, King Philip's War and Barbadian unrest had shaken the entire colonial project, a Dutchman, Heerman Abramsz, was at Sekondi along the Gold Coast, grumbling that the "English have crept in" and "in spite of promises to the contrary, the natives have allowed this," which was "quite contrary to their earlier promises"; in fact, "they trade every day with English, Portuguese and other ships and so we decided to abandon this lodge. The English had already abandoned theirs in 1650." His countrymen had preceded his fellow Western Europeans: "We even saw ourselves compelled, because of the bad behavior of the Blacks, to abandon the place in 1648." The "rowdiness" of Africans, he groused, indeed, the "nature of all the Blacks" meant they tended to "only stick to their promises as long as they see advantage in them; and so welcomed in 1648 the English." The "wars which the Blacks so often start for trifling reasons" meant that "trade is stopped" and "especially since musket and gunpowder have been introduced, things have become much worse"; that is, "the natives have become more war-like." As a consequence, "the whole Coast has come into a kind of state of wars. This started in the year 1658"; thus "slaves were very easy to get by on the Gold Coast, because of the wars. In Arder, on the contrary, the slave trade was entirely stopped because of war." This was tragic, Abramsz thought, given the "great importance of the slave trade."[76]

By 1684, the consensus was that "most of these Negroes remaining were brought here on the Gold Coast and are consequently inclined towards running away and seeking their freedom."[77]

By 1686 there was caviling about how "high-handed" Africans had become.[78] The next year there were protests indicating that the intended enslaved had become "not all that polite" and destroyed the Dutch flag. This was a "serious matter and the English and the French" were "quite happy about it." The Dutchman concluded that "our presence in this country is no longer brooked."[79]

By 1688 the notion was afloat that "Negroes are so bold as to compete in their trade even with the Company, trading on board of those interloper ships even when they are guarded." By 1688, not least because of the manipulation and arbitrage of Africans, there was a commercial competition, in particular with the English, which led to "innumerable squabbles." To that point, said one Dutchman with irritation, "the slave trade has well progressed but these days it seems to slow off a little as a result of the lack of wars in the interior."[80] And yes, fomenting wars would definitely resolve this nettlesome problem.

Just as colonialism, colonial merchants, and the wealth they generated—based on dispossession and enslavement—helped to propel the beheading of a king, the rise of Cromwell and the ultimate weakening of the Crown also catapulted the "Glorious Revolution" of 1688. At issue here, inter alia, was the demand of merchants that the Crown unfairly dominated the African Slave Trade not only to their detriment but to the detriment of the nation and of rights generally, including the rights of the demos. Their cause was to prevail and lead future generations of "Marxists" and "radicals" to hail the resultant growth of the productive forces. However, this "victory" was a staggering blow to Africans and Native Americans: it was the dawning of the apocalypse.

CHAPTER 8

The "Glorious Revolution" of 1688: Not So Glorious for Africans and the Indigenous

P ut simply, the "Glorious Revolution" of 1688 involved the deposing of King James II and the accession of William III and Mary II to the English throne. For purposes here, the import was a step toward Cromwell and away from the apparent repercussions of the royal restoration after he expired. More to the point, it involved a weakening of the Royal African Company and the monarch and the rise of merchants to the top ranks of this repugnant business, under the guise of strengthening the demos. Given the grimy origins of republicanism and "democracy" in the Anglo-American sphere, is it any wonder that even in today's United States, it remains difficult to extend the full bounty of rights to the descendants of the formerly enslaved or the indigenous?

BY 1680 BARBADOS WAS the richest colony in North America, sufficiently powerful to generate a "colony" of its own: South Carolina.[1] The future Palmetto State quickly developed a model of development comparable to that of this Caribbean island, including an often rebellious African majority. This restive majority's propensity for allying with indigenes and foreign invaders alike was to jeopardize all of London's holdings in North America.

Once the African Slave Trade accelerated after deregulation in 1688, however, Barbados simply could not absorb the massive influx of enchained Africans crossing the Atlantic, whereas the mainland could. Thus an enriching transformation of North America accelerated wildly, with Africa transformed also in an accelerative fashion, albeit in the opposing direction: impoverishment. This set the stage for a lurch toward secession in 1776. In that context, the recent thesis that 1776 represented a revolt against Parliament and not the monarch makes sense.[2] Now the merchants and planters of the mainland who had contributed to the 1688 deregulation by dint of weakening the monarchy went after the new power center that was Parliament. Moreover, 1776 was a kind of replay of the English civil wars of the 1640s when pro-royalists in Virginia opposed Cromwell, whose forces then began to lard Parliament. Colonial secession then was a "Royalist Revolution," as Virginia came to dominate the Republic in the pre-1861 era, representing as it did a lethal brew of feudalism, capitalism—and slavery.

Still, 1688 only served to ratify, as so often happens, changes already in motion, rather than mark a sharp line of demarcation. That is, freelance merchants had already begun to encroach on the wealth usually claimed by the Royal African Company, providing this rising class with a foretaste of riches that served to whet their ravenous appetites for more. Thus, by 1684, the authorities in Barbados were mulling over a statute involving "securing the possession of Negroes and slaves"; not coincidentally, also debated at this session was "an act for the settlement of the militia of this island."[3] By the next year, 1685, a levy was imposed on Negroes to pay for "fortifications,"[4] which was appropriate, in a way, since the presence of this oppressed group necessitated enhanced fortifying.

There was general instability in the vast territories under London's jurisdiction, and Africans had long displayed an ability to leverage it for their own purposes. In 1685 news was received on the island of the "disturbances" then unfolding in Scotland; these were caused by "traitors and others desperate of fortunes," said the Barbadian elite, and thus were viewed by them with both "abhorrence and detestation," showing how sensitive they were to arrival of such unsteadiness in the region.[5] But what the elite abhorred and detested potentially created more openings for Africans. Thus "rebellious subjects," "rebels" in fact, were "sent" to the island who had "taken up arms against us." The penalty of "death" was meted out to some, though "mercy" meant that others would be exempted. They were to be "kept as servants . . . for the space of two years,"[6] but it was possible that their demonstrated unmanageability would fit nicely with that of enslaved Africans.

The "traitorous practices and rebellion of the late Earl of Argyle" in Scotland was blamed easily, but harder to grapple with was the effect of dumping European rebels among often mutinous Africans.[7] Ultimately, as the African Slave Trade expanded, along with dispossession of indigenes on the mainland, the loyalty of more rebellious Scots could be purchased, stabilizing London, and further devastating Africans and Native Americans.

What was telling about this island was that as the number of Africans increased, so did their restiveness—and so did ever more ghoulish punishments of them, up to and including ghastly executions. African lives were devalued with the increase in their numbers, which was accompanied by a decline in deployment of European indentured servants, raising their scarcity value. Thomas Walrond was paid in mid-1685 "after a Negro man of his" was "executed"; received by this slaveholder was "four hundred thousand ponds of Muscovado Sugar," which appeared to establish an incentive for abusing Africans who demonstrated the slightest hint of rebelliousness.[8]

The Christmas holiday, when slaveholders may have been more inebriated and less alert than usual, was often a time for Africans to strike. With their numbers increasing and their executions rising, given economic incentives, a recipe for fiasco was created. In December 1685 Hugh Jones was paid "for a Negro of his executed"; Abraham Newell also was paid for a similar reason. Ditto for "Mary Sharp widow" and Captain William Burger, too, except he was paid "for the loss of two Negroes of his executed."[9]

Then, weeks later, it seemed that settlers' fear of insurrectionist Africans was real. For it was then that a "combination" of "the Negroes" and "some white servants," possibly recently arrived Scots, "designed" a plot to "destroy all the masters." A "strict search" was "to be made throughout all the Negro houses," seeking "arms, ammunition or other dangerous weapons." The prophylactic was to "keep good watch . . . over the Negroes both day and night and particularly on Sunday"—it was thought that on the latter day there was a tendency among "a great many" Africans to "meet on sundry places in order to consult and contrive their carrying on their bloody design."

But outnumbered slaveholders were forced to compromise in an unfortunately percipient manner. From then on there would be "keeping of a strict watch" over Africans "by such white servants as they can well trust and confide in."[10] This effectively drove a wedge between the two, as the pattern of effectively and seductively bribing poorer Europeans to monitor oppressed Africans took flight.

This diabolical strategy did not attain lift off instantaneously. A few weeks later "Irish servants" were jailed on "suspicion of their being concerned or privy to the late intended rising of the Negroes to destroy all masters and mistresses."[11] But soon "Irish servants" would be referred to as "white servants" who presumably shared an identity with "white" slaveholders. By April 1686 a dual list was drawn up. One concerned political prisoners from Europe to be shipped to Barbados and possibly other Caribbean islands.[12] The other was a list of African men to be executed.[13] As the number of Africans grew, the more uncontrollable they became and more were slated to be executed. This unruliness in turn necessitated more monitors, suggesting blandishments to arriving Europeans.

By 1687, this deteriorating environment had attracted the keen attention of Richard Blome, who was stunned by the "severity" accorded the enslaved. Inevitably, this "occasioned a great conspiracy against their Masters" that was barely blocked. "Many of them," meaning Africans, "were put to death" while "Terror" was doled out to the rest, "who being so numerous might prove dangerous." It was thought that the elite had a trump card, however, since the enslaved hailed from "different countries," and did "not understand one another's language,"[14] a complexity worthy of exploitation in the near future.

A similar process was developing in Jamaica. In 1681 it was ordered that "all owners of meat cattle shall keep one white man at each respective pen and at all pens" with more than "two hundred cattle, the owner of such pen shall keep two white men."[15] But "whites" were the coin of the realm, needed to reinforce settler colonialism and monitor Africans alike. That same year a law was passed "encouraging the importation of white servants."[16] But ordering this and actualizing it were two substantially different projects.

And yet, the overlords of slavery in Jamaica had to do something. In 1681 they were considering an act for "preventing fires," as fire was a frequent tactic employed by refractory Africans.[17]

By 1683 Jamaican settlers were optimistic, despite being besieged by Maroons, who were not opposed to allying with foreign invaders. Beaming, they had the sunny idea that as more settlers arrived, along with more enslaved Africans, "the trade and shipping will both increase." One reason for this misplaced cheeriness was that "in Jamaica the women after child[birth] are strong and lusty at three days end and about house again in a week," meaning higher productivity. And "nay, some Negro women are at work in the field the same day or next day." There was even confidence that the oppressed "were not a terror to us"; no, it was said shakily, "we are in no such fear or danger as in lesser islands" since "Jamaica is of too vast an extent for such surprise," though the very articulation betrayed nervousness. The rule was that "boats and ferries" were instructed to "carry no Negroes without a written ticket or license," as if promulgating a regulation magically shaped reality. "And if any slave be found wandering" about, then "any person may seize and carry him to his owner" and "receive a certain reward." Indeed, there was "safer living in Jamaica than England," with "rarely any house-breaking or robbery."

Yet this bullishness on Jamaica could not obscure the damning reality. Still, the idea that "any person"—meaning European—could "seize" an African, established a dangerous precedent, which on the mainland has yet to be extinguished.[18] Moreover, only a few years earlier it was acknowledged that there had been "several insurrections & Rebellions of our Negroes to the great disturbance of . . . peace & planting," necessitating "one white servant for every ten Negroes"—with nary an indication as to where or when this brave soul would arrive who would be capable of controlling ten Africans.[19]

In any case, in Jamaica during this time, a settler, Nicholas Scarlet, received "great and dangerous wounds" that were "received in pursuit of several Rebellious Negroes," meaning the "loss of the use of one of his limbs." He was to receive in compensation a "yearly salary" of "ten pounds during his residence" in Jamaica, a cost of conducting a bloody business. Limited options—and imagination—meant settlers could produce remedies more sophisticated than retaliatory terror and somehow import more Europeans. "Every master and owner of slaves shall have such quantity of white servants proportionable to the number of slaves," but left to the imagination was what enticements would be necessary to attract the guileless Europeans to a war zone. Simultaneously, settlers were creating a system that demanded more arrivals from the old continent. No Africans could be employed, for example, as "coopers or porters . . . under the penalty of twenty pounds" per offense, though this job restriction tended to compromise productivity. Inexorably, one of the lengthier pieces of legislation was one for "preventing fire," as arson remained the African's trusty friend.

London was pushed into a corner by the raucousness of European servants. Planters lusted after their cheap labor but were flummoxed by the prospect that they would rebel. Besides, there was a perceived need to continue to expel political dissidents and rebels from England and its environs. In 1685, for example, Jamaica—and other "parts of [the Crown's] Dominions in America"—received a directive to absorb at least "200 . . . servants" who would toil "for the space of ten years."[20]

Fortunately for London, 1685 also marked the Revocation of the Edict of Nantes, heightening religious repression against Protestants and Huguenots in France and opening the door for them to flee to more hospitable climes, such as London's possessions, thus increasing the importance of the developing "whiteness." Perhaps in objective retaliation, a French raid on Jamaica shortly thereafter resulted in a massive haul for French buccaneers of 1,900 enslaved Africans.[21]

Earlier, in 1683, before this monumental development became evident, Jamaican policymakers sought to contradict their earlier bullishness, when formulating words that went beyond official optimism. This concerned a life-and-death matter: the readiness of the militia. Conceded was the volatility of the vicinity, featuring "subtle, rich and potent nations," meaning "the necessity" of "being well armed and [being] trained [in] the art of military." Gunpowder and sharp swords were a must. Reluctantly admitted was that Africans could be deployed in the militia in an emergency—but must be "immediately discharged."[22]

Thus, with clockwork precision, by 1685 the aptly named "Council of War" in Jamaica was enmeshed in "consideration of the most proper means for the speedy suppressing and reducing of a party of rebellious Negroes."[23] The next year there was yet another "Negro rebellion" that was engendering conniptions.[24] The island, it was feared, was "infested at present with rebellious Negroes," and worse, there was a "very imminent danger from them."[25]

As ever, there was an organic tie between tumult on this island and trends in New England. Just as settlers in the Caribbean were wringing their hands about slavery, a French Protestant exile in 1687 commented that "there is not a house in Boston however small be its means that has not one or two" enslaved Africans, and "there are those that have five or six."[26] But given the problems in Boston with restive indigenes and rebellious Africans, was it really safe for settlers? Perhaps emoluments in the form of land seized from the indigenous and doled out to arriving European settlers, even poorer ones, could reverse these dangerous ratios.

Also in 1687 a typical event occurred when a settler in Jamaica met a vessel from New England, via Maryland, bound to Barbados. It was unclear if this ship was bringing newly enslaved indigenes, though it was conceded by this settler that "the Indians are of diverse nations brought hither," that is, from "Surinam, Florida, New England, etc., and are sold here for slaves." These indigenes were bound for an indomitable hell on earth. He conceded the use of "excessive torture" against these enslaved laborers, for example, "cutting off their ears and members and making . . . 'em eat them, by cutting out their tungs [*sic*] and cutting off their feet, etc." But this was insufficient because "still Negroes revolt and dayly run away from their masters into the woods and mountains, where they lurk together in parties, stealing at night from plantations" since "many of those vassals have gott arms . . . swords, etc." With a sigh, he confessed, "'tis a great trouble and expence to this island to keep continual parties out after 'em." But the Africans were armed and "well know the use of them; the rest are armed with bowes and launces."

How to respond? Again, "all gentlemen, merchants, planters" were urged to keep "one English servant in his house or plantation for every nine Negro slaves which he hath" and this would "strengthen" the island. It was also thought that "one faithful . . . Indian slave is as good as three Negro slaves," though it was unclear how this formula was devised. But settler colonialism was not for the fainthearted Harshness was mandatory when dealing with the enslaved, "for if you should be kinder to 'em they would so[o]ner cut . . . your throat than obey you."[27]

This acidulous rebuke seemingly could have been penned by William Blathwayt, the official with oversight of London's governors on the mainland and the Caribbean. His inbox was overflowing with hair-raising reports like the 1681 missive from Boston telling of African and indigenous slaves rebelling and seeking to burn down their "master's" house—and being executed in return.[28] Then it was Blathwayt's turn in 1682 to warn of "piratical Negroes" besieging settlements.[29] Nonetheless, the next year Blathwayt was informed by Jamaica's governor that a battleship should be sent to Africa's coast to repress those Africans interfering with the enslaving of Africans.[30] The situation was desperate, it was reported anxiously, as more manacled Africans were demanded.[31] Yet Jamaica continued to arrange for Spaniards to arrive on the island to buy the enslaved.[32] Thus, in a customary maneuver, Spaniards left Jamaica in 1683 with about 400 Africans,[33] and the next year a ship from Gambia arrived with about 200.[34] Either London had to restrain their Spanish competitors from denuding Jamaica of Africans or escalate the number brought from Africa. All the while, Jamaican Africans remained on the warpath, jeopardizing the entire colonial project.[35] Blathwayt may have been excused if he had concluded that the island he nominally supervised went by the name of "Rebellious Negroes" instead of Jamaica.[36]

If settlers had been paying attention, they might have noticed that Africans were not only rebelling upon arrival in the Americas, they were probably harder to manage in the immediate vicinity of Africa itself. In West Africa in 1686, it was reported somberly, they "rose on board and kill[ed] all the white men."[37] A few weeks later near Accra, the news was similar, it was noted with a grimace: the captain "and all his men were killed by the [Africans] which he had then aboard."[38]

The Royal African Company, nonetheless, was viewed as inadequate to the task at hand.[39] Yet in the run-up to the hinge moment that was 1688, the monarch was jealously guarding his control over the increasingly lucrative African Slave Trade, seeking to bar subjects from encroaching, with severe penalties meted out to those so audacious to try.[40]

In short, the RAC, which was to be eclipsed in the wake of the "Glorious Revolution," did not retreat willingly. The RAC's flacks wondered how a gaggle of freelance merchants could compete with the state power wielded by the Dutch in Africa. "This trade cannot be carried on," they said haughtily, "but by a constant maintaining of forts" along the coast and battleships to "protect the ships of trade" in morbid contestation "by reason of the natural perfidiousness of the Natives, who being a barbarous and heathen people, cannot be obliged by treaties without being awed by a continuing and permanent force." Moreover, European competitors—Dutch, French, Portuguese et al.—were "frequently instigating the Natives against us." These mere "private persons" were incapable of bearing the none too trivial cost and burden of this loathsome business.[41]

But the monarch and his retinue, as so often happens with a

beleaguered ruling elite, suffered from a failure of imagination. It was readily contemplatable that the monarch could be downgraded to the status of figurehead and with the added wealth brought by the African Slave Trade and dispossession of the indigenous, the talents of smart men could then be bought to administer a state apparatus with the strength to build forts in Africa and a prepossessing Royal Navy. However, the vanguard of change in 1688 did not necessarily contemplate 1776, when the decision was made to secede from London's rule altogether, and then challenge it forcefully in following decades.

The merchants had their own spinners of reality, who argued that if only the merchants were unleashed, with their animal spirts driving the magic of the marketplace, London would become great again.[42] Planters were groaning about taxes on imported Africans, which merged with their complaint that the RAC was derelict in supplying this labor force. "We must have them," cried Edward Littlejohn on Barbados, "we cannot be without them."[43]

Both sides could agree on the importance of enslaving Africans and the prosperity (for some) thereby generated; they just quarreled about who should be in control. One London propagandist in 1687 was gloating about the "growing greatness" of "distant colonies"; these territories had "already arrived" at a stature "so considerable" that it could easily "attract the emulation of the Neighbouring potentates. The Golden Peru," the pacesetter by some measures, was "hardly affording so great a treasure to the Catholick Crown, as these most flourishing plantations"—Barbados and Jamaica particularly—"produce to the Crown of England."[44]

That is, London had taken Jamaica in 1655 at a time when sugar began to boom, meaning a need for more Africans. By 1672 the Royal African Company had been organized to fill the breach, but in the following decade it was seen as inadequate to the task at hand. This meant deregulation of this hateful business, which meant reducing the powers of the Crown, which dominated the RAC. This blatant power and money grab by merchants was then dressed in the finery of liberty and freedom,[45] as the bourgeois revolution was conceived in a crass and crude act of staggering hypocrisy, which nevertheless bamboozled generations to follow, including those who styled themselves as radical.

AS THE "GLORIOUS REVOLUTION" in England was inaugurating a money and power grab by rising merchants in the name of liberty and freedom as they undermined the monarch's hegemony over the wildly profitable African Slave Trade, the intended victims—Africans—were in their usual bellicose posture. A "dreadful fire" devastated Barbados in April, and "in the space of two or three hours time," it was reported tremblingly, vast areas were "burnt and consumed almost all the buildings" extant. It was a "sad calamity," and the main suspect was a "little Negro, who lighted the candle" of destruction.[46]

That same year policymakers felt compelled to craft yet another "act for the governing of Negroes." Yes, "plantations and estates" could not be "fully managed" absent the "labour and service of great numbers and other slaves"; however, they were so "barbarous" and "wild" and of "savage natures," and besides that, it was "absolutely necessary to the safety of this place that all due care be taken to restrain" the "wandering and meetings of Negroes and other slaves at all times, more especially on *Saturday* nights and *Sunday* and other Holy days" (emphasis in original). In one of the lengthiest laws drafted during the colonial era on the island, lamented were "many heinous and grievous crimes," that is, "murders, burglaries, robbing in the highways, rapes, burning of houses or cane"—all of which were perpetrated by "Negroes and other Slaves," a veiled reference to the population of indigenes in this fraught category.[47]

The problem for London was that unrest was not just roiling the settlements; a similar process was unwinding in England itself. Indeed, one process was feeding the other in that a central issue was seeking to control the remunerative slave trade then dominated by the monarch. The conflict often took on a religious character in London, thereby heightening the intensity and fueling more shipments of dissident rebels to the Caribbean where they could continue their activism.[48]

After the *sturm und drang* had receded and the "Glorious Revolution" of 1688 registered success,[49] the already deteriorating monopoly of the Royal African Company eroded further, opening the door to a substantially larger trade in enslaved Africans and, notably, allowing Virginians to deploy even more Negro labor and reduce the reliance on European labor. In any event, Bacon's Rebellion was signaling such a change, allowing for exponential growth of the productive forces, creating a yawning gap with London that eventuated in the convulsion of 1776. This also laid the foundation for exponential growth of capitalism and its handmaidens: white supremacy and slavery.[50]

This process also involved, as noted, a religious conflict, and on the mainland in 1688 this meant a setback for Catholic Maryland. Just as in 1776, the fear of an African uprising, facilitated by the final colonial governor of Virginia—Lord Dunmore, reviled by republicans as a result—helped to galvanize settlers to overthrow London's rule, so too, there was a panic in 1688 that suggested Catholics had formed a conspiracy with indigenes to massacre Protestants, which galvanized Chesapeake settlers seeking to undermine the status quo.[51] This was a continuation of the 1640s and the civil war in England, when Catholics again were repressed.[52] The stakes were so large—swathes of land taken illicitly from indigenes, to then be "stocked" by enslaved Africans—and the ideology so suffused with lingering religious and accelerating racial bigotry that the victimized would ineluctably be numerous. Assuredly, "whiteness" or "race" was a more sturdy identity politics for implanting settler colonialism, than religion, which often served to split the settlers.

Maryland was being transformed by the after-effects of 1688. Recall the African named Anthony Johnson who during this century was able to accumulate a forty-four-acre tract with the telling name of "Angola." Quakers, who were beginning to exercise their abolitionist muscles, had migrated from the eastern shore of Virginia to Maryland (Johnson seems to have been affiliated with the Church of England). Also migrating to Somerset County, Maryland, from Virginia was a free Negro family surnamed Driggus. But as they were arriving, things were changing, transforming the Maryland they once knew. By 1681 the assembly passed a law imposing penalties on European indentured servant women who bore so-called bastard children by enslaved Africans, further driving a wedge through labor. Soon free Negroes were no longer permitted to testify against Europeans in civil and criminal cases, effectively handicapping their ability to climb the already unsteady class ladder. During most of the century, there were not that many enslaved Africans in the lower eastern shore region of Maryland, though afterward this changed dramatically.[53] Just as détente between London and the Ottoman Turks was not necessarily good news for Africans and the indigenous peoples, when Protestant and Catholic in Maryland moved to reconcile, it served to guarantee that they could focus their robust energy on further seizing of land and enslaving of the unfortunate.[54]

The wealth being generated in the slave labor camps of the Americas was often fed into ancillary industries such as shipbuilding, finance, banking, and insurance. As a proper colonialism should work, this benefited Liverpool, Bristol, and Manchester. After 1688 some economic theorists began to view the poor in these metropolises as a necessary resource for ensuring the prosperity of the nation; they were to provide a reservoir of labor that should be preserved for home use and not squandered on the colonies. (Admittedly, this was not a unanimously held viewpoint.) Correspondingly, this began to drain the settlements of Europeans as the number of Africans was rising, enhancing—in different ways—the value of both groups in the Americas: the enslaved produced wealth and the Europeans became more useful as occupiers of indigenous land and monitors of indigenes and the enslaved and the like.[55] This was taking place in the context of a shift from religion to "race" as an axis of society.

The unbridling of the flesh peddlers brought a tidal wave of Africans coursing across the Atlantic with untoward consequences rarely understood. As ever, policymakers focused on short-term approaches, for example, runaways committing depredations in Virginia, a primary site for their arrival. "Such Negroes, mulattoes or slaves, running away, or refusing to surrender," it was intoned

ominously, "may be killed and destroyed." As in Barbados there
would be "compensation to [the] master" for every slave "destroyed,"
providing an incentive to brook not the slightest hint of dissension.
As for a European man or woman, "bond or free intermarrying with a
Negro, mulatto or Indian,"[56] well, akin to Maryland, they were to be
"banished forever" as sharper racial lines were demarcated.

As Africans began to pour into South Carolina post-1688, the
"colony of the colony" continued this trend by copying the slave code
of Barbados. This code was unusually harsh, as the enslaved were
treated as less than human. Perhaps appropriately, Carolina's law of
slavery had more in common with the law of the Caribbean than that
of the mainland colonies to the north.[57]

At the source of supply in Africa, as was the custom, the coastlines
were aflame with revolt. A lodge there, wailed one Dutchman, was
"totally ruined by the Negroes and that all the factors [Europeans] are
said to have been murdered."[58]

It was not just Maryland and Virginia and South Carolina (and
Africa itself) that were shaken by 1688. There was Leisler's Revolt in
the region stretching outward from colonial New York with related
unsteadiness in Boston, too.[59] As with Bacon's Rebellion, London's
man in Boston, Sir Edmund Andros, was thought to be dangerously conciliatory toward indigenes, in a settlement where feelings
were still raw from the 1676 uprising of Native Americans.[60] In a
prelude to 1776, he was jailed in Boston.[61] In yet another precursor
to 1776, a merchant was furious with Sir Edmund since "people in
New England were all slaves and the only difference between them
and slaves is their not being bought and sold."[62] Thus the horrible
plight of actual slaves was trivialized, and thereby rationalized. Up
for grabs was a cornucopia of wealth and influence of which the
slave trade and the land of the indigenous represented a significant
portion. As in Maryland, there was a strain of anti-Catholicism in
Jacob Leisler's movement, along with resentment on the part of small
traders and artisans of rapidly enriching merchants.[63] An overlay of
religious conflict was the national one featuring Protestant England
versus Catholic France.[64] A precipitant of 1688 was the notion that the

monarch was seeking to oust Protestantism in favor of Catholicism, not least in North America.[65] Catholic recusants could save themselves, if not their souls, by bowing before the altar of the newest and still resonant creator: white supremacy.

This growing clash between London and Paris was to escalate post-1688[66] and created arbitrage opportunities for their various foes to lean against one, then the other, for the advancement of Africans and indigenes. Thus the Iroquois were accused of backing one power against another, while attacking the indigenous allies of that power.[67]

There was also religious conflict in London's neighborhood, with Scottish Presbyterians—in addition to Catholics—being the target. Quakers too often found themselves at odds with dominant religious elites. Many fled to the settlements as a result. The English at times viewed Scots with dislike and contempt, as the latter minority often found itself tortured to extort confessions for varied offenses. Repression of Presbyterians had been going on at least since the 1660 restoration; then the emergence of the Cameronian sect in 1680 led to their renouncing the Crown. As was the pattern, not least after the forging of the United Kingdom in 1707, many Scots migrated to sites such as East Jersey and other parts of the British Empire where they became key administrators and profiteers.[68] Effectively, their religious and nationalist dissidence was bought at the expense of indigenes— and enslaved Africans.

This was not an instant process, however. Some in Edinburgh had thought that the growth of settler colonialism was a detriment to Scotland, but their remedy was that Scots should cast aside doubts and plunge headlong into colonialism. This, it was said, would mean Scotland "will be rendered more rich and so better able to live like our Neighbours." Moreover, settlements would allow Scotland "to be free of our loose idle people without destroying them," since "it is evident our country cannot sustain the people it produceth and therefore our Youth in time of War . . . are forced abroad" to fight. Poland, for example, had "ten thousand Scots born and bred in Scotland"—why should they not seek fame and fortune westward, not eastward? For a "plantation would ease us all of all the Scum," including "our idle

Young Women." Besides, Scotland could export to the colonies.[69] What was not to like?

Toward the end of the seventeenth century, Africa became the direct source of imported Africans—as opposed to the Caribbean— as the number of indentured Europeans fell accordingly. Before 1650 there were more of the latter than the enslaved but by the 1690s this situation was altered conclusively. Anti-miscegenation laws meant that the prospect of "white slaves" or "Negro freemen" was pointedly circumscribed.[70]

During the same time in East Jersey, policymakers forbade the enslaved from hunting unless accompanied by their owners or owners' proxies; half of the fine would be given to the informer and half to the township for the use of poorer Europeans. Persons harboring the enslaved without the owner's consent were also fined. Any European could apprehend a runaway slave more than five miles from the master's house. Anyone supplying a pistol to a slave would forfeit the weapon to the master of the slave. Finally, in the 1690s, the entire slave code was enlarged,[71] at the same time that the naïve rhapsodized about the enlargement of bourgeois rights.

The year of 1688 also eased the transition from investments pouring into the Caribbean and being redirected to the mainland instead. Sending Africans to Jamaica, for example, was like sending troops to join the Maroons, who were threatening the entire settlement. By 1690 there was a revolt of the enslaved in Clarendon who then retreated to the interior of the island, evading colonial jurisdiction and creating havoc.[72]

CHAPTER 9

Apocalypse Now

I f one is searching for a year that marks the onset of the dawning of the apocalypse, 1688 is the date. For it was in that year the merchants completed what they had launched in the 1640s when the power and influence from settler colonialism propelled a revolt in London that led to the beheading of a king. By 1688, under the guise of "freedom" and "liberty," this same class had sliced—then ultimately beheaded— the dominance of the monarch in the growingly lucrative business of selling African bodies. The erosion of the strength of a feudal monarchy may have been a step forward, but this prize (for some) arrived with an apocalyptic price tag, a price at the expense of Africans and Native Americans. It is a sad commentary, and indicative of the steep climb ahead, that even those who have considered themselves radical have downplayed this latter factor, while hailing the "progressivism" of 1688 and its progeny. There is irony here, in that some of these same "radicals" have had little compunction about denouncing the price delivered by the arrival of socialism on the world stage in 1917, not to mention those who executed this earthshaking development.

As is so often the case, rivals engaged in unwise acts also explains London's post-1688 rise, a status then handed off to their North American cousins. For it was in 1688 that France found itself at war with both England and the Netherlands, as well as the armies of the Austrian and Spanish Hapsburgs. This devastating war lasted until 1697, leaving the hexagonal nation exhausted, and leaving Paris's Caribbean holdings vulnerable and hardly able to withstand the competition from Jamaica and Barbados. Of course, the other trend then was the opportunity presented to dissidents under London's jurisdiction; for example, when Irish uprisings on Saint-Christophe aided the—temporary—French triumph. But the English counterattacked vigorously and departed from the French Caribbean with the most valuable of commodities, enslaved Africans, who were to prove to be the decisive coin of the realm.[1]

UNSURPRISINGLY, IT WAS IN BARBADOS where one of the lengthiest laws to that point emerged detailing the encoding—or "governing"—of slavery. Anticipating apartheid, a kind of pass law was enacted for Africans when beyond the purview of their "masters." Forbidden was "using and carrying of clubs, wooden-swords or other mischievous and dangerous weapons or using or keeping drums, horns or other loud instruments which may call together or give sign or notice to one another, for their wicked designs and purposes." If such instruments were found, they were to be burned. Dwellings were to be searched "once every fourteen days for fugitive or runaway slaves," a growing problem, along with trading in "stolen goods." Special attention was accorded the "evil" ones who "attempted to steal away slaves by specious pretense of promising their freedom in another country." If found, they were to become a "servant for five years to the party injured" or fined severely. This was needed since there had been "many heinous and grievous crimes, as murder, burglaries, robbing in the high-ways, rapes, burning of houses or canes," all "many times committed by Negroes," who also had the temerity to "many times steal, willfully kill, maim or destroy one or more horses, mares, geldings, cattle, sheep," leaving the affected "family in terror, dread of jeopardy of their lives." The punishment for this latter crime was being "branded in the forehead with a hot iron." For repeated offenses, death was the penalty.

And "if any Negroes or other slaves"—a now familiar phrase—
"shall make Mutiny or Insurrection or rise in Rebellion" or "make
preparation of arms" or other "offensive weapons or [hold] any council
or conspiracy" or "rais[e] Mutiny or Rebellion," they too should receive
the death penalty. But, familiarly, masters were to be compensated in
such a circumstance, providing an incentive for a fierce crackdown on
slave resistance. Or, as the statute put it, since masters kept a "flock
of Negroes and other slaves whose desperate lives and great numbers
become dangerous to them and all other . . . inhabitants," this did
"increase the danger to this island" but these Africans—or at least their
labor—were needed to "hire out to others."

Still, at this late date, it was stressed that "no person of the *Hebrew*
nation residing in any sea-port town . . . shall keep or employ any
Negro or other slave," as if the two groups had dire plans in store.[2]

But accompanying this draconian law was a kind of amelioration
act concerning "poor Apprentices," or Europeans, as class conciliation between this group and the elite continued apace.[3] By 1692
an urgent appeal was made in the Leeward Islands designed for
"encouraging the importation of white servant men,"[4] which would
be repetitively invoked in coming decades. Security against the dual
threat of domestic insurrection accompanied by foreign invasion was
the driving force shaping settler colonialism—and, arguably, the successor state on the mainland, too. Barbados was not immune from this
trend for similar reasons. Also in 1692, London was informed curtly
that "the people of Barbados being in Great Fear and dread of their
Negroes and in great want of men" demanded at least a "regiment of
men" to be "posted" for "defence and safety," and ideally, more settlers. The "French" threat was stressed.[5] To put it bluntly, London
was told that "the people of the island were under very great fears, as
well from a conspiracy form'd against them by their Negroes, as from
the danger of a Foreign Enemy."[6]

Soon thereafter an act to organize a militia was devised, given the
"present war with *France*" (emphasis in original), meaning "every
poor Free man within this island . . . shall be [e]nlisted" and provided
arms. Every servant who performed adequately would be "declared

a free man," providing yet another opportunity for cross-class collaboration. By contrast, every African who performed adequately was to receive "yearly a Livery coat and a Hat," though many from this group were "worthy of great trust and confidence."[7] By mid-1696 London was once more seeking to attract "able White Men Servants" so as to overawe the enslaved, among other priorities.[8] Planters were "obliged" by London "to keep one white servant for every ten Negroes," though unhelpfully no instruction was provided as to their site of origin.[9]

By the turn of the eighteenth century, servants were rechristened as "white servants" and provided further "encouragement" in the form of "provisions and clothes."[10] War with France erupted in the Leeward Islands in 1690, as this Caribbean expression of a long-term trend provided Africans with numerous opportunities for arbitrage.[11]

By 1692, this legislative thumping had not seemed to have restrained Negro rebelliousness. Hence, though "subjects of the Kingdom of Spain" were "permitted to trade" in Barbados and "to buy and purchase Negroes," to facilitate sales—perhaps to oust the rebellious—all taxes against such sales would now be "absolutely null and void."[12]

That same year, yet another law had to be passed ordering death to runaways. Restricting Africans' consumption of the major export that was rum was also part of the agenda since it was thought that their drinking led to "many enormities" and "mischiefs hatched and contrived by Negroes and other slaves when . . . excessive drinking" occurs.[13]

In neighboring Jamaica there were similar problems, as more Africans arrived in the wake of "reforms" of the slave trade. Months after the successful conclusion of the "Glorious Revolution," Sir William Dains and other merchants were petitioning Parliament to allow them a share in the African Slave Trade and an erosion of the RAC monopoly.[14] As if on cue, the House of Assembly appropriated funds in 1696 to "pay parties to reduce Rebellious Negroes."[15] As in Barbados, Jamaica was haunted by an "invasion of the French, which meant more debt and, more fortifications, particularly at Port Morant."[16] The 1690s were an era of turmoil for Jamaica.[17]

Building fortifications in Kingston "for the better defending [of] this island" was a must given the multiple threats faced by the authorities.[18] That was primarily to blunt the danger of foreign invasion. However, the companion threat was an internal one, brought by the enslaved. By 1698 in Jamaica an act was passed for "raising parties to suppress rebellious and runaway Negroes" who "of late murdered several [settlers]," then "plundered and destroyed many of the small and out settlements. . . ."

Earlier, in 1692 a "most horrid, bloody, damnable and detestable rebellion, massacre, assassination and destruction" targeting "all the white inhabitants" of Barbados, at the hands of "Negroes and slaves"[19] was launched. A few years later there was yet another "horrid and detestable conspiracy formed and carried on by Papists and other wicked and traitorous persons . . . in order to encourage an invasion from France."[20] The similar language betrayed the objective interests that united foreign invaders and domestic insurrectionists.

As ever, Africans remained alert to tensions between and among the European powers and were keen to take advantage of same. Such was the case with the War of Spanish Succession of the early 1700s, which, said a Dutchman, "did not remain unnoticed" on the West African coast.[21]

Though defeated in war repeatedly, the Dutch caused repetitive anxiety for London. It was "feared" in Jamaica that these competitors had "quite carried away the whole [slave] trade from us"; they were "taking the best and choicest Negroes to furnish foreigners and strengthen them, while Your Majesty's poor subjects, the planters, must be content with the refuse or nothing." This meant the "poor planter" was "rendered incapable of paying his debts and several of them [were] forced to run off this island and others to put themselves into the service of foreign princes." It was pressure such as this that emerged in 1688, helping to determine the trailblazing events of this crucial year.[22]

There was like apprehension about the French. In 1692 in Jamaica it was felt that they had been "emboldened" and had been "conducted by some English Renegades and fugitives" who "traitorously" worked with "enemies" who "have lately landed a considerable body of men on the north side" of Jamaica.[23]

But the labor question had become so ensnarled that in 1699 in London there was a debate about the need for "encouraging the importation of white servants" to the settlements and "that a clause be inserted to prevent any more Negroes being brought up to trades," so as to prompt the "encouragement of white men." This too would be a constant, not least in the North American republic—that is, seeking to bar Negroes from certain skills while reserving same to "white men."[24] But this was not easy to do in the late seventeenth century, when most of the settlers were coming from England and its immediate vicinity. Antigua too was "encouraging & promoting the settling of the island" with "white people & promoting the importation of servants."[25] By late 1698, "encouraging the settlement" of Antigua with "white people and promoting the importation of servants" was still seen as necessary since "Christian people" had "decreased" due to "war" and "mortality." In other words, "white people" were the essential currency, and competition for their presence was stiff, meaning that the smaller Caribbean islands ineluctably would lose out to the mainland in the long run.[26] This also meant that the mainland was compelled as a matter of stiffened competition—and not necessarily Enlightenment discourse—to make itself more attractive to Europeans, who had a plethora of migration choices.

After 1776, when the scope of "whiteness" was extended to encourage the migration of those with roots in the sprawling region from the Atlantic to the Ural Mountains—and even dipping southward into the Arab world[27]—this would be an easier policy to execute.

As in Barbados as well, there was uneasiness in confronting what came to be called the "Jewish Question,"[28] a factor that enhanced the value of Christian [European] servants and served to foment class collaboration. "Privileges of this House," said the assembly in 1698, "had been broken by one Samuel Lopez, a Jew, by striking a servant of one of the members of this House at Port Royal."[29] In the 1690s, in the Leeward Islands, an act was passed "against Jews ingrossing [sic] commodities imported . . . and trading with the slaves belonging to the inhabitants." Yet it was also moved that the authorities should "prevent Papists and reputed Papists from settling," a double blow of bigotry that would have to make a tactical retreat as subsequent onlookers hailed what they considered to be "Enlightenment" taking hold, though it was more like a military maneuver.[30] In other words, it is to put the cart before the horse to insist that Enlightenment philosophy led to a retreat of religious chauvinism, particularly in the settlements, when actually the dire need of colonialism was primarily the movant party.

Contortion would be needed to label as "Enlightenment" a 1696 policy asserting that "no slave shall be free by becoming a Christian"; this was coupled with a provision that "no written title" was needed for the "legal purchases of slaves," which was a general invitation to chicanery and kidnapping of free Africans, wherever they might be found.[31] When a bill was debated in London in 1688 "prohibiting Jews from buying Christian servants," it was apparent that it would take the elite a while to work out the knotty tensions ensnaring class and religion.[32]

By the early eighteenth century the governor of the Leeward Islands was desperate, grumbling that his region was "still destitute of any support from the Queen's ships," despite the threat from Martinique, where an attack on Barbados was planned. He was reduced to hoping that this attack would occur so as to spare his jurisdiction, meaning their antagonist would "lose so many men there."[33] Feebly, official London could only confirm the "want of ships" and the imminent "arrival of several French men of war in those parts."[34]

In the long run, the Jamaican elite would feel compelled to make more fruitful entreaties to the Jewish community too (and even "Papists"), since the unruliness of the Africans meant that the rulers could ill afford to alienate wholly any who could loosely be termed "white." By 1698, as in Barbados, a policy was enacted for "raising parties to suppress rebellions and runaway Negroes," since the latter had "murdered" a number of settlers of late and had "plundered and destroyed many of the small . . . settlements and do still in great numbers" and "continue doing what robberies and other mischiefs they are able and daily increase their numbers by other Negroes running away and joining with them, which may be of fatal consequence." There was a felt need to "destroy all such Negroes," but this was easier articulated than executed.[35]

Maroons remained so formidable, aligned as they were with those known as "Madagascars," that by March 1, 1738, a treaty with them had to be negotiated, which was perceived widely in London as a "surrender." By the 1760s, this entente had broken down to an extent that London had less time and opportunity to focus on the mainland, which eased the way for the successful 1776 revolt.[36]

This unsteadiness in the Caribbean may have caught the attention of certain Virginians, for problems there were similar. In 1699 Virginia felt it necessary to restate a law that had been passed in 1680 and again in 1682 and enunciated in 1666—suggesting an escalating problem with little surcease. It was "for better preventing Insurrections by Negroes."[37]

In Massachusetts, the 1690s witnessed no letup in trade with Barbados, as this island continued to drive events on the mainland, implicating it directly in enslavement[38]—their own slaves set aside. The intimacy of ties was reflected when Rebecca Wansford of the Bay Colony married and indicated that her previous spouse was Barbadian.[39] This kind of matrimony was not unusual.[40]

Across the Atlantic in London there was grave concern about the threat in the Americas from the French, perched as they were in Quebec and in various islands southward. The threat was to London itself, as revealed in 1696 when there was a report of a "horrid and detestable conspiracy, formed and carried on by Papists and other wicked and traitorous persons for assassinating His Majesty's royal person in order to encourage an invasion from France."[41] In Boston this news reverberated, since their class comrades had largely emerged triumphant, post-1688. This was a "horrid and detestable plot and conspiracy against the life of His Sacred Majesty King William the Third."[42]

Paris was aware of this close tie and thus, near what is now Fall River, Massachusetts, "French ships of war" were detected days later[43] and they were said to "infest the Coast."[44] By the fall "French prisoners" were "in custody,"[45] and by December the "present war against the French" was well underway in the Bay Colony,[46] opening opportunities for leverage by the remaining indigenes and Africans alike. The presence of "French and Indian prisoners" in Massachusetts objectively provided such opportunities.[47]

In some ways, this late seventeenth-century conflict was a bloody rehearsal for the better known 1756–63 war with Paris and their indigenous allies, which caused London to impose more taxes to pay for this conflict, which was for the benefit of settlers but induced flowing resentment in that community, causing a revolt. "French prisoners of war" were treated like their indigenous allies to a degree in that they were shipped willy-nilly to "Europe, the Western Islands or the West Indies," then to "France or some of the French plantations."[48] There was a related fear that colonialism had to spread or be overwhelmed as "debtors, servants & Negroes" would seize the opportunity to flee to the embrace of London's antagonists—for example, the French.[49] For settler colonialism, the mantra seemed to be "expand or die," a point that London should have considered in 1763 when it issued its momentous Royal Proclamation seeking to bar further settler migration westward on the mainland, seizing land of the indigenous, and engendering murderous conflict, which so infuriated the colonists that they revolted and à la 1688 draped their mercantile motives in the finery of "liberty" and "freedom."

Intriguingly, this time, in the late seventeenth century, Massachusetts did not hesitate to impose an added tax for "prosecution of the Indian rebels" who were supposedly "committing . . . outrages and murder in the town of Andover."[50] "Suppressing of the Indian rebels" was a high priority,[51] as the Pequot slaughter and King Philip's War earlier in the century had not resolved the indigenous desire not to be ousted and liquidated. The presence in the region of the notorious freebooter "Captain Kidd," known to be both bloodthirsty and greedy, just arriving from a venture in Madagascar,[52] did not produce amicable interracialism.[53] (Captain Kidd may have had a hand in the 1698 proposal from New York demanding that unnamed parties "fetch as many Negroes from Madagascar as you can.")[54] It was known that this freebooter had perpetrated "divers piracy in the seas of India."[55] But since by 1699 Boston was "resisting the French enemy [from] landing" and since by 1700 there was a reputed "insurrection" miles away in Albany, which was "intended to be made by the Indians,"[56] the settlers needed all the help they could muster, no matter how ill-intentioned.

The ructions in New England were also driven by morbid concern about "witches," which apparently was a byproduct of the slave trade from the Caribbean in indigenes.[57] It was almost as if the settlers were enacting a drama that involved their justifiable persecution for the horribleness they had visited upon indigenes.

This barbarous encounter with the French and the indigenous had become so overpowering that there was even reconsideration of the presumed bedrock matter of religion. For it was at the "instigation" of French missionaries that "eastern Indians . . . murdered so many" and were now at the "devotion of the Jesuits to [en]act over again . . . another tragedy." Now these Jesuits wanted to do the same with the "Five Nations in the province of New York," yet another "execrable Treachery to England intended without doubt to serve the ends of Popery."[58] "Preventing abuses" of indigenes was viewed as a primary interest, too, as it merged effortlessly with the threat from Paris.[59] But after London had beaten back France in 1763, the settlers then craftily brokered a deal with Paris against the interests of Great Britain.

The problem for settlers in Massachusetts was not just with the rebelling indigenous, as formidable as that was. By 1700 Samuel Sewall was similarly griping about the "numerousness of slaves at this day in the province and the uneasiness of them under slavery." As ever, he yearned for more attention "to the welfare [of] White Servants." It was true that "their continual aspiring after their forbidden liberty, renders them Unwilling Servants"; perhaps this desire could be assuaged somehow, which might mean a more severe crackdown on Africans and Native Americans. Sewall wrung his hands about the "horrible" nature of slave ships, the "uncleanness, mortality, if not

189

murder" that delivered "great crowds of miserable men and women," though other than crocodile tears, he had no concrete proposals to arrest this terribleness.[60] For Sewall well knew about the vociferous resistance of the enslaved in the Caribbean and what that might portend for settlements.

The mainland, in sum, did not evade the tribulations delivered by the deregulation of the African Slave Trade and the subsequent flooding onto these shores of the enslaved.[61] In 1696 the House of Commons received a petition lambasting the purported monopoly of the Royal African Company from a group of merchants and traders from Virginia and Maryland. They felt their plantations were capable of producing more tobacco and that bringing more enslaved Africans would deliver this result.[62]

Between 1664 and 1698 the African population of what became the renowned New York City nearly doubled, along with the restiveness they routinely delivered.[63] By 1690, Isaac Morrill, an African, was arrested for allegedly enticing other Negroes to follow him to Canada and join an invading force launched by the French and returning to New England—along with indigenous allies—with conquest in mind. Since Africans in that region often had ties to Madagascar and the Persian Gulf, they were not oblivious to the reality that regimes could be easily unsettled by militancy.[64]

Still, the fact remained that apart from a single importation from Africa in the 1690s, all of the enslaved Africans in neighboring Rhode Island and their ancestors had been brought from Barbados.[65] New York City was not sui generis. By 1693, the eastern shore of Virginia was astir with febrile rumors of a slave uprising.[66]

By 1709 in Surry County, Virginia, the authorities were in an uproar since "Negro and Indian slaves" were "concerned in a Late Dangerous Conspiracy formed and carried on by great numbers"; their aim was "making their Escape by force" and then "destroying and cutting off such of [the monarch's] subjects" that had "opposed their design."[67] The very next year in Virginia worried reports emerged about "some Negroes going away with arms."[68] There was an "intended insurrection of the Negroes," which mandated a felt need to "prevent the meetings and consultations of the Negroes."[69]

Intensifying the horrors inflicted upon indigenes and Africans was the fact that immoral and amoral pirates played such a primary role in driving the process of dispossession and enslavement. Many of these men came from the elite of society, though their underlings often did not, but, in an embodiment of the "American Dream," could climb the class ladder rapidly by emulating their "betters," helping to forge a cross-class solidarity grounded in racial and economic solidarity that has yet to disappear. On the road to becoming the premier metropolis of the early Republic, Philadelphia embodied this trend: here pirates found a haven. Invoking religious principles to protect pocketbook interests was a hallmark of this town that has yet to dissolve. Other religionists who believed in predestined salvation were then incentivized, according to their foes, to "do what a beast might do," which proved to be a quite useful trait to possess when conducting the foul business of enslavement and dispossession. Unsurprisingly, this colony and Rhode Island too began to surge in the post-1688 era as the slave trade was deregulated, which in turn provided impetus for further dispossession and wealth accumulation. Bristol and Liverpool were thus hoisted on their own petards, as the piracy that buoyed these English towns provided a worthy model for republicans to emulate.[70]

THE DIE HAD BEEN CAST in 1688 with the "Glorious Revolution" and the rise of the merchants who proceeded to build vast fortunes on the backs of enslaved Africans and dispossessed indigenes while shouting from the rooftops about the "liberty" and "freedom" they were demanding at the expense of the monarch.

Of course, hypocrisy from self-interested tycoons is nothing new, though the question remains as to why so many in subsequent generations—including, as we have noted, even those who consider themselves radical—should have credited this sham. This pretense toward "freedom" continued in 1776 when settlers revolted when

London seemed to be loath to continue funding their wars of dispossession against indigenes and the constant conflict with enslaved
Africans that was an adjunct of that process.

Even today in the United States there seems to be shock and surprise when billionaires claim to be the tribunes of the "little guy," and
many of the latter seem to go along with this dissimulation in a replay
of past cross-class coalitions when the high and mighty joined with
poorer Europeans in mutually feasting upon the misery of those not
defined as "white."

Fortunately, the world has changed and the room for maneuver for
white supremacy and capitalism in the United States is not as capacious as it was in North America and the Caribbean in the seventeenth
century. This raises the distinct possibility for a decisive turning of
the tide against this malignant force at some point in the twenty-first
century. If this is to occur, it will require at least the acknowledgment
that the escalation of settlement in the Americas hundreds of years
earlier may have been a great leap forward for those Europeans who
were enriched. But for Africans and the indigenous, it was nothing
short of an apocalypse.

THROUGH THE CENTURIES, the Republic that eventuated in
North America has maintained a maximum of chutzpah and a mini-
mum of self-awareness in forging a creation myth that sees slavery and
dispossession not as foundational but inimical to the founding of the
nation now known as the United States. But, of course, to confront
the ugly reality would induce a persistent sleeplessness interrupted by
haunted dreams, so thus far this unsteadiness has prevailed.

Fortunately, with the unstinting contribution of the Haitian
Revolution,[71] a general crisis of the entire slave system was ignited,
which could only be resolved with its collapse. With that monumental event, a corollary crisis for white supremacy was fomented,
which continues to unfold. This tendency was compounded by the
Bolshevik Revolution of 1917, which—at least—thrust the question of class onto center stage, and this, reflexively, helped to erode
the capitalist world's maniacal obsession with "race."[72] Like falling

dominoes, the ascendancy of Moscow forced Washington to work out an entente with China some four odd decades ago, which bids fair to place this sprawling nation led by a communist party in the passing lane.[73] This represents a crisis for all aspects of the hydra-headed monster that arose in the seventeenth century—white supremacy and capitalism not least.

This impact of global currents on nefarious domestic trends should remind today's strugglers that their interests would be better served by spending less time debating with the American Civil Liberties Union about the "rights" of fascists and more time conversing with potential and actual allies in Beijing, Moscow, Havana, Brussels, Pretoria and elsewhere. This admonition is directed particularly to descendants of enslaved Africans and dispossessed indigenes in North America.

For more work needs to be done in an attempt to repair the immense damage inflicted over the centuries, not least on Africa, Africans, and Native Americans. This mandates a massive program of reparations that—I trust—will accelerate in coming decades.

Notes

Introduction

1. Christopher Hill, *The Century of Revolution, 1603–1714*, Edinburgh: Nelson, 1961, 2.

2. The overwhelming majority of the thirteen colonies that seceded from the British Empire to form the United States of America were founded before 1688; the thirteenth—Georgia—which was founded in principle as an "all white" settlement in about 1733, in some ways represents the epitome of the resultant republic, which has privileged white supremacy: the 2010 Census revealed that this U.S. state contained the largest population of African descent within the nation: this—ironically—meant that this state maintained, perhaps, the highest stage of white supremacy as reflected, for example, in lynchings, the density of racist chain gangs, etc. In other words, the fundamental framework for today's republic was formed—arguably—as early as 1688, thus underscoring scrutiny of this pivotal century. See e.g. Gerald Horne, *The Counter-Revolution of 1776: Slave Resistance and the Origins of the United States of America*, New York: New York University Press, 2014; W. Fitzhugh Brundage, *Lynching in the New South: Georgia and Virginia, 1880–1930*, Urbana: University of Illinois Press, 1993.

3. Wendy Warren, *New England Bound: Slavery and Colonization in Early America*, New York: W. W. Norton, 2016, 4–5. See most recently Graham Allison, *Destined for War: Can America and China Escape Thucydides' Trap*, Boston: Houghton Mifflin, 2017, 239: Citing the historian Niall Ferguson, the author suggests there were 6 "killer apps" that led to the ascendancy of the North Atlantic nations, including competition; scientific revolution; property rights; modern medicine; consumer society; and work ethic. Slavery, colonialism and the ideology of white supremacy which enabled the two is left unmentioned.

4. Andres Resendez, *The Other Slavery: The Uncovered Story of Indian Enslavement in America*, New York: Houghton Mifflin Harcourt, 2016, 5–6, 149.

5. Joyce Rockwood Hudson, *Looking for De Soto: A Search Through the South for the Spaniard's Trail*, Athens, GA: University of Georgia Press, 1993.

6. Paul Kelton, *Epidemics and Enslavement: Biological Catastrophe in the Native Southeast, 1492–1715*, Lincoln: University of Nebraska Press, 2007; and *Cherokee Medicine, Colonial Germs: An Indigenous Nation's Fight Against Smallpox, 1518–1824*, Norman: University of Oklahoma Press, 2015.

7. Terri L. Snyder, *The Power to Die: Slavery and Suicide in British North America*, Chicago: University of Chicago Press, 2015.

8. David Eltis et al., "Atlantic History and the Slave Trade to Spanish America," *American Historical Review*, 120/2 (April 2015): 433–61, 440.

9. Christian J. Koot, *Empire at the Periphery: British Colonists, Anglo-Dutch Trade and the Development of the British Atlantic, 1621–1713*, New York: New York University Press, 2011, 22.

10. Walter Rodney, *How Europe Underdeveloped Africa*, Dar es Salaam: Tanzania Publishing House, 1972.

11. William Pettigrew, *Freedom's Debt: The Royal African Company and the Politics of the Atlantic Slave Trade, 1672–1752*, Chapel Hill: University of North Carolina Press, 2013, 11, 39, 218.

12. L. H. Roper, *Advancing Empire: English Interests and Overseas Expansion, 1613–1688*, New York: Cambridge University Press, 178.

13. See Douglas R. Burgess, Jr., *The Politics of Piracy: Crime and Civil Disobedience in Colonial America*, Lebanon, NH: University Press of New England, 2014.

14. See Gerald Horne, *Class Struggle in Hollywood, 1930–1950: Moguls, Mobsters, Stars, Reds and Trade Unionists*, Austin: University of Texas Press, 2001.

15. Harvey Cox, *The Market as God*, Cambridge, MA: Harvard University Press, 2016.

16. *The Economist*, 17 December 2016.

17. Roger Crowley, *Conquerors: How Portugal Forged the First Global Empire*, New York: Random House, 2015, 78, 148, 305.

18. Edgar Tristram Thompson, *The Plantation*, Columbia: University of South Carolina Press, 2010, 25. See also Derek Hughes, ed., *Versions of Blackness: Key Texts on Slavery from the Seventeenth Century*, New York: Cambridge University Press, 2007.

19. Ellen Meiksins Wood, *The Origin of Capitalism: A Longer View*, New York: Verso, 2017, 142.

20. L. H. Roper, *Advancing Empire: English Interests and Overseas Expansion, 1613–1688*, New York: Cambridge University Press, 2017, 168.

21. Karen Ordahl Kupperman, "The Seventeenth Century: Expansion and Consolidation," in *The Princeton Companion to Atlantic History*, ed. Joseph Miller, Princeton: Princeton University Press, 2015, 26–35, 29.

22. See, for example, Lynn T. Ramey, *Black Legacies: Race and the European Middle Ages*, Tallahassee: University Press of Florida, 2014; Rotem Kowner,

From White to Yellow: The Japanese in European Racial Thought, 1300-1735, Montreal: McGill-Queens University, 2014, 347. According to this analyst, the term "race" emerged in English as early as 1508, just as the African slave trade was taking off. Arguably, English attempts to enslave Japanese in the pivotal seventeenth century contributed to this nation's self-imposed isolation and emergence in the late nineteenth century as a power bent on upsetting the white supremacy that had strangled Africa. See also Gerald Horne, *Race War! White Supremacy and the Japanese Attack on the British Empire*, New York: New York University Press, 2003.

23. Geoffrey Parker, *The Cambridge History of Warfare*, New York: Cambridge University Press, 2005.

24. Samuel Willard Crompton, "Military Technologies," in Miller, *The Princeton Companion to Atlantic History*, 333–36, 334.

25. Peter Frankopan, *The Silk Roads: A New History of the Road*, New York: Knopf, 2016, 253.

26. David Boyle, *Toward the Setting Sun: Columbus, Cabot, Vespucci and the Race for America*, New York: Walker, 2008, 361.

27. Alan Taylor, *American Colonies: The Settling of North America*, New York: Penguin, 2001, 257.

28. Tonio Andrade, *The Gunpowder Age: China, Military Innovation and the Rise of the West in World History*, Princeton: Princeton University Press, 2016.

29. Peter Frankopan, *The Silk Roads: A New History of the Road*, New York: Knopf, 2016, 261.

30. Eduardo de Mesa, *The Irish in the Spanish Armies in the Seventeenth Century*, Rochester, NY: Boydell Press, 2014. See also Igor Perez Tostado, *Irish Influence at the Court of Spain in the Seventeenth Century*, Dublin: Four Courts Press, 2008; Oscar Recio Morales, *Ireland and the Spanish Empire, 1600–1825*, Dublin: Four Courts Press, 2010; Grainne Henry, *The Irish Military Community in Flanders, 1586–1621*, Dublin: Irish Academic Press, 1992.

31. David Worthington, *Scots in the Hapsburg Service, 1618–1648*, Boston: Brill, 2014.

32. L. H. Roper, *Advancing Empire*, 140, 150.

33. H. R. Trevor-Roper, "The General Crisis of the 17th Century," *Past & Present* 16 (November 1959): 31–64, 31.

34. E. J. Hobsbawm, "The General Crisis of the European Economy in the 17th Century," *Past & Present* 5 (May 1954): 33–53, 33, 37, 38.

35. Parker, *Global Crisis*, xvii, 105, 327, 351.

36. John Miller, *The English Civil Wars: Roundheads, Cavaliers and the Execution of the King*, London: Constable & Robinson, 2009, 112, 119, 128.

37. Audrey Horning, *Ireland in the Virginian Sea: Colonialism in the British Atlantic*, Chapel Hill: University of North Carolina Press, 2013, 267. See "The Rebellion of 1641," in *Irish Historical Documents, 1172–1922*, ed. Edmund Curtis and R. B. McDowell, New York: Barnes & Noble, 1968, 148–52. See also J. P. Kenyon, ed., *The Stuart Constitution, 1603–1688: Documents and Commentary*, London: Cambridge University Press, 1966.

38. *The Articles of the Treaty of Peace Signed and Sealed at Munster in Westphalia the 24th of October 1648...*, Huntington Library, San Marino, CA.

39. Derek Croxton, *Westphalia: The Last Christian Peace*, New York: Palgrave, 2013.

40. Gerald Horne, *The Counter-Revolution of 1776: Slave Resistance and the Origins of the United States of America*, New York: New York University Press, 2014.

41. Matthew S. Hopper, *Slaves of One Master: Globalization and Slavery in Arabia in the Age of Empire*, New Haven: Yale University Press, 2015, 32, 33.

42. Richard Allen Blair, *European Slave Trading in the Indian Ocean, 1500–1850*, Athens: Ohio University Press, 2014, 10.

43. Benjamin Madley, *An American Genocide: The United States and the California Indian Catastrophe, 1846–1873*, New Haven: Yale University Press, 2016.

44. Horne, *The Counter-Revolution of 1776*.

45. Richard Gott, *Britain's Empire: Resistance, Repression and Revolt*, London: Verso, 2011, 5.

46. Andrew Woolford et.al., eds., *Colonial Genocide in Indigenous North America*, Durham, NC: Duke University Press, 2014.

47. Sylvester A. Johnson, *African-American Religions, 1500–2000: Colonialism, Democracy and Freedom*, New York: Cambridge University Press, 2015.

48. Susan Dwyer Amussen, *Caribbean Exchanges: Slavery and the Transformation of English Society, 1640–1700*, Chapel Hill: University of North Carolina Press, 2007, 12. See also Roxann Wheeler, *The Complexion of Race: Categories of Difference in Eighteenth Century British Culture*, Philadelphia: University of Pennsylvania Press, 324: "As opposed to *African* current since the ninth century *European* was a relatively new term; the OED lists the first citation in the early seventeenth century. Its first meaning reveals the way its usage emerged in response to colonialism.... The first entry appeared in 1698." Bernard Bailyn and Patricia L. Denault, eds., *Soundings in Atlantic History: Latent Structures and Intellectual Currents, 1500–1830*, Cambridge, MA: Harvard University Press, 2009.

49. Edmund Abaka, *House of Slaves and 'Door of no Return': Gold Coast/Ghana Slave Forts, Castles and Dungeons and the Atlantic Slave Trade*, Trenton, NJ: Africa World Press, 2012, 3.

50. Joseph E. Inikori, *Forced Migrations: The Impact of the Export Slave Trade on African Societies*, London: Hutchinson, 1982; and *The Chaining of a Continent: Export Demand for Captives and the History of Africa South of the Sahara, 1450–1870*, Mona, Jamaica: Institute of Social and Economic Research, University of the West Indies, 1992.

51. Joseph E. Inikori, *Africans and the Industrial Revolution in England: A Study in International Trade and Economic Development*, New York: Cambridge University Press, 2002. See also Eric Eustace Williams, *Capitalism and Slavery*, Chapel Hill: University of North Carolina Press, 1994.

52. Theodore Allen, *The Invention of the White Race*, New York: Verso, 2012. See also Theodore William Allen, *Class Struggle and the Origin of Racial Slavery:*

The Invention of the White Race, Hoboken, NJ: H.E.P., 1974: The thesis that traces the crucible of "whiteness" and its accompanying "racial slavery" to the late seventeenth century is instructive. I argue in these pages that other factors must be considered in explicating this troublesome phenomenon, for example, civil wars in the British Isles; the rise of merchants; the opportunity for "racial slavery" and maniacal profiteering opened by the taking of Jamaica in 1655 and Manhattan (along with what are now the U.S. Mid Atlantic states) in 1664; the decline of the Ottomans, relieving pressure on Western Europe and allowing a fuller turn to plunder of Africa and the Americas. All culminate in the "Glorious Revolution" of 1688, that is, the retreat of the royals and the advance of the merchants, leading to deregulation of the African Slave Trade and the linking of parliamentary power with resultant racism, which in the United States then takes the form of an identity of interests between the construction of whiteness and conservatism, a linkage that persists to this very day. This involved reducing indentured servitude for poorer Europeans and heavier reliance on enslaved labor. Then the former were elevated as a more conscientious effort to seize the land of indigenes was launched with redistribution to poorer Europeans, culminating appropriately enough in the Homestead Act during the U.S. Civil War. This elevation was to include voting rights and was also a way to entice poorer Europeans to defend the North American regime against internal challenges from indigenes and the enslaved, and foreign invasion too. Obviously, this complicates the class question mightily. See also Peter Abrahams, *The Black Experience in the 20th Century: An Autobiography and Meditation*, Bloomington: Indiana University Press, 2000, 350–351. Abrahams, a South African-born writer of Ethiopian descent, opined that "the depth of the anger against each other of the poor who are white and the poor who are black has been one of the crueler factors in the relations between the lighter and darker peoples of the earth." Arguably, this tragic trend, which sheds light on the results of the November 2016 election in the United States, was forged in the fiery crucible of the seventeenth century.

53.   Caroline Finkel, *Osman's Dream: The History of the Ottoman Empire, 1300–1923*, New York: Basic Books, 2005, 446, 553. See also Rhoads Murphey, *Ottoman Warfare, 1500–1700*, New Brunswick, NJ: Rutgers University Press, 10–11; and Khaled El–Rouayheb, *Islamic Intellectual History in the Seventeenth Century: Scholarly Currents in the Ottoman Empire and the Maghreb*, New York: Cambridge University Press, 2015.

54.   Wendy Laura Belcher and Michael Kleiner, eds., *The Life and Struggles of Our Mother Walatta Petros: A Seventeenth-Century African Biography*, Princeton: Princeton University Press, 2015, xiii, 201. See also C. F. Beckingham and G. W. B. Huntingford, eds., *Some Records of Ethiopia, 1593–1646, Being Extracts from the History of Ethiopia...by Manuel de Almeida*, London: Hakluyt Society, 1954; and Lord Stanley, ed., *Narrative of the Portuguese Embassy to Abyssinia During the Years 1520–1527 by Father Francisco Alvareza*, London: Hakluyt Society, 1881.

55.   Salih Ozbaran, ed., *The Ottoman Response to European Expansion: Studies on*

Ottoman-Portuguese Relations in the Indian Ocean and Ottoman Administration in the Arab Lands During the Sixteenth Century, Istanbul: ISIS, 1994, 193n.

56. Brendan Simms, *Europe: The Struggle for Supremacy from 1453 to the Present*, New York: Basic Books, 2013, 36, 57.

57. *Narrative of Joshua Gee, 1680–1687*, Hartford, CT: Wadsworth Athenaeum, 1943, 7: This important document can be found at the Massachusetts Historical Society, Boston.

58. Steven Karl Flogstad Heise, "'Whether It Be Lawful': The Debate Over Slavery in the Atlantic World, 1550–1750," Ph.D. diss., Clark University, 2014, 202.

59. Jean Houbert, "Creolisation and Decolonization in the Changing Geopolitics of the Indian Ocean," in Richard Parkhurst, ed., *The African Diaspora in the Indian Ocean*, Trenton: Africa World Press, 2003, 123–149, 130. See also Lorenzo Veracini, *Settler Colonialism: A Theoretical Overview*, New York: Palgrave, 2010. Settler colonialism as it evolved in what became the United States, involved the violent implantation of settlers accompanied by the ouster of indigenes and the increasing installation of enslaved Africans as a primary labor force. Overwhelmingly, most of the settlers had roots in the sprawling region stretching from the Atlantic Ocean to the Urals, allowing the United States to draw upon the energy and ingenuity of what was then the rising continent. However, the scope of the identity politics that was "whiteness" also headed southward into Lebanon, some parts of the Arab world, and even Persia. See, for example, Neda Maghbouleh, *The Limits of Whiteness: Iranian Americans and the Everyday Politics of Race*, Stanford: Stanford University Press, 2017. (Despite the subsequent entrance into the hallowed halls of whiteness of those without—apparent—roots in Europe, I will use nonetheless the term "Euro-Americans" to describe this entire group.) The broad scope of "whiteness" allowed the majority to assume that the bludgeoning of indigenes and Africans was an anomaly, not an essential aspect of how the republic evolved. This elision is also reflected in the unofficial republican slogan—supposedly—describing the U.S.: "a nation of immigrants." See also Karen Brodkin, *How Jews Became White Folks and What that Says About Race in America*, New Brunswick: Rutgers University Press, 1998.

60. Nabil Matar, *Turks, Moors and Englishmen in the Age of Discovery*, New York: Columbia University Press, 1999, 93.

61. Minutes of the Council, 12 December 1676, Jamaica Archives and Records Department, Spanish Town, Jamaica.

62. Philip Barbour, ed., *The Complete Works of Captain John Smith (1580–1631)*, vol. 3, Chapel Hill: University of North Carolina Press, 1986, 193–96.

63. John D. Krugler, *English and Catholic: The Lords Baltimore in the Seventeenth Century*, Baltimore: Johns Hopkins University Press, 2004, 21.

64. Richard Dale, *Who Killed Sir Walter Raleigh?*, Gloucestershire, MA: AA History Press, 2011, 17. See also Peter C. Mancall, ed., *The Atlantic World and Virginia, 1550–1624*, Chapel Hill: University of North Carolina Press, 2007.

65. David Potter, ed., *A Knight of Malta at the Court of Elizabeth I: The*

Correspondence of Michel De Seure, French Ambassador, 1560–1561, New York: Cambridge University Press, 2014, 39n.

66. Boyle, *Toward the Setting Sun*, 359.

67. Eid Abdallah Dahiyat, *Once Upon the Orient Wave: Milton and the Arab World*, London: Hesperus, 2012, 32, 87–88.

68. Ibid., 211, 212. Philip P. Boucher, *France and the American Tropics to 1700: Tropics of Discontent?* Baltimore: Johns Hopkins University Press, 2008, 211, 212.

69. See e.g. Carolyn Chappell Lougee, *Facing the Revocation: Huguenot Families, Faith and the King's Will*, New York: Oxford University Press, 2016.

70. Malcolm Gaskill, *Between Two Worlds: How the English Became Americans*, New York: Basic Books, 2014, 198.

71. A. C. Grayling, *The Age of Genius: The 17th Century and the Birth of the Modern Mind*, New York: Bloomsbury, 2016, 108.

72. Yda Schreuder, "A True Global Community: Sephardic Jews, the Sugar Trade and Barbados in the Seventeenth Century," *Journal of the Barbados Museum and Historical Society* 50 (December 2004): 166–94, 168, 170, 172. Arguably the impact of sugar on the health of those consuming this product has been similarly apocalyptic, contributing to obesity, diabetes, heart disease, and related maladies. See, for example, Gary Taubes, *The Case Against Sugar*, New York: Knopf, 2016.

73. Samuel Oppenheim, *The Early History of Jews in New York, 1654–1664*, New York: 1909, 39. See also Jeroen Dewulf, *The Pinkster King and the King of Kongo: The Forgotten History of America's Dutch–Owned Slaves*, Jackson: University Press of Mississippi, 2017.

74. George Francis Zook, *The Company of Royal Adventurers of England Trading into Africa, 1660–1672*, New York: Negro Universities Press, 1969 [originally published in 1919], 134–35.

75. Graham Russell Hodges, *Root & Branch: African Americans in New York and East Jersey*, Chapel Hill: University of North Carolina Press, 1999, 25, 29.

76. Karel Schoeman, *Early Slavery at the Cape of Good Hope, 1652–1717*, Pretoria, SA: Protea Book House, 2007, 122.

77. Ibid., 158.

78. Frankopan, *The Silk Roads*, 235.

79. Leslie M. Harris, *In the Shadow of Slavery: African Americans in New York City, 1626–1863*, Chicago: University of Chicago Press, 2003, 28–30.

80. Ibid., 195, 202.

81. Georg Norregard, *Danish Settlements in West Africa, 1658–1850*, Boston: Boston University Press, 1966, 42.

82. Parker, *Global Crisis*, 275.

83. Wim Klooster, *The Dutch Moment: War, Trade and Settlement in the Seventeenth Century*, Ithaca, NY: Cornell University Press, 2016, 30.

84. James Conget to East India Company, 27 December 1658; and "Agent and Factors at Fort Cormantine" to East India Company, 10 June 1661, in Margaret Makepeace, ed., *Trade on the Guinea Coast, 1657–1666: The Correspondence*

of the English East India Company, Madison: University of Wisconsin African Studies Program, 1991, 27–30, 94–99.

85. "Agent and Factors at Fort Cormantine," in ibid., 135–37.
86. The Council Book, 23 October 1663, CO140/1, National Archives of the United Kingdom, London.
87. L. H. Roper, *Advancing Empire*, 184.
88. Statute, 27 October 1692, in *Acts Passed in the Island of Barbados from 1643 to 1762*, London: Richard Hall, 1764, 129–30, Barbados National Archives.
89. J. Kehaulani Kauanui, "Tracing Historical Specificity: Race and the Colonial Politics of (In)Capacity," *American Quarterly*, 69(Number 2, June 2017): 257–265, 262.
90. See Gerald Horne, *The End of Empires: African Americans and India*, Philadelphia: Temple University Press, 2009; Gerald Horne, *From the Barrel of a Gun: The United States and the War Against Zimbabwe, 1965–1980*, Chapel Hill: University of North Carolina Press, 2000; Gerald Horne, *Mau Mau in Harlem? The United States and the Liberation of Kenya*, New York: Palgrave, 2000; Gerald Horne, *Race to Revolution: The U.S. and Cuba During Slavery and Jim Crow*, New York: Monthly Review Press, 2014.
91. Peter Frase, *Four Futures: Life after Capitalism*, New York: Verso, 2016.

1. Beginning

1. Nell Irvin Painter, *The History of White People*, New York: Norton, 2010, 34. Reportedly, there were 13, 000 Slavic slaves in Cordoba in 961, Christian Era. (CE).
2. Michael Guasco, *Slaves and Englishmen: Human Bondage in the Early Modern Atlantic World*, Philadelphia: University of Pennsylvania Press, 2014, 25. See also Steven Karl Flogstad Heise, 58, citing Heise dissertation in previous chapter. "Estimates taken from the Domesday Book suggest that roughly one-tenth of the English population were slaves in 1086; in that same century, the port city of Bristol carried out a slave trade to the European continent"; then there were the "Viking raids" into the Isles for purpose of enslavement.
3. Peter Frankopan, *The Silk Roads*, 115, 117, 211. This image neatly encapsulated the ties linking Pan-Europeanism, religious liberty, and an ascending capitalism, lessons all developed further by the North American republic
4. Ibid., 115.
5. Edmund Abaka, *House of Slaves and 'Door of No Return': Gold Coast/Ghana Slave Forts, Castles and Dungeons and the Atlantic Slave Trade*, Trenton, NJ: Africa World Press, 2012, 230.
6. Wendy Warren, *New England Bound*, 28.
7. Francisco Bethencourt, *The Inquisition: A Global History, 1478–1834*, New York: Cambridge University Press, 2009, 1.
8. Andres Resendez, *The Other Slavery: The Uncovered Story of Indian Enslavement in America*, New York: Houghton, Mifflin, Harcourt, 2016, 3–4.
9. David Boyle, *Toward the Setting Sun: Columbus, Cabot, Vespucci and the Race for America*, New York: Walker, 2008, 15, 16, 106, 112, 121, 167, 172. See also

David B. Quinn, ed., *From Concept to Discovery: Early Exploration of North America*, vol. 1, New York: Arno Press, 1979; and Samuel Eliot Morison, ed., *Journals and Other Documents on the Life and Voyages of Christopher Columbus*, New York: Heritage, 1963.

10. Gonzalo Fernandez de Oviedo, *Writings from the Edge of the World: The Memoirs of Darien, 1514–1527*, Tuscaloosa: University of Alabama Press, 2006. See also T. F. Earle and K. J. P. Lowe, eds., *Black Africans in Renaissance Europe*, New York: Cambridge University Press, 2005.

11. P. C. Emmer, *The Dutch Slave Trade, 1500–1850*, New York: Berghan, 2006, 9.

12. Graham Russell Hodges, *Root and Branch: African Americans in New York & East Jersey, 1613–1863*, Chapel Hill: University of North Carolina Press, 1999, 6.

13. Frankopan, *The Silk Roads*, 213.

14. Pieter de Marres, *Description and Historical Account of the Gold Kingdom of Guinea Coast (1602)*, New York: Oxford University Press, 1987, 91, 205.

15. Georg Norregard, *Danish Settlements in West Africa, 1658–1850*, 42. See also Cassander Smith, *Black Africans in the British Imagination: English Narratives of the Early Atlantic World*, Baton Rouge: Louisiana State University Press, 2016, 31. As early as 1530, Englishmen were trading for ivory in West Africa.

16. Kenneth R. Andrews, *Trade, Plunder and Settlement: Maritime Enterprise and the Genesis of the British Empire, 1480–1630*, New York: Cambridge University Press, 1984, 117. Edmund Abaka, *House of Slaves and 'Door of No Return': Gold Coast/Ghana Slave Forts, Castles and Dungeons and the Atlantic Slave Trade*, Trenton, NJ: Africa World Press, 2012, 230; Linda M. Heywood and John K. Thornton, *Central Africans, Atlantic Creoles and the Foundation of the Americas, 1585–1660*, New York: Cambridge University Press, 2007, 11.

17. George Zook, *The Company of Royal Adventurers of England Trading into Africa, 1660–1672*, New York: Negro Universities Press, 1969 (originally published 1919), 138.

18. Frankopan, *The Silk Roads*, 241.

19. Note in R. A. Brock., ed., *Miscellaneous Papers, 1672–1865, Now First Printed from the Manuscript in the Collections of the Virginia Historical Society*, Richmond: Virginia Historical Society, 1887, 2.

20. Cassander Smith, 31, 47.

21. David Wheat, *Atlantic Africa and the Spanish Caribbean, 1570–1640*, Chapel Hill: University of North Carolina Press, 2016, 55.

22. Guasco, *Slaves and Englishmen*, 60, 66, 67.

23. Richard Hakluyt, "Discourse of Western Planting," in Clarence L. Ver Steeg and Richard Hofstadter, eds., *Great Issues in American History: From Settlement to Revolution, 1584–1776*, New York: Vintage, 1969, 18–21, 20, 21.

24. Prefatory Note in *Miscellaneous Papers, 1672–1865, now First Printed from the Manuscript in the Collections of the Virginia Historical Society*, ed. R. A. Brock, Richmond: Virginia Historical Society, 1887, 2, 4, 5.

25. Guasco, *Slaves and Englishmen*, 87.

26. P. E. H. Hair, ed., *Hawkins in Guinea, 1567–1568*, Leipzig: University of Leipzig, Papers on Africa, 2000, 53.

27. J. Brent Morris, ed., *Yes, Lord, I Know the Road: A Documentary History of African Americans in South Carolina, 1526–2008*, Columbia: University of South Carolina Press, 2017, ix.

28. Eid Abdallah Dahiyat, *Once Upon the Orient Wave: Milton and the Arab Muslim World*, London: Hesperus, 2012, 87.

29. Gerald A. John Kelly, *Celts, Germans, Jews and Other Surprises at Roanoke: The Beginning of Multi-Ethnic America*, Seaford, NY: Druid Press, 2013, 58.

30. Peter Mancall, *Hakluyt's Promise: An Elizabethan's Obsession for an English America*, New Haven: Yale University Press, 2007, 168. See also James Horn, *A Kingdom Strange: The Brief and Tragic History of the Lost Colony of Roanoke*, New York: Basic Books, 2010.

31. Michael Leroy Oberg, *The Head in Edward Nugent's Hand: Roanoke's Forgotten Indians*, Philadelphia: University of Pennsylvania Press, 2008, 102. See also Robbie Franklyn Ethridge, *From Chicaza to Chickasaw: The European Invasion and the Transformation of the Mississippian World, 1540–1715*, Chapel Hill: University of North Carolina Press, 2010.

32. *An Answer to Certaine Spanish Lies*, London, 1589, Huntington Library, San Marino, CA.

33. Captain Henry Saville, *A Libel of Spanish Lies*, London, 1596, New-York Historical Society, Manhattan.

34. Charles Carlton, *This Seat of Mars: War and the British Isles, 1485–1746*, New Haven: Yale University Press, 2011, 44.

35. Frankopan, *The Silk Roads*, 251, 254.

36. Diego Fernandez de Quinones to King Philip II, September 1586, in David B. Quinn., ed., *New American World: A Documentary History of North America to 1612*, vol. 5: *The Extension of Settlement in Florida, Virginia and the Spanish Southwest*, New York: Arno Press, 1979, 50–51. In the same volume, see reference to enslavement of Africans in Florida in P. M. Marques to King Philip II, 17 July 1586, 47.

37. Report, 22 June 1587, in ibid., 58. See also *A Libel of Spanish Lies: Found at the Sacke of Cales, Discoursing the Fight in the West Indies, Twixt the English Navie...*, London: Windet, 1596, Huntington Library, San Marino, CA.

38. Diego Fernandez de Quinones to President of Casa de Contratacion, 22 March 1587 in Quinn, *New American World*, 58.

39. Kenneth R. Andrews, ed., *English Privateering Voyages to the West Indies, 1588–1595*, Cambridge: Cambridge University Press, 1959, 184n.

40. Ibid., 245n.

41. Guasco, *Slaves and Englishmen*, 115, 122.

42. Evelyn Berckman, ed., *Victims of Piracy: The Admiralty Court, 1575–1678*, London: Hamilton, 1979, 15n.

43. Kris Lane, "Raiders," in Joseph C. Miller et al., eds., *The Princeton Companion to Atlantic History*, 390–95, 392. See also Christina Snyder, *Slavery in Indian*

Country: The Changing Face of Captivity in Early America, Cambridge, MA: Harvard University Press, 2010.

44. Paul Baepler, ed., *White Slaves, African Masters: An Anthology of American Barbary Captivity Narratives*, Chicago: University of Chicago Press, 1999, 3n.

45. *By the King: A Proclamation Declaring the Kings Majesties Royall Pleasure Concerning the Inhabitants of Algiers, Tunis, Sallie and Tituan in the Parts of Africa*, 1628, Huntington Library, San Marino, CA.

46. Francis Bacon, also known as Fracis Lo, *Verulam Considerations Touch a Warre with Spaine*, 1629, Brown University, Providence, RI.

47. Charles Sumner, *White Slavery in the Barbary States*, Boston: Jewett, 1853, 11, 14, 28, 37, 110.

48. *Narrative of Joshua Gee, 1680–1687*, Hartford, CT: Wadsworth Athenaeum, 1943, 7.

49. Painter, *The History of White People*, 38. See fn 1.

50. Hill, *The Century of Revolution, 1603–1714*, 212. See Introduction

51. Emily C. Bartels, "Imperialist Beginnings: Richard Hakluyt and the Construction of Africa," *Criticism*, 34 (Fall 1992): 517–38, 527–30, 532, 533. See also Emory Washburn, *Slavery as It Once Prevailed in Massachusetts, A Lecture for the Massachusetts Historical Society at the Lowell Institute*, 22 January 1869, Boston: Wilson, 1869. African slavery is dated herein from Spain in 1508 and domesticated in England by 1553.

52. Jerry Broxton, *This Orient Isle: Elizabethan England and the Islamic World*, London: Allen Lane, 2016, 13.

53. Caroline Finkel, *Osman's Fortune: The History of the Ottoman Empire, 1300– 1923*, 177.

54. Clarence L. Ver Steeg and Richard Hofstadter, eds., *Great Issues in American History: From Settlement to Revolution, 1584–1776*, New York: Vintage, 1969, 4n.

55. E. H. Carter and R. A. F. Mears, *A History of Britain*, vol. 4: *The Stuarts, Cromwell and the Glorious Revolution, 1603–1714*, London: Stacey, 2010, 21.

56. Peter C. Mancall, *Hakluyt's Promise: An Elizabethan's Obsession for an English America*, New Haven: Yale University Press, 2007, 71, 81, 238..

57. Thomas Vaughan et al., eds., *Russian Penetration of the North Pacific Ocean, 1700–1799: A Documentary Record*, vol. 2, Portland: Oregon Historical Society, 1988, xxxi.

58. Thomas Vaughan et al., eds., *Russia's Conquest of Siberia, 1558–1700: A Documentary Record*, vol. 1, Portland: Oregon Historical Society, 1985.

59. John E. Willis, *1688: A Global History*, New York: Norton, 2001, 99.

60. Robert Brenner, *Merchants and Revolution: Commercial Change, Political Conflict and London's Overseas Traders, 1550–1653*, Princeton: Princeton University Press, 1993.

61. Wendy Warren, *New England Bound: Slavery and Colonization in Early America*, New York: W. W. Norton, 2016, 17.

62. Comment, no date, Van Cortlandt Family Papers, Columbia University, New York.

63. Gerald Horne, *Race War! White Supremacy and the Japanese Attack on the British Empire*, New York: New York University Press, 2003.

64. Carter and Mears, *The Stuarts, Cromwell and the Glorious Revolution, 1603–1714*, 22.

65. J. Sears McGee, *An Industrious Mind: The Worlds of Sir Simond D'ewes*, Stanford, CA: Stanford University Press, 2015, 275, 276.

66. See *Orders and Constitutions, Partly Collected out of His Majesties Letters, Patents...for the Plantation of the Summer Islands...6 February 1621...*, London: Kyngston, 1622, 82. See Article 30 concerning relations with Virginia, Huntington Library, San Marino, CA.

67. Recommendation to Madrid, 5 May 1611, in Quinn, *New American World*, 141.

68. Edward Waterhouse, *A Declaration of the State of the Colony and Affaires in Virginia with a Relation of the Barbarous Massacre in the Time of Peace and League, Treacherously Executed by the Native Infidels Upon the English, the 22nd of March Last...*, London: Mylbourne, 1622; and *The Native Infidels Upon the English, the 22nd of March Last...*, London: Mylbourne, 122, University of Virginia, Charlottesville. See also H. R. McIlwaine, ed., *Minutes of the Council and General Court of Colonial Virginia, 1622–1632*, Richmond, 1924, University of Virginia, Charlottesville.

69. Increase Mather, *A Relation of the Troubles Which Have Happened in New England by Reason of the Indians There from the Year 1614 to the Year 1675*, University of Virginia, Charlottesville. At the same site see also Louis des Cognets, Jr., *English Duplicates of Lost Virginia Records*, Princeton, 1958.

70. *Algiers Voyage in a Journall or Briefe...Fleet of the Ships Sent out by the King His Most Excellent Majestie, as Well Against the Pirates of Algiers as Others*, 1621, Huntington Library–San Marino: The backdrop included "Spanish ships and galleys, Turkish pirates, as we encountered with at sea..."

71. *A True Relation of the Late Cruel and Barbarous Tortures and Execution, Done Upon the English at Amboya in the East Indies by the Hollanders there Residing*, 1623, Huntington Library, San Marino, CA.

72. A. C. Grayling, *The Age of Genius: The Seventeenth Century and the Birth of the Modern Mind*, New York: Bloomsbury, 2016, 39.

73. Vivienne L. Kruger, "Born to Run: The Slave Family in Early New York, 1626–1827," Ph.D. diss., Columbia University, 1985, 34. See also Jaap Jacobs and L. H. Roper, eds., *The Worlds of the Seventeenth-Century River Valley*, Albany: State University of New York Press, 2014.

74. Edgar Tristram Thompson, *The Plantation*, Columbia: University of South Carolina Press, 2010, 25.

75. Captain J. Smith, *Historie of Virginia*, London, 1624, 78, 148, Huntington Library, San Marino, CA.

76. Karine V. Walther, *Sacred Interests: The United States and the Islamic World, 1821–1921*, Chapel Hill: University of North Carolina Press, 2015, 11.

77. J. Sears McGee, *An Industrious Mind: The Worlds of Sir Simond D'Ewes*, Stanford, CA: Stanford University Press, 2015, 155, 157. See also John Wood

Sweet and Robert Appelbaum, eds., *Envisioning an English Empire: Jamestown and the Making of the North Atlantic World*, Philadelphia: University of Pennsylvania Press, 2005.

78. Parker, *Global Crisis*, 293, 289.

79. Sue Peabody, *'There Are No Slaves in France': The Political Culture of Race and Slavery in the Ancien Regime*, New York: Oxford University Press, 1996, 5.

80. Edmund Abaka, *House of Slaves*, 231.

81. Comment in Warren M. Billings, ed., *The Old Dominion in the Seventeenth Century: A Documentary History of Virginia, 1606–1689*, Chapel Hill: University of North Carolina Press, 1975, 148. See also Cognets, *English Duplicates of Lost Virginia Records*.

82. Karl Polyani, *Dahomey and the Slave Trade: An Analysis of an Archaic Economy*, Seattle: University of Washington Press, 1966, 19.

83. *A Declaration of the State of the Colony and Affaires in Virginia with a Relation of the Barbarous Massacre in the Time of Peace League, Treacherously Executed by the Native Infidels Upon the English...1622*, Huntington Library, San Marino, CA. See Alden T. Vaughan, "'Expulsion of the Savages': English Policy and the Virginia Massacre of 1622," *William and Mary Quarterly* 35(1978): 57–84; *The Inconveniences that Have Happened to Some Persons which Have Transported Themselves from England to Virginia*, London: Kyngston, 1622, Boston Public Library.

84. Bernard Bailyn, *The Barbarous Years: The Conflict of Civilizations*, New York: Vintage, 2012, 174. See also Peter C. Mancall, ed., *The Atlantic World and Virginia, 1550–1624*, Chapel Hill: University of North Carolina Press, 2007.

85. Alan Gallay, ed., *Indian Slavery in Colonial America*, Lincoln: University of Nebraska Press, 2011.

86. Wesley Frank Craven, *The Southern Colonies in the Seventeenth Century, 1607–1689*, Baton Rouge: Louisiana State University Press, 1949, 218. See also Kathleen Donegan, *Seasons of Misery: Catastrophe and Colonial Settlement in Early America*, Philadelphia: University of Pennsylvania Press, 2014.

87. Richard Jobson, *The Golden Trade or a Discovery of the River Gambia and the Golden Trade of the Aethiopians also the Commerce with a Great Blacke Merchant, Called Buck or Sano and His Report of the Houses Covered with Gold and Other Strange Observations for the Good of our Owne Country...*, London: Okes, 1623, Huntington Library, San Marino, CA.

88. David L. Kent, ed., *Barbados and America*, Arlington, VA: Kent, 1980, 8. Kristen Block, *Ordinary Lives in the Early Caribbean: Religion, Colonial Competition, and the Politics of Profit*, Athens: University of Georgia Press, 2012.

89. Yda Schreuder, "The Influence of the Dutch Colonial Trade on Barbados in the Seventeenth Century," *Journal of Barbados Museum and Historical Society* 48(November 2002): 43–63, 50. See also William Duke, *Some Memoirs of the First Settlement on the Island of Barbados and other Carribbee Islands...*, 1741, Brown University, Providence.

90. Philip P. Boucher, 132.

91. Thomas E. Davidson, *Free Blacks on the Lower Eastern Shore of Maryland: The Colonial Period, 1662 to 1775*, Crownsville, MD: Maryland Historical and Cultural Publications, 1991, 5, 25. See also T. H. Breen and Stephen Innes, *'Myne Owne Ground': Race and Freedom on Virginia's Eastern Shore, 1640–1676*, New York: Oxford University Press, 2004, 12; Lorena Walsh, *Motives of Honor, Pleasure and Profit: Plantation Management in the Colonial Chesapeake, 1607–1763*, Chapel Hill: University of North Carolina Press, 2010, 115;

92. Audrey Horning, *Ireland in the Virginian Sea: Colonialism in the British Atlantic*, Chapel Hill: University of North Carolina Press, 267.

2. No Providence for Africans and the Indigenous

1. E. H. Carter and R. A. F. Mears, *A History of Britain*, vol. 4: *The Stuarts, Cromwell, and the Glorious Revolution, 1603–1714*, London: Stacey, 2010, 24. See also Jenny Shaw, *Everyday Life in the Early English Caribbean: Irish, Africans and the Construction of Difference*, Athens: University of Georgia Press, 2013.

2. John Barry, *Roger Williams and the Creation of the American Soul*, New York: Viking, 2012; Edwin S. Gaustad, *Roger Williams*, New York: Oxford University Press, 2005.

3. Margaret Ellen Newell, *Brethren by Nature: New England, Indians, Colonists and the Origins of American Slavery*, Ithaca: Cornell University Press, 2015, 37.

4. Jon C. Blue, *The Case of the Piglet's Paternity: Trials from the New Haven Colony, 1639–1663*, Middletown, CT: Wesleyan University Press, 2015, 64.

5. Geoffrey Parker, *Global Crisis*, 325.

6. Dated 25 September 1634, in N. B. Shurtleff, ed., *Records of the Governor and Company of the Massachusetts Bay in New England*, vol. 1: *1628–1641*, Boston: White, 1853, 129n.

7. Dated 13 May 1640, in ibid., 295.

8. Protest, 1659, Box 1, MS 2018, Colonial Records Collection, Maryland Historical Society, Baltimore.

9. Memorandum from Lords' Commissioners for Foreign Plantations, 3 July 1633, in Clarence L. Ver Steeg and Richard Hofstadter, eds., *Great Issues in American History: From Settlement to Revolution, 1584–1776*, New York: Vintage, 1969, 57–60.

10. Remarks by Sir Edward Giles, 26 November 1641, in Ann Hughes, ed., *Seventeenth Century England: A Changing Culture*, vol. 1: *Primary Sources*, London: Ward and Lock, 1988, 31–34.

11. John D. Krugler, *English and Catholic: The Lords Baltimore in the Seventeenth Century*, Baltimore: Johns Hopkins University Press, 2004, 3.

12. Reverend William P. Treacy, *Old Catholic Maryland and Early Jesuit Missionaries*, Swedesboro, NJ: St. Joseph's Rectory, unclear date, Maryland Historical Society, Baltimore.

13. "Instructions to the Colonists by Lord Baltimore," 1633, in Clayton Colman Hall, ed., *Narratives of Early Maryland, 1633–1684*, New York: Scribner's, 1910, 16–23.

14. Memorandum, 4 April 1638, in Ver Steeg and Hofstadter, *Great Issues in American History*, 53–57.

15. J. Hall Pleasants, "Religious Intolerance in Early Maryland," n.d., Box 2, MS, 2018, Colonial Records Collection, Maryland Historical Society, Baltimore. See also Margaret Lucille Kekewich, ed., *Princes and Peoples: France and the British Isles, 1620–1714*, Manchester, UK: Manchester University Press, 1994.

16. Michael J. Rozbicki, *Transformation of the English Cultural Ethos in Colonial America*, Lanham, MD: University Press of America, 75. See also Howard Bradstreet, *The Story of the Pequot War of 1637*, Hartford, CT: Polygon, 1930.

17. Parker, *Global Crisis*, 500.

18. P. C. Emmer, *The Dutch Slave Trade, 1500–1850*, New York: Berghan, 2006, 23, 24, 26, 75.

19. *A True Relation of the Late Battel Fought in New England Between the English and the Salvages...with the Present State of Things There*, London: Butters, 1637, Huntington Library, San Marino, CA. At the same site, see also W. Hubbard, *A Narrative of the Troubles with the Indians in New England from the First Planting Thereof in the Year 1607 to the Present Year 1677... A Discourse About the Warre with the Pequods in the Year 1637*, Boston: Foster, 1677; Shurtleff, *Records of the Governor and Company of the Massachusetts Bay*, 192.

20. Note in ibid., N.B. Shurtleff, 392.

21. Wendy Warren, *New England Bound*, 5.

22. Philip Boucher, 262, 282.

23. David Silverman, *Thundersticks: Firearms and the Violent Transformation of Native America*, Cambridge: Harvard University Press, 29, 68.

24. Yda Schreuder, "A True Global Community: Sephardic Jews, the Sugar Trade and Barbados in the Seventeenth Century," *Journal of the Barbados Museum and Historical Society* 50(December 2004): 166–94, 182.

25. Richard Sheridan, "The Plantation Revolution and the Industrial Revolution, 1625–1775," *Caribbean Studies* 9 (October 1969): 5–25. See also *Tobacco Battered & the Pipes Shattered...Barbarous a Weed...Loathsome, 1617*, Huntington Library, San Marino, CA.

26. Mordecai Arbell, *The Portuguese Jews of Jamaica*, Kingston: Canoe Press, 2000, 1.

27. Willie F. Page, *The Dutch Triangle: The Netherlands and the Atlantic Slave Trade, 1621–1644*, New York: Garland, 1997,

28. Emmer, *The Dutch Slave Trade*, 18, 22, 23.

29. Sir Benjamin Rudyerd, "A Speech Concerning a West Indies Association at a Committee of the Whole House in the Parliament," 1641, Brown University, Providence, RI.

30. "A Brief Report on the State That is Composed of the Four Conquered Captaincies, Pernambuco, Itamaraca, Paraiba and Rio Grande, Situated in the North of Brazil," ca. 1654, in Stuart B. Schwartz, ed., *Early Brazil: A Documentary Collection to 1700*, New York: Cambridge University Press, 2010, 234–64, 234.

31. Jonathan Israel, *Diasporas within a Diaspora: Jews, Crypto Jews and the World Maritime Empires, 1540–1740*, Leiden: Brill, 2002, 292.

32. Robert Brenner, *Merchants and Revolution: Commercial Change, Political Context and London's Overseas Traders, 1550–1653*, Princeton: Princeton University Press, 1993, 164, 92.

33. Joseph Schumpeter, *Capitalism, Socialism and Democracy*, London: Routledge, 1994.

34. Charles Spencer, *Killers of the King: The Men Who Dared to Execute Charles I*, New York: Bloomsbury, 2014, 159.

35. George H. Moore, *Additional Notes on the History of Slavery in Massachusetts*, 1866, Huntington Library, San Marino CA. See also Christina Snyder, *Slavery in Indian Country: The Changing Face of Captivity in Early America*, Cambridge, MA: Harvard University Press, 2010.

36. Margaret Ellen Newell, *Brethren by Nature: New England Indians, Colonists and the Origins of American Slavery*, Ithaca, NY: Cornell University Press, 2015, 6, 7, 168, 179.

37. Ibid., 45. See also Carolyn Thomas Foreman, *Indians Abroad, 1493–1938*, Norman: University of Oklahoma Press, 1943.

38. John Donoghue, "Out of the Land of Bondage: The English Revolution and the Atlantic Origins of Abolition," *American Historical Review* 115 (October 2010): 943–74, 950.

39. Law of 1640, in Warren M. Billings, ed., *The Old Dominion in the Seventeenth Century: A Documentary History of Virginia, 1606–1689*, Chapel Hill: University of North Carolina Press, 1975, 172–73.

40. David Silverman, *Thundersticks: Firearms and the Violent Transformation of Native America*, Cambridge: Harvard University Press, 2016, 103.

41. Alan Taylor, *American Colonies: The Settling of North America*, New York: Penguin, 2001, 206.

42. Vincent T. Harlow, *A History of Barbados, 1625–1685*, Oxford: Clarendon Press, 1926, 268. See also Richard S. Dunn, *Sugar & Slaves: The Rise of the Planter Class in the English West Indies, 1624–1713*, Chapel Hill: University of North Carolina Press, 1972.

43. Bernard Bailyn, *The Barbarous Years: The Peopling of North America: The Conflict of Civilizations 1600–1675*, New York: Knopf, 2012, 490–91.

44. A. C. Grayling, *The Age of Genius: The 17th Century and the Birth of the Modern Mind*, New York: Bloomsbury, 2016, 56.

45. Steven Karl Flogstad Heise, 64.

46. Newell, *Brethren by Nature*, 49. See also Karen Ordahl Kupperman, *Providence Island, 1630–1641: The Other Puritan Colony*, New York: Cambridge University Press, 1995.

47. Jon Latimer, *Buccaneers of the Caribbean: How Piracy Forged an Empire*, Cambridge, MA: Harvard University Press, 2009, 84.

48. Memorandum, 28 March 1636, in W. Noel Sainsbury, ed., *Calendar of State Papers, Colonial Series, 1574–1660*, London: Her Majesty's Stationery Office, 1860, 229.

49. Company of Providence Island to Captain Hunt, Governor, 19 March 1637, in ibid.,247.

50. Company of Providence Island to Governor and Council, 29 March 1637, in ibid., 249.
51. Minutes, 22 June 1637, in ibid., 255.
52. Company of Providence Island to the Governor and Council, 3 July 1638, in ibid., 277–78.
53. John Donoghue, "Out of the Land of Bondage: The English Revolution and the Atlantic Origins of Abolition," *American Historical Review*, 115 (October 2010): 943–974, 961.
54. Warren, *New England Bound*, 34, 12.
55. Company of Providence Island to Governor and Council, 7 June 1639, in Sainsbury, *Calendar of State Papers*, 296.
56. Andrea Stuart, *Sugar in the Blood: A Family's Story of Slavery and Empire*, New York: Knopf, 2013, 10.
57. Warren, *New England Bound*, 77.
58. Richard Pares, *Yankees and Creoles: The Trade between North America and the West Indies Before the American Revolution*, Cambridge, MA: Harvard University Press, 1956.
59. Comment in David L. Kent, ed., *Barbados and America*, Arlington, VA: Kent, 1980, 7.
60. *A Relation of Seven Years Slaverie Under the Turks of Argeire Suffered by an English Captive Merchant...with a Description of the Sufferings of the Miserable Captives under That...Tyrannie...*, London: Sparke, 1640, Huntington Library, San Marino, CA.
61. *The Arrivall and Intertainements of the Embassador Alkaid Jaurar Ben Abdella with His Associate Robert Blake, from the High and Mighty Prince, Mulley Mahamed Sheque, Emperor of Morocco, King of Fez...*, London: Okes, 1637,Huntington Library, San Marino, CA..
62. Orest and Patricia Ranum, eds., *The Century of Louis XIV*, New York: Walker, 1972.
63. See, for example, "The Rebellion of 1641," in Edmund Curtis and R. B. McDowell, eds., *Irish Historical Documents, 1172–1922*, New York: Barnes & Noble, 1968, 148–52. See also J. P. Kenyon, ed., *The Stuart Constitution, 1603–1688: Documents and Commentary*, London: Cambridge, 1966.
64. *A Perfect Declaration of the Barbarous and Cruel Practices Committed by Prince Robert, the Cavalier and Others in His Majesties Army, from the Time of the Kings Going from His Parliament Until this Present Day. Also the Names and Places of All Those Whose Houses Have Bin Plundered and Lost Their Lives and Estates, Compared with the Bloody Cruelties of Rebells in Ireland, Whose Examples they Follow...and Make Use of Them as Their Agent to Act Their Cruelties in England...*, London, 1642, Huntington Library, San Marino, CA. At the same archive, see Sir John Temple, *The Irish Rebellion: Or an History of the Beginnings and First Progress of the General Rebellion Raised within the Kingdom of Ireland...in the Year 1641...Together with the Barbarous Cruelties and Bloody Massacres which Ensued Thereupon*, London: White, 1646.

3. The Rise of the Merchants and the Beheading of a King

1.   Theodore Roosevelt, *Oliver Cromwell*, New York: Scribner's, 1900, 1, 14.

2.   John Miller, *The English Civil Wars: Roundheads, Cavaliers and the Execution of the King*, London: Constable & Robinson, 2009, 16, 112, 119, 128. See also Robert Ashton, *Counter-Revolution: The Second Civil War and Its Origins, 1646–1648*, New Haven: Yale University Press, 1994; and Carla Gardina Pestana, *The English Atlantic in an Age of Revolution, 1640–1661*, Cambridge: Harvard University Press, 2004.

3.   E. H. Carter and R. A. F. Mears, *A History of Great Britain*, vol. 4: *The Stuarts, Cromwell and the Glorious Revolution, 1603–1714*, London: Stacey, 2010, 48.

4.   Adam Jones, ed., *West Africa in the Mid-Seventeenth Century: An Anonymous Dutch Manuscript*, Atlanta, GA: African Studies Association Press, 1995, 3.

5.   J. Sears Mc Gee, *An Industrious Mind: The Worlds of Sir Simond D'Ewes*, Stanford, CA: Stanford University Press, 2015, 156, 157.

6.   William Pettigrew, "Commercialization," in Joseph C. Miller, ed., *The Princeton Companion to Atlantic History*, 111–16, at 115.

7.   *Good Newes from Ireland...Two Great Victories Obtained Against the Rebels There...*, London: Wright, 1642, Huntington Library, San Marino, CA.

8.   Malcolm Gaskill, *Between Two Worlds: How the English Became Americans*, New York: Basic Books, 2014, 194.

9.   Karine V. Walther, *Sacred Interests: The United States and the Islamic World, 1821–1921*, Chapel Hill: University of North Carolina Press, 2015, 12.

10. Don Jordan and Michael Walsh, *White Cargo: The Forgotten History of Britain's White Slaves in America*, New York: New York University Press, 2008.

11. John D. Krugler, *English and Catholic: The Lords Baltimore in the Seventeenth Century*, Baltimore: Johns Hopkins University Press, 2004, 194.

12. Gerald Horne, *Negro Comrades of the Crown: African Americans and the British Empire Fight the United States before Emancipation*, New York: New York University Press, 2012; and *Confronting Black Jacobins: The U.S., the Haitian Revolution and the Origins of the Dominican Republic*, New York: Monthly Review Press, 2015.

13. Cromwell, 17 September 1949, in *Oliver Cromwell, Letters from Ireland: Relating to the Several Great Successes it Hath Pleased God to Give Unto the Parliaments Forces there in the Taking of Drogheda, Trym, Dundalk, Caelingford and the Nury*, London: Field, 1649, 53.

14. Nicholas Foster, *A Briefe Relation of the Late Horrid Rebellion Acted in the Island of Barbados, in the West Indies Wherein Is Contained, Their Inhumane Acts and Actions, in Fining and Banishing the Well-Affected to the Parliament of England (both Men and Women)...*, London: Unwin, 1879 (originally published ca. 1650), Massachusetts Historical Society, Boston.

15. Foster, *A Briefe Relation of the Late Horrid Rebellion...*, London: Lowndes, 1650, Huntington Library, San Marino, CA.

16. *A True and Exact Narrative of the Proceedings of the Parliament's Fleet, Against the Island of Barbadoes with the Manner of Reducing Thereof: Together with*

the Submittings of the Islands of St. Christophers, Antego, and St. Nevis to the Commonwealth of England, Written by an Eye-Witnesse, Mr. T.H. from Aboard the Amity, London: Harper, 1650, Brown University, Providence, RI.

17. *Articles of Agreements Made and Concluded the 11th Day of January 1651, By and Between the Commissioners of the Right Honourable the Lord Willoughby of Parrham on the One Part and the Commissioners in the Behalfe of the Commonwealth of England on the Other Part, Being in Order to the Rendition of the Island of Barbadoes*, London: Coles, 1652, Brown University, Providence, RI.

18. *An Act Prohibiting Trade with the Barbada's, Virginia, Bermudas and Antego*, London: Husband and Field, 1650, University of Virginia, Charlottesville.

19. *Ordinance on Duties on Exports to Virginia*, 1646, Huntington Library, San Marino, CA.

20. Nicholas Darnell Davis, *Cavaliers and Roundheads in Barbados, 1650–1652*, British Guiana, 1887, v.

21. Matthew Neufeld, "From Peacemaking to Peacebuilding: The Multiple Endings of England's Long Civil Wars," *American Historical Review* 120/5 (December 2015): 1709–23.

22. Timothy B. Riordan, *The Plundering Time: Maryland and the English Civil War, 1645–1646*, Baltimore: Maryland Historical Society, 2004, 3, 5.

23. Malcolm Gaskill, *Between Two Worlds: How the English Became Americans*, New York, 2014.

24. *Virginia and Maryland or the Lord Baltimore's Printed Case Uncased and Answered. Shewing the Illegality of His Patent and Usurpation of the Royal Jurisdiction...Also a Short Relation of the Papists Late Rebellion Against the Government of His Highness, the Lord Protecter*, London, 1655, 155, Huntington Library, San Marino, CA.

25. Brenner, *Merchants and Revolution*, 171.

26. Parker, *Global Crisis*, 375, 377, 380.

27. "Act in Parliament, 3 October 1650," in N. B. Shurtleff, ed., *Records of the Governor and Company of the Massachusetts Bay in New England*, vol. 3, 224.

28. Note, 14 October 1651, in ibid., 240.

29. *An Act for the Redemption of Captives*, London: Husband and Field, 1650, University of Virginia, Charlottesville.

30. John Langdon Sibley, ed., *Biographical Sketches of Graduates of Harvard University in Cambridge, Massachusetts*, vol. 1, Cambridge: Sever, 1873, 31, 32, 40, 41.

31. Parker, *Global Crisis*, 450, 451.

32. Lemuel A. Welles, *The History of Regicides in New England*, New York: Grafton Press, 1927, 11, 21. 25.

33. Chandler Robbins, *The Regicides Shelter in New England: A Lecture*, Boston: Wilson, 1869, Massachusetts Historical Society, Boston.

34. Margaret Ellen Newell, *Brethren by Nature*, 58.

35. Parker, *Global Crisis*, 380.

36. Ibid., 381.

37. Entry, 4 November 1646, in N. B. Shurtleff, ed., *Records of the Governor and Company of Massachusetts Bay in New England*, vol. 2: *1642–1649*, Boston: White, 1853, 168.

38. Note, 1 October 1645, in ibid., 136.

39. Note, 4 November 1646, in ibid., 176.

40. Ibid., 136.

41. Note, 14 October 1645, in Shurtleff, *Records of the Governor and Company*, vol. 3,

42. *The Code of 1650…of the General Court of Connecticut*, Hartford, CT: Andrus, 54, Huntington Library, San Marino, CA

43. Entry, September 1646, in *Records of the Colony of New Plymouth in New England*, Boston: White, 1861…., vol. 1: *1643–1651*, 71.

44. *The Second Part of the Tragedy or Amboyna: Or a True Relation of a Most Bloody, Treacherous and Cruel Design of the Dutch in the New Netherlands in America. For the Total Ruining and Murthering of the English Colonists in New England, Being Extracted from one of the Several Letters Very Lately Written from New England to Several Gentlemen and Merchants in London*, London: Matthews, 1653, Huntington Library, San Marino. CA .

45. *The Second Part of the Tragedy or Amboyna*, Brown University.

46. John Quarles, *The Tyranny of the Dutch Against the English*, London, 1653, Huntington Library, San Marino, CA.

47. Jean Houbert, "Creolisation and Decolonization in the Changing Politics of the Indian Ocean," in Richard Parkhurst et.al., eds., *The African Diaspora in the Indian Ocean*, Trenton: Africa World Press, 2003, 123–149, 130.

48. Note, 27 May 1652, in Shurtleff, *Records of the Governor and Company*, vol. 3, 269; and Note, 26 May 1652, in Shurtleff, *Records of the Governor and Company*, vol. 4, 86.

49. Wendy Warren, *New England Bound*, 190.

50. Nicholas Darnell Davis, *Cavaliers and Roundheads in Barbados, 1650–1652*, British Guiana: Argosy, 1883, 5, 125.

51. Malcolm Gaskill, *Between Two Worlds: How the English Became Americans*, New York: Basic Books, 2014, 186, 188, 234.

52. Robert Emmett Curran, *Papist Devils: Catholics in British America, 1574–1783*, Washington, D.C.: Catholic University of America Press, 2014, 83.

53. Stuart B. Schwartz, "Looking for a New Brazil: Crisis and Rebirth in the Atlantic World after the Fall of Pernambuco," in *The Legacy of Dutch Brazil*, ed. Michael van Groesen, New York; Cambridge University Press, 2014, 41–58, 47, 48.

54. Russell R. Menard, "The Sugar Industry in the Seventeenth Century: A New Perspective on the Barbadian 'Sugar Revolution'," in *Tropical Babylons: Sugar and the Making of the Atlantic World, 1450–1680*, ed. Stuart B. Schwartz, Princeton: Princeton University Press, 2004, 289–320.

55. Mordecai Arbell, *The Portuguese Jews of Jamaica*, Kingston, Jamaica: Canoe Press, 2000, 1.

56. Alan Taylor, *American Colonies: The Settling of North America*, New York: Penguin, 2001, 220.

57. Jerome S. Handler, ed., "A German Indentured Servant in Barbados in 1652: The Account of Heinrich von Uchteritz," *Journal of the Barbados Museum and Historical Society*, 1970, Brown University.

58. Brycchan Carey, *From Peace to Freedom: Quaker Rhetoric and the Birth of American Antislavery, 1657–1761*, New Haven: Yale University Press, 2012, 10.

59. Richard Ligon, *A True & Exact History of the Island of Barbados*, London: Moseley, 1657, 46.

60. Horne, *Confronting Black Jacobins*, passim.

61. Horne, *The Counter-Revolution of 1776*, passim.

62. Ligon, *A True & Exact History*, 46.

63. Marion Gleason McDougall, *Fugitive Slaves (1619–1865)*, Boston: Ginn, 1891, 9, 10.

64. Margaret Lillian Mitchell, "Slavery in Colonial Delaware," B.A. thesis, Smith College, 1970, 16.

65. *The Laws of Jamaica Comprehending All the Acts in Force Passed Between the Thirty-Second Year of the Reign of King Charles the Second and the Thirty-Third*, vol. 1, St. Jago de la Vega, Jamaica: Aikman, 1792, xxix, National Library of Jamaica, Kingston.

66. *1652 Acts and Statutes of the Island of Barbados...Set forth the Seventh Day of September in the Year of Our Lord ...*, London: Bentley, 1652, British Library, London.

67. Kwasi Konadu, *The Akan Diaspora in the Americas*, New York: Oxford University Press, 2010, 7.

68. John Donoghue, "Out of the Land of Bondage: The English Revolution and the Atlantic Origins of Abolition," *American Historical Review* 115 (October 2010): 943–74, at 947.

69. Warren, *New England Bound*, 11.

70. Charles Spencer, *Killers of the King*, 266.

71. *Resolution*, London: Hunscott, 1642, Boston Public Library.

72. Nuala Zahedieh, *The Capital and the Colonies: London and the Atlantic Economy, 1660–1700*, New York: Cambridge University Press, 2010, 246.

73. Edmund Abaka, *House of Slaves and Door of No Return*, 6, 205, 208.

74. Brenner, *Merchants and Revolution*, 171.

75. Richard Boothby, *The Discovery or Description of the Most Famous Island of Madagascar or St. Laurence in Asia Neare unto...India*, London: Hardesty, 1646.

76. Walter Hamond, *Madagascar, the Richest and Most Fruitfull Island in the World...Dedicated to the Honourable John Bond, Governor of the Island*, London: Bourne, 1643.

77. Lt. Colonel Robert Hunt, *The Island of Assada Neare Madagascar...Plenary Description of the Situation, Fertility and People Therein Inhabiting...*, London: Bourne, 1650.

78. Li Anshan, *A History of Overseas Chinese in Africa to 1911*, New York: Diasporic Africa Press, 2012, 1.

79. Warren, *New England Bound*, 54. For more on Anglo-Dutch conflict, see, for

example, Frances Henderson, ed., *The Clarke Papers: Further Selections from the Papers of William Clarke, Secretary to the Council of the Army, 1647–1649 and to General Monck and the Commanders of the Army in Scotland, 1651–1660*, Chapel Hill: University of North Carolina Press, 2005.

4. Jamaica Seized from Spain

1. James Evans, *Emigrants: Why the English Sailed to the New World*, London: Weidenfeld & Nicolson, 2017. See also Geoffrey Parker, pages denoted in note 2.
2. Geoffrey Parker, *Global Crisis*, 327, 381, 447, 452, 464.
3. Note in Warren M. Billings, ed., *The Old Dominion in the Seventeenth Century: A Documentary History of Virginia, 1606–1689*, Chapel Hill: University of North Carolina Press, 1975, 148–49, 153.
4. *The Lawes [sic] Now in Force*, London: Cotes, 1662, 59, Brown University, Providence.
5. Carla Gardina Pestana, *The English Conquest of Jamaica: Oliver Cromwell's Bid for Empire*, Cambrridge: Harvard University Press, 2017, 248.
6. Charles Long, "Names of the Principal Planters and Settlers in Jamaica, 1633," New-York Historical Society, Manhattan. It is possible that this list contained Irishmen, thus vitiating any advantage for London.
7. Cassander Smith, *Black Africans in the British Imagination*, 110, 103.
8. *The History and State of Jamaica under Lord Vaughan*, n.d., ca. early seventeenth century, MS 159, National Library of Jamaica, Kingston.
9. *A True Copy of Oliver Cromwell's Manifesto Against Spain Dated October 26, 1655. Containing Authentic Accounts of Many Pyracies, Robberies, Murders, and Cruelties Committed by the Spaniards upon the English during the Pacific Reign of James I and Perplext Reign of Charles I*, London: Cooper, 1741, Huntington Library, San Marino, CA. At the same site, see also *A Declaration of His Highness by the Advice of his Council; Setting Forth on the Behalf of this Commonwealth the Justice of their Cause Against Spain*, ca. 1655.
10. *A Brief and Perfect Journal of the Late Proceedings and Success of the English Army in the West Indies, Continued Until June the 24th 1655*, London, 1655, Huntington Library, San Marino, CA.
11. Vice-Admiral Edward Vernon, *A New History of Jamaica from the Earliest Accounts to the Taking of Porto Bello*, London: Hodges, 1740, 39, 66, 76, New-York Historical Society. At the same site, see also *The History of Jamaica or General Survey of the An[c]ient and Modern State...*,vol. 1, London: Lowndes, 1774.
12. S. A. G. Taylor, "The Odyssey of James Martin: A Story of Life in Jamaica Under the Spaniards," MS 1954A, National Library of Jamaica, Kingston. See also Vincent T. Harlow, ed., *The Voyages of Captain William Jackson (1642–1645)*, London: Offices of the Society, 1923.
13. Mordechai Arbell, *The Portuguese Jews of Jamaica*, Kingston: Canoe Press, 2000, 9.
14. *Narrative of the Great Success God Hath Been Pleased to Give His Highness Forces in Jamaica Against the King of Spain's Forces...Published by His Highness*

Special Command, London: Hills and Field, 1658, Jamaica National Library, Kingston.

15.   Irene Wright, *The English Conquest of Jamaica: An Account of What Happened in the Island of Jamaica, from May 20 of the Year 1655, When the English Laid Siege to It, up to July 3 of the Year 1656 by Captain Julian de Castilla*, 1923, 11, Huntington Library, San Marino, CA.

16.   *A Brief and Perfect Journal of the Late Proceedings and Success of the English Army.*

17.   "Instructions" in *Calendar of State Papers, Colonial Series, 1574–1660*, ed. W. Noel Sainsbury, London: Her Majesty's Stationery Office, 1860, 429.

18.   William Haller, ed., *The Leveller Tracts, 1647–1653*, Gloucester, MA: Peter Smith, 1964. See also *The Anti–Levellers Antidote Against he Most Venomous of the Serpents, the Subtillest Monopolizers*, n.d., Boston Public Library.

19   See, for example, Jenny Shaw, *Everyday Life in the Early English Caribbean: Irish, Africans and the Construction of Difference*, Athens: University of Georgia Press, 2013.

20.   Henry Barham, "An Account of the Island of Jamaica, 1492–1722," 1722, MS4, Jamaica National Library, Kingston.

21.   Carla Gardina Pestana, *The English Conquest of Jamaica*, 191.   Ultimately, Cuba as the key to the emergent slave trade was borne out by the emergence of the United States in that as early as the tenure of George Washington, U.S. nationals were dominating the odious commerce that gripped the "Pearl of the Antilles": see Gerald Horne, *Race to Revolution: The U.S. and Cuba During Slavery and Jim Crow*, New York: Monthly Review Press, 2014.

22.   Bev Carey, *The Maroon Story: The Authentic and Original History of the Maroons in the History of Jamaica, 1490–1880*, St. Andrew, Jamaica: Agouti, 1997, 84.

23.   Richard Blome, *A Description of the Island of Jamaica; with the Other Isles and Territories in America, to Which the English Are Related, viz. Barbadoes*, London: Milbourn, 1672, 47–48.

24.   Ibid., Carla Gardina Pestana, 238.

25.   Parker, *Global Crisis*, 557.

26.   Wim Klooster, *The Dutch Moment: War, Trade and Settlement in the Seventeenth Century*, Ithaca, NY: Cornell University Press, 2016, 30, 167,

27.   Mark L. Thompson, *The Contest for the Delaware Valley: Allegiance, Identity and Empire in the Seventeenth Century*, Baton Rouge: Louisiana State University Press, 2013, 97.

28.   Gerald Horne, *The Counter-Revolution of 1776*, 200.

29.   John Donoghue, " 'Out of the Land of Bondage': The English Revolution and the Atlantic Origins of Abolition," *American Historical Review* 120 (October 2010): 943–74, at 965.

30.   Parker, *Global Crisis*, 383.

31.   S. A. G. Taylor, *The Western Design: An Account of Cromwell's Expedition to the Caribbean*, Kingston: Institute of Jamaica, 1965, 75, 98, 99–100, 102–3, 112, 133–34, 181. See also C. H. Firth, ed., *The Narrative of General Venables:*

With an Appendix of Papers Relating to the Expedition to the West Indies and the Conquest of Jamaica, 1654–1655, New York: Longmans, Green, 1900.

32. Charles Spencer, *Killers of the King: The Men Who Dared to Execute Charles I*, New York: Bloomsbury, 2014, 76. See also David Farr, *John Lambert, Parliamentary Soldier and Cromwellian Major-General, 1619–1684*, Rochester, NY: Boydell, 2003. On the transitions in Texas, see Gerald Horne, *Negro Comrades of the Crown: African Americans and the British Empire Fight the U.S. before Emancipation*, New York: New York University Press, 2012.

33. *A Brief and Perfect Journal of the Late Proceedings and Success of the English Army in the West Indies, Continued until June the 24th 1655, Together with Some Queries Inserted and Answered. By I.S, an Eyewitness*, London, 1655, Boston Public Library. This publication can also be found at Brown University.

34. Thomas Gage, *A New Survey of the West Indies: Or the English Thousand and Three Hundred Miles Within the Main Land Area of America…*, London: Sweeting, 1655, Boston Public Library. See also *A Narrative of the Great Success God Hath Been Pleased to Give His Highness Forces in Jamaica, Against the King of Spain's Forces…*, London: Hills and Field, 1658, Brown University, Providence.

35. Carey, *The Maroon Story*, 84.

36. Yda Schreuder, "The Influence of the Dutch Colonial Trade on Barbados in the Seventeenth Century," *Journal of the Barbados Museum and Historical Society* 48 (November 2002): 43–63, 54, 56.

37. Caroline Finkel, *Osman's Dream: The History of the Ottoman Empire, 1300–1923*, New York: Basic Books, 2007, 213.

38. Yda Schreuder, "A True Global Community: Sephardic Jews, the Sugar Trade and Barbados in the Seventeenth Century," *Journal of the Barbados Museum and Historical Society* 50 (December 2004): 166–94, 168, 178, 180, 182, 185, 190.

39. Philip B. Boucher, *France and the American Tropics to 1700*, 92, 297, 298.

40. Mordechai Arbell, *The Portuguese Jews of Jamaica*, Kingston: Canoe Press, 2000, 1, 9, 11, 37, 44, 48. 52. See also Peter Mark and Jose da Silva Horta, *The Forgotten Diaspora: Jewish Communities in West Africa and the Making of the Atlantic World*, New York: Cambridge University Press, 2011, 69. Note the comment on the slave trade database developed by David Eltis and others: "Contraband voyages are missing and there were a lot of them." See also Toby Green, *The Rise of the Trans-Atlantic Slave Trade in Western Africa, 1300–1589*, New York: Cambridge University Press, 2010, 7, 135. Philip Curtin is accused of underestimating the sixteenth-century slave trade. The role of the Iberian community grew in Africa following the "1391 riots," when some Iberians got involved in the early slave trade.

41. Karl Watson, "The Iconography of Tombstones in the Jewish Graveyard, Bridgetown, Barbados," *Journal of the Barbados Museum and Historical Society* 50 (December 2004): 195–212, 198.

42. Boucher, 115.

43. Yda Schreuder, "The Influence of the Dutch Colonial Trade on Barbados in

the Seventeenth Century," *Journal of the Barbados Museum and Historical Society* 48 (November 2002): 43–63, 49.

44. "Instructions," *Calendar of State Papers, Colonial Series, 1574–1660*, 429.

45. Entry, in Richard S. Dunn et al., eds., *The Journal of John Winthrop, 1630–1649*, Cambridge, MA: Harvard University Press, 1996, 362.

46. Tobias Payne, "History of the Family and Descendants of Tobias Payne," *Remarkable Providences, 1600–1760*, ed. John Demos, New York: Braziller, 1972, 175–88, at 175.

47. John Cotton to Oliver Cromwell, 28 July 1651, in Sargent Bush, Jr., ed., *The Correspondence of John Cotton*, Chapel Hill: University of North Carolina Press, 2001, 458, 461, 463.

48. E. H. Carter and R. A. F. Mears, *A History of Britain*, vol. 4: *The Stuarts, Cromwell and the Glorious Revolution, 1603–1714*, London: Stacey, 2010, 115.

49. *The Popish Inquisition Newly Erected in New England and Whereby their Church Is Manifested to Be a Daughter of Mysterie Babylon, which Did Drink the Blood of the Saints...*, London: Simmons, 1659, Brown University, Providence.

50. Gerald Horne, *Race War!*, passim.

51. Vincent T. Harlow, *A History of Barbados, 1625–1685*, 277.

52. Matthew Mulcahy, *Hubs of Empire: The Southeastern Low Country and British Caribbean*, Baltimore: Johns Hopkins University Press, 2014, 44. See also Chad van Dixhoorn, ed., *The Minutes and Papers of the Westminster Assembly, 1643–1652*, vol. 1, New York: Oxford University Press, 2012.

53. Note, 14 May 1656, in N. B. Shurtleff, ed., *Records of the Governor and Company of the Massachusetts Bay in New England*, vol. 4, 273.

54. Ibid.. See also Gordon Donaldson, ed., *Scottish Historical Documents*, New York: Barnes & Noble, 1970.

55. *A Declaration of Former Passages and Proceedings Between the English and the Narroganset, with their Confederates...Published by Order of the Commissioners for the United Colonies at Boston, the 11th of the Sixth Month 1645*, Brown University, Providence.

56. *Britain Triumphs, or a Brief History of the Warres and Other State Affairs of Great Britain, from the Death of the Late King to the Third Year of the Government of the Lord Protector*, London: Farnham, 1656, Brown University, Providence.

57. Ray A. Kea, *Settlements, Trade and Polities in the Seventeenth Century Gold Coast*, Baltimore: Johns Hopkins University Press, 1982, 201, 209.

58. Mark L. Thompson, *The Contest for the Delaware Valley: Allegiance, Identity and Empire in the Seventeenth Century*, Baton Rouge: Louisiana State University Press, 2013, 73.

59. *Articles of Peace Between...Charles the Second...And the Most Excellent Signors, Mahomet Bashaw, the Duan of the Noble City of Tunis...Concluded 5 October 1662, Renewed and Confirmed the Fourth of February 1675*, Brown University, Providence.

60. Nabil Matar, *Turks, Moors and Englishmen in the Age of Discovery*, New York: Columbia University Press, 1999, 3, 16.

61. *The Several Declarations of the Company of Royal Adventurers of England Trading into Africa. Inviting All His Majesties Native Subjects in General to Subscribe and Become Sharers in the Joynt-Stock...*, 1667, i, National Library of Australia-Canberra.

62. Daina Ramey Berry, *The Price for Their Pound of Flesh: The Value of the Enslaved, from Womb to Grave, in the Building of a Nation*, Boston: Beacon Press, 2017, 11.

63. *Bloody Newes From the Barbadoes, Being a True Relation of a Great and Terrible Fight Between the Parliaments Navie...and the King of Scots Forces...*, London: Horton, 1652, Brown University, Providence.

64. David L. Kent, ed., *Barbados and America*, Arlington, VA: Kent, 1980, 8, 10, 11.

65. Parker, *Global Crisis*, 448, 675.

66. Oliver Cromwell to "Commissioners of Maryland," 26 September 1655, in *Oliver Cromwell's Letters and Speeches: With Elucidations by Thomas Carlyle*, vol. 2, London: Chapman and Hall, 1845, 374–75.

67. C. H. Firth, ed., *The Narrative of General Venables*, New York: Longmans, Green, 1900.

68. Statute, 4 April 1655, in Richard Hall, ed., *Acts Passed in the Island of Barbados from 1643 to 1762*, London, 1764, 21–22, Barbados National Archives, St. James.

69. Statute, 27 September 1661, in ibid., 35–42, 36.

70. Request, 20 January 1666, Box 19, *David Parrish Slavery Transcripts*, New York Historical Society, Manhattan.

5. The Dutch Ousted from the Mainland

1. James Delbourgo, *Collecting the World: The Life and Curiosity of Hans Sloane*, London: Allen Lane, 2017.

2. Malcolm Gaskill, *Between Two Worlds*, 317.

3. Charles Wilson, *Profit and Power: A Study of England and the Dutch Wars*, London: Longmans, Green, 1957, 115. See also Maurice Exwood and H. L. Lehmann, *The Journal of William Schellink's Travels in England, 1661–1663*, London: Royal Historical Society, 1993.

4. Karel Schoeman, *Early Slavery and the Cape of Good Hope, 1652–1717*, Pretoria: Protea, 2007, 58, 108,

5. See Malyn Newitt, *The Portuguese in West Africa, 1415–1670: A History*, New York: Cambridge University Press, 2010.

6. Willie F. Page, *The Dutch Triangle: The Netherlands and the Atlantic Slave Trade, 1621–1664*, New York: Garland, 1997, 197.

7. Steven C. A. Pincus, *Protest and Patriotism: Ideologies and the Making of English Foreign Policy, 1650–1668*, New York: Cambridge University Press, 1996, 245–46, 247, 248,

8. Wendy Warren, *New England Bound*, 196.

9. A. J. F. Van Laer, ed., *Documents Relating to New Netherland, 1624–1626*, 1924, Huntington Library, San Marino, CA.

10. Graham Russell Hodges, *Root & Branch*, 38.

11.   Bernard Bailyn, *The Barbarous Years: The Conflict of Civilizations*, 174, 175.
12.   F. W. Payn, *Cromwell on Foreign Affairs*, London: Clay, 1901.
13.   William Prynne, *The Subjection of All Traytors*, London, 1658, Huntington Library, San Marino, CA.
14.   *A Relation of the Inhumane and Barbarous Sufferings of the People Called Quakers in the City of Bristol...,Commencing From the 29 of the 7 Month to the 29 Day of the Month, 1664, 1665*, Huntington Library, San Marino, CA.
15.   Geoffrey Parker, *Global Crisis*, 675.
16.   Nuala Zahedieh, *The Capital and the Colonies: London and the Atlantic Economy, 1660–1700*, New York: Cambridge University Press, 2010, 542.
17.   Charles Spencer, *Killers of the King*, 291.
18.   Entry, ca. 1656, in John Towill Rutt, ed., *Diary of Thomas Burton...Member of the Parliaments of Oliver and Richard Cromwell, From 1656–1659*, vol. 3, London: Colburn, 1828, 103.
19.   *By the King. A Proclamation for the Encouraging of Planters in His Majesties Island of Jamaica in the West Indies*, 14 December 1661, Huntington Library, San Marino, CA.
20.   Cornelius Burrough to Commissioners of the Navy, 20 June 1660, in W. Noel Sainsbury, ed., *Calendar of State Papers, Colonial Series, America and West Indies, 1661–1668*, London: Her Majesty's Stationery Office, 1880, 482.
21.   Proposals, November 1660, in ibid., 491.
22.   Jan Glate, *Navies and Nations: Warships, Navies and State Building in Europe and America, 1500–1800*, Stockholm: Almquist & Wiksell, 1993; Charles Carlton, *This Seat of Mars: War and the British Isles, 1485–1746*, New Haven: Yale University Press, 2011, 187–88.
23.   Robert Brenner, *Merchants and Revolution*, 712.
24.   Instructions to Captain George Swanley, 23 June 1659, in Margaret Makepeace, ed., *Trade on the Guinea Coast, 1657–1666: The Correspondence of the English East India Company*, Madison: University of Wisconsin African Studies Program, 1991, 41.
25.   East India Company to Agent, Fort Cormantine, 11 July 1662, in ibid., 118.
26.   Note, 15 July 1658, in ibid., 14.
27.   James Conget to East India Company, 4 February 1660, in ibid., 50.
28.   *Instructions to Governors, Commissions & Other Papers Respecting the Colonies*, ca. 1660s, Huntington Library, San Marino, CA.
29.   East India Company to Fort Cormantine, 10 June 1661, in Makepeace, *Trade on the Guinea Coast*, 94.
30.   Sarah Barber, *The Disputatious Caribbean: The West Indies in the Seventeenth Century*, New York: Palgrave, 18.
31.   John Lisle to Williamson, 19 September 1667, in Sainsbury, *Calendar of State Papers, Colonial Series*, 499.
32.   Note, unclear provenance, December 1667, in ibid., 529.
33.   Memorandum, November 1667, in Leo Francis Stock, ed., *Proceedings and Debates of the British Parliaments Respecting North America*, vol. 1: *1542–1688*, Washington, D.C.: Carnegie, 1924, 342–43.

34. Statute, 27 September 1661, Box 1, William Blathwayt Papers, Huntington Library, San Marino, CA.

35. Entry, March 1659, in John Towill Rutt, ed., *Diary of Thomas Burton... Member of the Parliaments of Oliver and Richard Cromwell from 1656–1659*, vol. 4, London: Colburn, 1828, 270, 271, 272.

36. Edmund Abaka, *House of Slaves and Door of No Return,*, Trenton: Africa World Press, 2012, 78, 231.

37. Brodie Cruickshank, *Eighteen Years on the Gold Coast off Africa Including an Account of the Native Tribes And their Intercourse with Europeans*, London: Hurst and Blackett, 1853, 19.

38. George Zook, "The Royal Adventurers in England," *Journal of Negro History* 4/2 (April 1919): 143–62.

39. Mark L. Thompson, *The Contest for the Delaware Valley: Allegiance, Identity and Empire in the Seventeenth Century*, Baton Rouge: Louisana State University Press, 181, 182.

40. Philip Boucher, 181.

41. Minutes of the Council, 3 July 1661, 1B/5/3/1, Jamaica Archives, Spanish Town.

42. Ibid., 27 August 1661, 1B/5/3/1.

43. Ibid., 10 October 1662, 1B/5/3/1.

44. Ibid., 19 November 1662, 1B/5/3/1.

45. Ibid., memorandum from Sir Charles Lyttleton, 1 February 1662.

46. Ibid., 26 July 1664.

47. Ibid., 31 March 1665.

48. Ibid., 23 October 1663, 1B/5/3/1.

49. Ibid., 23 October 1663.

50. Ibid., 11 June 1664.

51. Bev Carey, *The Maroon Story*, 93, 103.

52. Minutes of the Council, 1 September 1665, Jamaica Archives, Spanish Town.

53. Ibid., 2 February 1665.

54. Mordechai Arbell, *The Portuguese Jews of Jamaica*, Kingston: Canoe Press, 2000.

55. See, for example, Alan Taylor, *American Colonies: The Settling of North America*, New York: Penguin, 2001; Jaap Jacob, *New Netherland: A Dutch Colony in Seventeenth-Century America*, Leiden: Brill, 2005.

56. Ethan A. Schmidt, *The Divided Dominion: Social Conflict and Indian Hatred in Early Virginia*, Boulder: University Press of Colorado, 2015, 138, 153. See also *To Friends in Barbados, Virginia, Maryland, New England and Elsewhere, 29 September 1666*, Brown University, Providence.

57. Journal of a Slaver, 1663, *David Parrish Slavery Transcripts*, New-York Historical Society.

58. Report, 24 June 1664, ibid.

59. Mark L. Thompson, *The Conquest for the Delaware Valley*, 5.

60. Steven Karl Flogstad Heise, 195.

61. Ellen Smith and Jonathan D. Saran, "The Jews of Rhode Island," in *The Jews*

of Rhode Island, ed. George M. Goodwin and Ellen Smith, Waltham, MA: Brandeis University Press, 2004, 1–12, at 1. See also Michiel van Groesen, ed., *The Legacy of Dutch Brazil*, New York: Cambridge University Press, 2014. Centuries later, it was reported that one of Stuyvesant's first acts upon arriving in Manhattan was organizing a police force, which was designed as little more than a force to capture slave runaways. *New York Observer*, 24 February 2015.

62. Samuel Oppenheim, *The Early History of the Jews in New York, 1654–1664*, New York: n.p., 1909, 39.

63. Anthony Julius, *Trials of the Diaspora: A History of Anti-Semitism in England*, New York: Oxford University Press, 2010.

64. John M. McCusker and Russell R. Menard, "The Sugar Industry in the Seventeenth Century: A New Perspective on the Barbadian 'Sugar Revolution,'" in *Tropical Babylons: Sugar and the Making of the Atlantic World, 1450–1680*, ed. Stuart B. Schwartz, Princeton: Princeton University Press, 2004.

65. See Henry Adid, *A Letter Sent from Syrranam to His Excellency, the Lord Willoughby of Parham, General of the Western Islands and of the Continent of Guianah...then Residing at Barbados...*, London, 1664, Brown University, Providence.

66. Report, 9 March 1660, in Berthold Fernow, ed., *The Records of New Amsterdam from 1653 to 1674*, vol. 1, New York: Knickerbocker, 1897, 44.

67. Charles Wilson, *Profit and Power: A Study of England and the Dutch Wars*, London: Longmans, Green, 1957, 1.

68. Leslie Harris, *In the Shadow of Slavery: African Americans in New York City, 1626–1863*, Chicago: University of Chicago Press, 2003, 15, 21.

69. Lisa Jardine, *Going Dutch: How England Plundered Holland's Glory*, London: Harper, 2008, 127.

70. Julie A. Fisher and David J. Silverman, eds., *Ninigret, Sachem of the Niantics and Narragansetts: Diplomacy, War and the Balance of Power in Seventeenth Century New England and Indian Country*, Ithaca, NY: Cornell University Press, 2014, 29, 73.

71. See Harman Bogaest, *A Memorial of the Principal Events that Happened During the Journey to the Maquas and Sinnekens Indians, 1634–1635*, Huntington Library, San Marino, CA. In the same library see also Dingman Versteeg, *Manhattan in 1628: As Described in the Recently Discovered Autograph Letter of Jonas Michaelius Written from the Settlement on the 8th of August of that Year and Now First Published*, New York: Dodd Mead, 1924. See also Charles T. Gehring et al., eds., *A Journey into Mohawk and Oneida Country*, Syracuse, NY: Syracuse University Press, 1988.

72. T. Astley Atkins, "Indian Wars and the Uprising of 1655," *Journal of Yonkers Historical and Library Association*, 18 March 1892, Huntington Library, San Marino, CA. At the same library, see also *The Founding of New York City by the Dutch, 1624–1626*.

73. John E. Pomfret, *The Province of East Jersey, 1609–1672: The Rebellious Proprietary*, Princeton: Princeton University Press, 1962, 11, 16.

74. Willie F. Page, *The Dutch Triangle: The Netherlands and the Atlantic Slave Trade, 1621–1664*, New York: Garland, 1997, 191.

75. Calvin Schermerhorn, "Slavery, U.S.," in *The Princeton Companion to Atlantic History*, ed. Joseph C. Miller, 420–23, 421. See Andrew Lipman, *The Saltwater Frontier: Indians and the Contest for the American Coast*, New Haven: Yale University Press, 2015, 219.

76. Graham Russell Hodges, *Root and Branch*, 40.

77. Jonathan Israel, *European Jewry in the Age of Mercantilism, 1550–1750*, London: Littman, 1998, 114, 146. See also David Hancock, *Citizens of the World: London Merchants and the Integration of the British Atlantic Community, 1735–1785*, New York: Cambridge University Press, 1995.

78. Linda Briggs Biemer, *Women and Property in Colonial New York: The Transition from Dutch to English Law, 1643–1727*, Ann Arbor: UMI Research Press, 1983, 75.

79. Boucher, 118.

80. *Treaty of Peace, Commerce and Alliance Between the Crowns of Great Britain and Spain Concluded in a Treaty of Madrid the 13–23 of May...in 1667*, Huntington Library, San Marino, CA.

81. Thomas Philipot, *The Original and Growth of the Spanish Monarchy United with the House of Austria...*, London: Taylor, 1664, Brown University, Providence.

82. *The Arraignment of Popery: Being a Short Collection, Taken Out of the Chronicles, and Other Books, of the State of the Church in the Primitive Times*, London, 1669, Brown University, Providence.

83. *Articles of Peace and Alliance Between the Most Serene and Mighty Prince, Charles the Second, by the Grace of God, King of England and Scotland and France and Ireland and Defender of the Faith...and the Most Serene and Mighty Prince Lewis XIV, the Most Christian King...*, 21–31 July 1667, Huntington Library, San Marino, CA.

84. *Articles of Peace and Alliance Between the Most Serene ... King of England, etc... and the High and Mighty Lords, the States General of the United Netherlands*, 21–31 July 1667, Huntington Library, San Marino, CA.

85. J. P. Kenyon, ed., *The Stuart Constitution, 1603–1685: Documents and Commentary*, New York: Cambridge University Press, 1966.

86. Nuala Zahedieh, *The Capital and the Colonies: London and the Atlantic Economy, 1660–1700*, New York: Cambridge University Press, 2010.

6. More Enslaved Africans Arrive in the Caribbean

1. Gerald Horne, *The Counter-Revolution of 1776*, 92–93.

2. Gerald Horne, *Race to Revolution: The United States and Cuba During Slavery and Jim Crow*, New York: Monthly Review Press, 2014.

3. John Spurr, ed., *Anthony Ashley Cooper, First Earl of Shaftesbury, 1621-1683*, Burlington: Ashgate, 2011. Cf. Alexander Livingston, *Damn Great Empires! William James and the Politics of Pragmatism*, New York: Oxford University

Press, 2016. See also Addison Moore, "Pragmatism and Its Critics," *The Philosophical Review*, 14 (Number 3, 1905): 322-343.

4. Speech of Charles II, ca. 1663, in Andrew Browning, ed., *English Historical Documents, Volume VIII, 1660–1714*, London: Eyre & Spttiswoode, 1953, 349–50.

5. Account by John Oldmixon, 1741, in ibid., 577–79.

6. Richard Blome, "Account of Jamaica and Other West India Settlements," 1672, in ibid., 559–67.

7. *An Answer of the Company of Royal Adventurers of England Trading into Africa to the Petition and Paper of Certain Heads...and Others Concerned in His Majesties Plantations in America*, 1667, Brown University, Providence.

8. *To the Right Honourable the Knights, Citizens and Burgesses Assembled in Parliament. The Humble Petition of Sir Paul Painter Knight, Fernando Gorges, Henry Baston, Gentlemen and Benjamin Skutt...Merchants in Behalf of Themselves and Others Concerned in His Majesties Plantations in America*, ca. 1667, Brown University, Providence.

9. *Petition*, 1667, by Paul Painter, Ferdinand Gorges, Henry Batson, Benjamin Skutt, and Thomas Knight, Daniel Parrish Transcripts.

10. Vivienne L. Kruger, "Born to Run: The Slave Family in Early New York, 1626–1827," Ph.D. diss., Columbia University, 1985, 78.

11. Charter of Royal African Company, 27 September 1672, in W. Noel Sainsbury, ed., *Calendar of State Papers, Colonial Series, America and West Indies, 1669–1674*, London: Her Majesty's Stationery Office, 1889, 409.

12. Broadside: "By the King, A Proclamation," London: Bill and Barker, 1674, New-York Historical Society.

13. Nuala Zahedieh, *The Capital and Colonies: London and the Atlantic Economy, 1660–1700*, New York: Cambridge University Press, 2010, 116.

14. Whitehall Proclamation, 25 November 1674, in Sainsbury, *Calendar of State Papers*, 626.

15. See, for example, Henry B. Dawson, ed., *Records of the City of New Amsterdam in New Netherland*, vol. 1, Morrisania, New York: Bradstreet, 1867.

16. Kevin P. McDonald, *Pirates, Merchants, Settlers and Slaves: Colonial America and the Indo-Atlantic World*, Berkeley: University of California Press, 2015, 46–47, 50, 54–55. See also *The King of Pirates: Being an Account of the Famous Enterprises of Captain....the Mock King of Madagascar with his Rambles and Piracies*, London: Bettesworth, 1720, Massachusetts Historical Society, Boston, and Huntington Library, San Marino, CA.

17. *The Fundamental Constitutions of Carolina*, 1670, Brown University, Providence.

18. Russell R. Menard, *Sweet Negotiations: Sugar, Slavery and Plantation Agriculture in Early Barbados*, Charlottesville: University of Virginia Press, 2006, 108.

19. Jason T. Sharples, "A Priest at the Bottom of Every Plot: Catholic, Indian and Irish Contexts for Discovering Slave Conspiracies in the Seventeenth Centuries," 6 March 2010, .https://africandiasporaphd.com/category/jason-t-sharples/

20. Trevor Burnard, *Planters, Merchants and Slaves: Plantation Societies in British America, 1650–1820*, Chicago: University of Chicago Press, 2015, 65, 68, 70. See also Michael Craton and James Walvin, *A Jamaican Plantation: The History of Worthy Parker, 1670–1970*, London: Allen, 1970, Virginia Historical Society, Richmond.

21. Statute, 3 July 1661, CO140/1, National Archives of the United Kingdom, London (henceforth, NAUK).

22. Statute, 23 October 1663, CO140/1.

23. Statute, 23 October 1663,

24. Statute, 9 June 1664, CO140/1.

25. Statute, 15 August 1665, CO140/1.

26. Minutes of the Council of Jamaica, 2 May 1670, in Sainsbury, *Calendar of State Papers*, 64–66.

27. Minutes of the Council, 2 May 1670, 1B/5/3/1, Jamaica Archives, Spanish Town.

28. Minutes of the Council, 9 November 1671.

29. Minutes of the Council, 28 November 1671.

30. Minutes of the Council, 2 July 1672.

31. Statute, May 1670, CO140/1, NAUK.

32. Minutes of the Council, 26 September 1672, 1/B/5/3/2.

33. Statute, 9 November 1671, CO140/1, NAUK.

34. Statute, 2 July 1672, CO140/1.

35. Statute, 21 March 1673, CO140/1.

36. Minutes of the Council, 11 March 1673, 1/B/5/3/2, Jamaica Archives, Spanish Town.

37. Minutes of the Council, 3 September 1675, 1/B/5/3/2.

38. Statute, 2 November 1675, CO 140/1, NAUK.

39. Minutes of the Council, 15 December 1675, 1/B/5/3/2, Jamaica Archives, Spanish Town.

40. Nell Irvin Painter, *The History of White People*, New York: W. W. Norton, 2010, 263.

41. William Byam to William Lord Willoughby, Governor of Barbados, ca. 1670, in Sainsbury, *Calendar of State Papers*.

42. Sir Charles Wheeler, Governor of Leeward Islands to Council for Foreign Plantations, ca. 1670s, in ibid., 291.

43. Report, September 1672, in ibid., 413.

44. David Wheat, *Atlantic Africa and the Spanish Caribbean, 1570-1640*, Chapel Hill: University of North Carolina Press, 2016, 71.

45. John Style to Secretary Sir William Morrice, 14 January 1669, in Sainsbury, *Calendar of State Papers*, 5.

46. Report, 22 January 1970, in ibid., 52–53.

47. Minutes of the Council, 24 April 1677, 1/B/5/3/2, Jamaica Archives, Spanish Town.

48. Minutes of the Council, 27 April 1677, 1/B/5/3/2.

49. Minutes of the Council, 23 January 1676, 1/B/5/3/2.

50.   Minutes of the Council, 12 December 1676.

51.   Minutes of the Council, 27 July 1677, 1/B/5/3/2.

52.   John Esquemeling, *Bucaniers of America: Or a True Account of the Most Remarkable Assaults Committed of Late Years Upon the Coasts of the West Indies*, London: Crooke, 1684, 60.

53.   Minutes of the Council, 5 April 1678, 1/B/5/3/2, Jamaica Archives, Spanish Town.

54.   David Wheat, *Atlantic Africa and the Spanish Caribbean, 1570-1640*, Chapel Hill: University of North Carolina, 2016, 143, 154, 263.

55.   Philip Boucher, 189, 261.

56.   Pedro Welch, "Jews in a Caribbean Colonial Society: Resistance and Accommodation in Bridgetown, Barbados, 167–1834," *Journal of the Barbados Museum And Historical Society* 44 (November–December 1998): 54–64, 54–55, 57, 59, 61, 62. See also N. Darnell Davis, "Notes on the History of the Jews in Barbados," *Publications of the American Jewish Historical Society* 18 (1909): 133, Virginia Historical Society, Richmond.

57.   Sir Thomas Lynch to Secretary Lord Arlington, 17 December 1671, in Sainsbury, *Calendar of State Papers*, 298.

58.   Statute, 27 September 1661, CO30/1, NAUK.

59.   Statute, 29 April 1668, CO30/1, NAUK.

60.   Report, December 1667, in Sainsbury, *Calendar of State Papers*, 529.

61.   Statute, 11 August 1670, in Richard Hall, ed., *Acts Passed in the Island of Barbados from 1643 to 1762*, London, 1764, 77, Barbados National Archives.

62.   Statute, 9 May 1672, in ibid., 87–93.

63.   Statute, 4 July 1671, in ibid., 83–84.

64.   *Narrative of the Late Dreadful Fire Which Happened at Bridgetown in the Barbadoes, April 28, 1668*, London: Lillicrap, 1668, British Library, London.

65.   President and Council of Barbados to Council for Trade and Plantations, 28 May 1673, in Sainsbury, *Calendar of State Papers*, 493.

66.   Statute, 1674, in Hall, *Acts Passed in the Island of Barbados*. 94 "An Act appointing how the testimony of the Hebrew nation shall be admitted in all Courts and Causes...."

67.   Statute, 21 April 1676, in ibid., 97–98.

68.   Statute, 17 April 1678, in ibid., 102–3.

69.   *Great Newes from the Barbadoes or a True and Faithful Account of the Grand Conspiracy of the Negroes Against the English and the Happy Discovery of the Same with the Number of Those That Were Burned Alive, Beheaded and Otherwise Executed for their Horrid Crimes*, London: Curtis, 1676, British Library.

70.   *A Continuation of the State of New England; Being a Partner Account of the Indian Warr . . . 19th of December 1675 . . . Together with an Account of the Intended Rebellion of the Negroes in the Barbadoes*, London: Newman, 1676, Brown University, Providence.

71.   *The Case of John Wilmore Truly and Impartially Related or a Looking Glass for all Merchants and Planters That Are Concerned in the American Plantations*, London: Powell, 1682, University of Virginia, Charlottesville.

72. Mark G. Hanna, *Pirate Nests and the Rise of the British Empire, 1570–1740*, Chapel Hill: University of North Carolina Press, 2015, 18.

73. William Dampier, *A New Voyage Around the World: The Journal of an English Buccaneer*, London: Hummingbird, 1697.

74. Ellen Smith and Jonathan Saran, "The Jews of Rhode Island," in *The Jews of Rhode Island*, ed. George M. Goodwin and Ellen Smith, Waltham, MA: Brandeis University Press, 1–12, 1.

75. Note, in Richard S. Dunn et al., eds., *The Papers of William Penn*, vol. 2: *1680–1684*, Philadelphia: University of Pennsylvania Press, 1981, 542.

76. William Penn to Ralph Fretwell, 3 April 1684, in ibid., 546–47.

77. Brycchan Carey, *From Peace to Freedom: Quaker Rhetoric and the Birth of American Antislavery, 1657–1761*, New Haven: Yale University Press, 2012, 13.

78. Kenneth J. Banks, "Contraband," in *The Princeton Companion to Atlantic History*, ed. Joseph C. Miller et al., 119–23, 121.

79. Alan Gallay, "Slaving, Europeans, of Native Americans," in ibid., 433–37, at 436.

80. *A Relation of the Coasts of Africk Called Guinee...Being Collected in a Voyage...*, London: Starkey, 1670, Huntington Library, San Marino, CA.

81. *A True Relation of the Late Action Between the French and Dutch at Tobago in the West Indies, Giving an Account of What Happened There...*, London: W.D., 1677. "Very great slaughter" occurred on all sides. "The Dutch loss is very great, for all the captains of their ships save one are killed and wounded."

82. Stephen Saunders Webb, *1676: The End of American Independence*, New York: Knopf, 1984, xvi.

7. The Spirit of 1676

1.   W. Hubbard, Minister of Ipswich, *A Narrative of the Troubles with the Indians in New England...Chiefly of the Late Troubles in the Two Years 1675 and 1676*, Boston: Foster, 1677, Huntington Library, San Marino, CA. This document can also be found at the University of Virginia, Charlottesville.

2.   *The General Laws and Liberties of the Massachusetts Colony...*, Cambridge, MA: Green, 1672, 75, 76, 67, Huntington Library, San Marino, CA.

3.   *A New and Further Narrative of the State of New England from Being a Continued Account of the Bloody Indian War From March Till August 1676...*, London: Dorman Newman, 1676, Huntington Library, San Marino, CA.

4.   *New England's Present Sufferings Under their Cruel Neighboring Indians...*, London, 1675, Huntington Library, San Marino, CA.

5.   Increase Mather, *A Relation of the Troubles Which Have Hapned [sic] in New England, By Reason of the Indians There: From the Year 1614 to the Year 1675...*, Boston: Foster, 1677, Huntington Library, San Marino, CA, This document can also be found at the University of Virginia, Charlottesville.

6.   John E Morris and George W. Ellis, *King Philip's War*, New York: Grafton, 1906, 12, 201. See also Charles H. Lincoln, ed., *Narratives of the Indian Wars, 1675–1699*, New York: Scribner's, 1913.

7.   Memorandum, 5 June 1667, in *Records of Plymouth Company Court Records*,

vol. 3: *1651–1661*, Boston: White, 1855, 151. See Julie A. Fisher and David J. Silverman, eds., *Ninigret, Sachem or the Niantics and Narragansetts*, 129: It is probable that the Dutch and the French supported the indigenes in their conflict with settlers.

8.   George Fox, *An Answer to Several New Laws and Orders Made by the Rulers of Boston in New England, the Tenth Day of the Eighth Month, 1677*, 1678, Brown University, Providence.

9.   Proclamation, 9 August 1676, MS 1695, National Library of Jamaica, Kingston.

10.   Proclamation, 12 September 1676, MS 1695, National Library of Jamaica, Kingston.

11.   Index entry, ca. 1676, "Royal African Company" box, Daniel Parish Papers, New-York Historical Society.

12.   *A Continuation of the State of New England; Being a Farther Account of the Indian Warr...19th of December 1675...,Together with an Account of the Intended Rebellion of the Negroes in the Barbadoes*, London: Newman, 1676, Brown University, Providence. This document can also be found at the University of Virginia, Charlottesville, and the Boston Public Library, which is indicative of its circulation on the mainland.

13.   Toni Morrison, *The Origin of Others*, Cambridge: Harvard University Press, 2017.

14.   Nathaniel Bacon et al., *The Declaration of the People Against William Berkeley and Present...Governors of Virginia...August 1676*, PH00, Rockefeller Library, Williamsburg, Virginia.

15.   *The Beginning, Progress and Conclusion of Bacon's Rebellion in Virginia in the Years 1675 and 1676*, 1897, Huntington Library, San Marino, CA.

16.   Bacon's Declaration, 30 July 1676, in Clarence Ver Steeg and Richard Hofstadter, eds., *Great Issues in American History: From Settlement to Revolution, 1584–1776*, New York: Vintage, 1969, 104–7, at 107.

17.   Statement by Robert Beverley, 1704, in ibid., 94–100, 98.

18.   Broadside, *By the King: A Proclamation for the Suppressing of a Rebellion Lately Raised Within the Plantation of Virginia*, London: Bill and Barker, 1676, University of Virginia, Charlottesville.

19.   Frank P. Brent, *Some Unpublished Facts Relating to Bacon's Rebellion on the Eastern Shore of Virginia, Gleaned from the Court Records of Accomac County*, 1891, Huntington Library, San Marino, CA.

20   *Strange News from Virginia; Being a Full and True Account of the Life and Death of Nathaniel Bacon Esquire Who Was the Only Cause and Original of All the Late Troubles in that Country, with a Full Relation of All the Accidents Which Have Happened in the Late War There between the Christians and Indians*, London: Harris, 1677, Brown University, Providence.

21.   "More News from Virginia," 1677, and comment in Harry Firestone, ed., *Bacon's Rebellion: The Contemporary News Sheets*, Charlottesville: University of Virginia Press, 1956, 7–18, 19–27, 29–32. See also Charles M. Andrews, ed., *Narratives of the Insurrections, 1675–1690*, New York: Scribner's, 1915.

22.   Geoffrey Parker, *Global Crisis*, 454.

23. "Indian Treaty," 1677, Box 1, Miscellaneous Indian file, Huntington Library, San Marino, CA.

24. Malcolm Gaskill, *Between Two Worlds: How the English Became Americans*, New York: Basic Books, 2014, 324.

25. "The Secretary of Virginia Reports on Self-Regulation Without Benefit of Legislation," 8 May 1682, in. Ver Steeg and Hofstadter, *Great Issues in American History*, 241–43.

26. Statute, 1682, in William Waller Hening, ed., *The Statutes at Large, Being a Collection of All the Laws of Virginia from the First Session of the Legislature in the Year 1619*, vol. 2, New York: Barlow, 1823, 492.

27. See Hening, *The Statutes at Large, Being a Collection of All the Laws of Virginia*, vol. 3, pp. 86, 87, 179, 210, 277.

28. Lorena S. Walsh, *Motives of Honor, Pleasure and Profit: Plantation Management in the Colonial Chesapeake, 1607–1763*, Chapel Hill: University of North Carolina Press, 2010, 250, 2003, 204, 201.

29. "Intelligence of the Discovery of a Negro Plot," 24 October 1687, in H. R. McIlwaine, ed., *Executive Journals of the Council of Colonial Virginia*, vol. 1: *11 June 1680–22 June 1689*, Richmond: Public Printing, 1925, 186. University of Virginia,Charlottesville.

30. R. F., *The Present State of Carolina with Advice to the Settlers*, London: Bringhurst, 1682, Brown University, Providence; also see here *Friendly Advice to the Gentlemen Planters of the East and West Indies*, 1684.

31. *A Narrative of Affairs Lately Received from His Majesties Island of Jamaica: Viz. His Excellency the Governour Sir Thomas Linch's Speech to the Assembly Met September 21, 1682...*, London: Raylor, 1683, Brown University, Providence.

32. *A Letter from Jamaica to a Friend in London Concerning Kid-Napping*, 30 December 1681, Brown University, Providence.

33. *At the Court of Whitehall*, 13 December 1682, Huntington Library, San Marino, CA.

34. Morgan Godwyn, *The Negro's & Indian's Advocate Suing for Their Admission into the Church or a Persuasive to the Instructing and Baptizing of the Negro[e]s and Indians in Our Plantations*, London: MG, 1680, Huntington Library, San Marino, CA.

35. "An Act to Prevent Runaways," 1683, Box 1, Daniel Parrish Slavery Transcripts, New-York Historical Society.

36. John Peter, *A Relation of the Diary of the Siege of Vienna...Judge Advocate of the Imperial Army*, London: Nott, 1684, Huntington Library, San Marino, CA.

37. *A True Account of the Heroic Actions and Enterprises of the Confederate Princes Against the Turks and Hungarian Rebels During the Last Glorious Campaign*, London: Thackery, 1686, Boston Public Library.

38. Caroline Finkel, *Osman's Dream*, 167, 197, 221, 231, 232, 300, 301, 325, 341, 358, 359, 446. See also Abraham Browne, *Volume of Reminiscences, 1653–1668*, Massachusetts Historical Society, Boston. Another account by a prisoner of North Africans.

39. "Final Treaty of Capitulations: The Ottoman Empire and England," September 1675, in J. C. Hurewitz, ed., *Diplomacy in the Near and Middle East: A Documentary Record, 1535–1914*, vol. 1, Princeton: Nostrand, 1956, 25–32, 28, 30.

40. John Towill Rutt, ed., *Diary of Thomas Burton*, vol. 3, cxxxvii.

41. Daniel Goffman, *Britons in the Ottoman Empire, 1642–1660*, Seattle: University of Washington Press, 1998, 144, 156.

42. Comment in Paul Baepler, *White Slaves, African Masters: An Anthology of American Barbary Captivity Narratives*, Chicago: University of Chicago Press, 1999, 1.

43. Sonia P. Anderson, *An Englishman Consul in Turkey: Paul Rycaut at Smyrna, 1667–1678*, New York: Oxford University Press, 1989, 194, 276. See also Sir Paul Ricaut, Late Consul of Smyrna, *The History of the Present State of the Ottoman Empire*, London: Brome 1686, New-York Historical Society. See Francis Brooks, *Barbarian Cruelty: Being a True History of the Distressed Condition of the Christian Capitol Under the Tyranny of Mully Ishmael Emperor of Morocco and King of Fez and Macqueness in Barbary...*,Boston: Phillips, 1700, Massachusetts Historical Society. The "Shack of the Jews" offers to take Christians to "build the Jews Town" in North Africa. Then there was the "Emperor who immediately sent out his Negroes to drive back the Christians."

44. *The History of Algiers and Its Slavery with Many Remarkable Particulars of Africa Written by Emanuel D'Aranda, Sometime a Slave There....*, London: Starkey, 1666, Boston Public Library.

45. *Articles of Peace Between The Most Serene and Mighty Prince Charles II by the Grace of God, King of Great Britain, France and Ireland, Defender of the Faith... and the Most Excellent Signors Mahot Bashaw, the Duan of the Noble, City of Tunis...*, London: John Bill, 1677, Huntington Library, San Marino, CA.

46. *Articles of Peace Between the Most Serene and Mighty Prince, Charles the Second, by the Grace of God, King of Great Britain, France....and the Most Excellent Signors, Mahomet Bashaw, the Duan of the Noble City of Tunis... Concluded by Sir John Lawson, the Fifth of October 1662 and Confirmed the Fourth of February 1674...*, Huntington Library, San Marino, CA.

47. *Capitulations and Articles of Peace Between the Majesty of King of Great Britain, France and Ireland...and the Sultan of the Ottoman Empire...*, September 1675, Brown University, Providence.

48. *Articles of Peace and Commerce Between the Most Serene and Mighty Prince, Charles the Second...and the Most Illustrious Lords, the Bashaw, Dey, Aga, Divan and Governors of the City and Kingdoms of Tripoli....*5 May 1676, Huntington Library, San Marino, CA.

49. *Articles of Peace and Commerce Between the Most Serene and Mighty Prince Charles the Second...and the Most Illustrious Lords, the Bashaw, Dey Aga and Governors of the Famous City and Kingdom of Algiers in Barbary...*,10 April 1682, Huntington Library, San Marino, CA.

50. Entry, ca. 1661, in Henry B. Wheatley, ed., *The Diary of Samuel Pepys*, vol. 1, London: Bell, 1924, 319.

51. Entry, ca. 1661, in ibid., vol. 2, 135. See also *The Moores Baffled: Being a Discourse Concerning Tangier Especially When It Was Under the Earl of Teviot*, London: Crookee, 1681, Brown University, Providence. Also at Brown, see section on return of slaves and servants to St. Christopher's, Antigua, etc. "taken by the Arms of the foresaid Most Christian King," in *Articles of Peace and Alliance Between the Most Serene and Mighty Prince, Charles the Second, by the Grace of God, King of England, Scotland, France and Ireland, Defender of the Faith...and the Most Serene and Mighty Prince, Lewis XIV, the Most Christian King...July 1667, in Several Treaties of Peace and Commerce Concluded Between the King of Blessed Memory Deceased and Other Princes and States*, London, 1685..

52. *A History of the Captivity and Restoration of Mrs. Mary Rowlandson, a Minister's Wife in New England...the Cruel and Inhumane Usage She Underwent Among the Heathens for Eleven Weeks Time...*, London, 1682, Huntington Library, San Marino, CA.

53. *A True Account of the Captivity of Thomas Phelps at Machaness in Barbary and of his Strange Escape...Thirteenth Day of June 1685*, London: Hills, 1685, Brown University, Providence.

54. Charles Sumner, *White Slavery in the Barbary States*, Boston: Jewett, 1853, 46.

55. John Ogilby, *Africa: Being an Accurate Description of the Regions of Egypt, Barbary, Libya and Billedulgerid, the Land of Negroes, Guinee, Aethiopia, and the Abyssines...*, London: Johnson, 1670, 161, 253. Huntington Library, San Marino, CA.

56. *Articles of Peace Concluded and Agreed Between the Excellency the Lord Bellaysyse, His Majesties Governour of His City and Garrison of Tangier in Africa...and Cidid Hamet Haden Ben Ali Gayland, Prince of West Barbary.the Second of April 1666*, London, 1666, Huntington Library, San Marino, CA.

57. *A Treaty for the Composing of Differences, Restraining of Depredations and Establishing Peace in America Between the Crown of Great Britain and Spain, Concluded at Madrid, 8–18 ...July...1670...*, Huntington Library, San Marino, CA. Included was the desire for "universal peace in America as well as elsewhere.... English to keep what they possess at present in America."

58. *The Adventures of Mr. T.S. an English Merchant Taken Prisoner by The Turks of Algiers and Carried into the Inland Country of Africa...*, London: Pitt, 1670, Huntington Library, San Marino, CA.

59. Ibid. Also at the Huntington Library, see Abraham Lloyd, *Journal of a Voyage, 1675–1686*.

60. Michael Wansleben, *A Brief Account of the Rebellions and Bloodshed Occasioned by the Anti-Christian Practices of the Jesuits and other Popish Emissaries in the Empire of Ethiopia*, London: Foster, 1677, Huntington Library, San Marino, CA. Also here, see *A History of Ethiopia...Vulgarly Though Erroneously Called the Empire of Prester John*, London: Smith, 1684; and *Friendly Advice to the Gentlemen Planters of the East and West Indies... the Complaints of the Negro Slaves Against the Hard Usages and Barbarous*

Cruelties Inflicted Upon Them...A Discourse in Way of Dialogue Between an Ethiopian or Negro Slave and a Christian that Was His Master in America, 1684.

61. *The Voyage and Travels of John Struys Through Italy, Greece, Muscovy, Tartary, Media Persia, East India, Japan and Other Countries in Europe, Africa and Asia...*, London: Swale, 1684, Huntington Library, San Marino, CA.

62. *The English Acquisitions in Guinea and East India*, unclear date, Huntington Library, San Marino, CA. Reference is made to the "hatred" between and among Moslems.

63. Sir John Narbrough, *A Particular Narrative of the Burning in the Port of Tripoli, Four Men of War, Belonging to the Corsairs*, 1676, Huntington Library, San Marino, CA

64. *A Treatise Wherein It Is Demonstrated that the East India Trade Is the Most National of all Foreign Trades. That the Clamors, Aspersions and Objections Made Against the Present East India Company Are Sinister, Selfish or Groundless...that the Trade of the East Indies Cannot be Carried to National Advantage in Any Other Way than by a General Joynt-Stock. That the East India Trade Is More Profitable and Necessary to the Kingdom of England, than to Any Other Kingdom or Nation in Europe*, London: Boulter, 1681, Brown University, Providence, RI.

65. *Articles of Peace and Commerce...between Charles the Second...and the Most Illustrious Lords, the Bashaw, Dey, Agan and Governors of the Famous City and Kingdom of Algiers in Barbary...*, 10 April 1682, Brown University, Providence.

66. See *A Letter Sent by the Emperor of Morocco and King of Fez to His Majesty of Great Britain and Delivered by His Ambassador in January 1681*, London: Jones 1681, Huntington Library, San Marino, CA: "To confirm the peace and treaty that we have made with you...let us not make the same terms as had in the beginning of the war, wherein so many dyed by the Sword when we were Enemies.... If any Renegade shall run away from us to Tangier you shall be obliged to send him back again.... We expect that you should furnish us with Six Thousand pieces of Eight yearly."

67. *The Case of Many Hundreds of Poor English Captives in Algiers, Together with Some Remedies to Prevent their Increase, Humbly Represented to Both Houses of Parliament*, n.d., ca. 1680, Huntington Library, San Marino, CA.

68. See also *A True Account of the Captivity of Thomas Phelps at Machaness in Barbary and of His Strange Escape...Thirteenth Day of June 1685*, London: Hills, 1685, Brown University, Providence. After being held, Phelps issued a blistering philippic of "the accursed Jews...the stench and pest of the Nations of the Earth, malicious to all mankind and loathsome and abominable wherever they come, who not only have the blood of the Saviour of the World Lying upon their heads, but are accountable for the blood of many Thousands of his Members.... Wicked enemies of Christianity, brought back these poor Christians into the house of bondage." See also *The History of Algiers and Its Slavery with Many Particulars of Africa...*: At Ceuta in North Africa "a Jew, a man of great reputation for his wealth," was quite prominent. See also Anderson, *An English Consul in Turkey: Paul Rycaut at Smyrna, 1667–1678*, 24, 211: Rycaut left "the principal surviving account of Cromwell's speech

in favour of their admission," meaning those of the Jewish community and a "public conference on the resettlement of the Jews in England." This community, says the author, were "on an equal footing with other subjects of the Crown, a situation without parallel in Europe."

69.   Pedro Welch, "Jews in a Caribbean Colonial Society: Resistance and Accommodation in Bridgetown, Barbados, 1675–1834," *Journal of the Barbados Museum and Historical Society* 44 (November–December 1998): 54–64, 56.

70.   "An Act for the Effectual Putting in Execution a Statute of England..." 1678, in Richard Hall, ed., *Acts Passed in the Island of Barbados from 1643 to 1762*, London, 1764, 103–4, Barbados National Archives, St. James.

71.   Marilyn Delevante, *The Knell of Parting Day: A History of the Jews of Port Royal and the Hunt's Bay Cemetery*, Kingston. Jamaica: Kimberley, 2008, 33, 40, 46, 67.

72.   George Fox, *An Answer to the Speech...Declaration of the Great Turk, Sultan Mahomet, which He Sent to Leopold Emperor of Germany*, 1688, Brown University, Providence

73.   Susan Alice Westbury, "Colonial Virginia and the Atlantic Slave Trade," Ph.D. diss., University of Illinois, Urbana, 1981, 145.

74.   Georg Norregard, *Danish Settlements in West Africa, 1658–1850*, Boston: Boston University Press, 1966, 31.

75.   "Memoir of Trade Within the Present Limits of the Charter of the WIC, 1670," in A. Van Dantzig, ed., *The Dutch and Guinea Coast, 1674–1742: A Collection of Documents from the General State Archive at The Hague*, Accra, Ghana: GAAS, 1978, 31–32, 10–11.

76.   Report by Heerman Abramsz, 23 November 1679, in ibid., 13–20, 16, 17, 18.

77.   Memorandum, 7 August 1684, in ibid., 44.

78.   Report by Van Hoolwerff, 8 December 1686, in ibid., 22–23.

79.   Report by Van Hoolwerff, 31 January 1687, in ibid., 29–30.

80.   Van Hoolwerff to the Directors of the Chamber, Amsterdam, 10 February 1688, in ibid., 9.

8. "The Glorious Revolution" of 1688

1.   Richard S. Dunn, "The Barbados Census of 1680: Profile of the Richest Colony in North America," *William and Mary Quarterly* 36 (1969): 3–29.

2.   Eric Nelson, *The Royalist Revolution: Monarchy and the American Founding*, Cambridge, MA: Harvard University Press, 2014.

3.   Council Minutes, 10 December 1684, Barbados National Archives, St. James.

4.   Council Minutes, 1 September 1685, ibid.

5.   Council Minutes, 15 September 1685, ibid..

6.   Council Minutes, 29 December 1685, ibid..

7.   Council Minutes, 4 January 1686, ibid.

8.   Council Minutes, 17 June 1685, ibid.

9.   Council Minutes, 15 December 1685, ibid.

10.   Council Minutes, 16 February 1686, ibid.

11.   Council Minutes, 16 March 1686, ibid.

12.   Council Minutes, 13 April 1686, ibid.

13.   Council Minutes, 11 May 1686, ibid.

14.   Richard Blome, *The Present State of His Majesties Isles and Territories in America...*, London: Clark, 1687, Huntington Library, San Marino, CA.

15.   Act, 1681, in *The Laws of Jamaica Comprehending All the Acts in Force Passed Between the Thirty-Second Year of the Reign of King Charles the Second and the Thirty-Third*, vol. 1, St. Jago de la Vega, Jamaica: Aikman, 1792, 9. National Library of Jamaica, Kingston.

16.   Act 1681, in ibid., 13.

17.   Act, 1681, in ibid., 18.

18.   See Kevin Alexander Gray et al., eds., *Killing Trayvons: An Anthology of American Violence*, Petrolia, California: Counterpunch Books, 2014.

19.   Statute, 15 December 1675, CO140/3, National Archives of the United Kingdom, London.

20.   Directive, October 1685, MS41, *State Papers, Colonial Series*, National Library of Jamaica, Kingston.

21.   Philip Boucher, 205, 209.

22.   All of the foregoing concerning Jamaica in 1683 comes from *The Laws of Jamaica Passed by the Assembly and Confirmed by His Majesty in Council, February 27, 1683...*, London: Harper, 1683, Boston Public Library. Also see in this archive *A Narrative of Affaires Lately Received from His Majesties Island of Jamaica*, London: Taylor, 1683.

23.   Minutes of the Council of War, 1 August 1685, CO140/4, National Archives of the United Kingdom, London.

24.   Report, 3 June 1686, CO140/4, ibid..

25.   Report, circa 1686, CO140/4, ibid.

26.   Report, 1687, Box 19, Daniel Parrish Slavery Transcripts, New-York Historical Society.

27.   David Buissert, ed., *Jamaica in 1687: The Taylor Manuscript at the National Library of Jamaica*, Kingston: University of West Indies Press, 2008, 14.

28.   Richard Wharter to William Blathwayt, 22 September 1681, William Blaythwayt Papers, Rockefeller Library, Williamsburg.

29.   William Blathwayt to Thomas Lynch, 20 May 1682, ibid..

30.   Thomas Lynch to William Blathwayt, 26 April 1683, ibid.

31.   Thomas Lynch to William Blathwayt, 14 August 1683, ibid.

32.   Thomas Lynch to William Blathwayt, 6 October 1683, ibid.

33.   Thomas Lynch to William Blathwayt, 2 May 1683, ibid.

34.   Thomas Lynch to William Blathwayt, 8 April 1684, ibid..

35.   See Hender Molesworth to William Blathwayt, 16 February 1685, ibid.,; and Molesworth to Blathwayt, 25 March 1684; Molesworth to William Blathwayt, 9 April 1686; Molesworth to Blathwayt, 6 August 1686.

36.   Hender Molesworth to William Blathwayt, 9 February 1686; Molesworth to Blathwayt, 12 March 1686; Molesworth to Blathwayt, 16 June 1687, ibid.

37.   Report from Mark Whiteing, 24 January 1686, in Robin Law, ed., *The English*

in *West Africa, 1685–1688: The Local Correspondence of the Royal African Company of England, 1681–1699*, Part 2, New York: Oxford University Press, 2001, 268.

38. Report from Mark Whiteing, 2 February 1686, in ibid., 269.

39. Thomas Lynch to William Blathwayt, 21 October 1683, William Blathwayt Papers.

40. Broadside, *By the King. A Proclamation to Prohibit His Majesties Subjects to Trade Within the Limits Assigned to the Royal African Company of England Except Those in the Company*, London: Bill and Hillis, 4 April 1685, Brown University, Providence.

41. *Certain Considerations Relating to the Royal African Company of England to which the Original Growth and National Advantages of the Guiney Trade, are Demonstrated...*, 1680, New York Historical Society.

42. William Wilkinson, Mariner, *System Africanum or a Treatise Discovering the Intrigues and Arbitrary Proceedings of the Guiney Company. And Also How Prejudicial they are to the American Planters, the Woollen and Other English Manufactures: To the Visible Decay of Trade and Consequently Greatly Impairing the Royal Revenue which Would Be Infinitely Increased Provided Merchants and Mariners Were Encouraged, Who Can Discover Several Places not Yet Known or Traded Unto by the African Company*, London, 1690, Brown University, Providence.

43. Edward Littlejohn, *The Groans of the Plantations, or, a True Account of their Grievous and Extreme Suffering, by the Heavy Impositions upon Sugar and Other Hardships...Barbados*, London: Clark, 1689, Duke University, Durham, NC.

44. Richard Blome, *The Present State of His Majesties Isles and Territories in America...*, London: Clark, 1687, n.p., Huntington Library, San Marino, CA.

45. William A. Pettigrew, *Freedom's Debt: The Royal African Company and the Politics of the Atlantic Slave Trade, 1672–1752*, Chapel Hill: University of North Carolina Press, 2013.

46. *A True and Perfect Narrative of the Late Dreadful Fire Which Happened at Bridgetown in the Barbadoes, April 18, 1688, as the Same Was Communicated in Two Letters from Mr. John Bushel and Mr. Francis Bond, Two Eminent Merchants There, to Mr. Edward Bushel, Citizen and Merchant of London*, London: Lilicrap, 1688, Duke University, Durham, NC.

47. Statute, 8 August 1688, *Acts of Assembly Passed in the Island of Barbados from 1648 to 1718*, London: Basket, 1732, 118, New-York Historical Society.

48. Anna Keay, *The Last Royal Rebel: The Life and Death of James, Duke of Monmouth*, London: Bloomsbury, 2016. See also *A Brief History of the Succession of the Crown of England...*, London: Janeway, 1688, Boston Public Library. At the latter site see also *The Prince of Orange, His Declaration Shewing the Reasons why he Invaded England with a Short Preface and Some Modest Remarks*, London: Taylor, 1688.

49. *A Brief History of the Succession of the Crown of England...*, London: Janeway, 1688, Boston Public Library.

50. Susan Alice Westbury, "Colonial Virginia and the Atlantic Slave Trade," 24.

51. Gerald Horne, *The Counter-Revolution of 1776*, passim. See also Treacy and Davidson cited immediately below.

52. Reverend William P. Treacy, *Old Catholic Maryland and Early Jesuit Missionaries*, Swedesboro, New Jersey: St. Joseph's Rectory, 1889, passim.

53. Thomas E. Davidson, *Free Blacks on the Lower Eastern Shore of Maryland: The Colonial Period, 1662 to 1775*, Crownsville, MD: Maryland Historical Trust Press, 1991, 6,

54. *A Law of Maryland Concerning Religion*, 1689, Huntington Library, San Marino, CA.

55. Westbury, "Colonial Virginia and the Atlantic Slave Trade," 29.

56. Statute, April 1691, in William Walker Henning, ed., *The Statutes at Large; Being a Collection of the Laws of Virginia from the First Session of the Legislature of the Year 1619*, vol. 3, New York: Bartow, 1823.

57. William E. Nelson, *The Common Law in Colonial America*, vol. 2: *The Middle Colonies and the Carolinas, 1660–1730*, New York: Oxford University Press, 83.

58. Report, 9 December 1692, in A. Van Dantzig, 54.

59. Dennis J. Maika, "Commerce and Community: Manhattan Merchants in the Seventeenth Century," Ph.D. diss., New York University, 1995. See also *Records of the Particular Court of the Colony of Connecticut Administration of Sir Edmund Andros, Royal Governor, 1687–1688*, Hartford, 1935, Massachusetts Historical Society, Boston.

60. William Stoughton, ed., *Narrative of the Proceedings of Sir Edmond Andros and His Complices...Who Acted by Illegal and Arbitrary Commission from the Late K. James During his Government in New England*, Boston, 1691, Massachusetts Historical Society, Boston.

61. Geoffrey Parker, *Global Crisis*, 455.

62. *An Account of the Late Revolution in New England Together with the Declaration of the Gentlemen, Merchants and Inhabitants of Boston...*, 18 April 1689, Huntington Library, San Marino, CA.

63. Kees-Jan Waterman, "Leisler's Rebellion, 1689–1690: Being Dutch in Albany," *Maryland Historian* 22/2 (December 1991): 21–40.

64. E. E. Rich, ed., *Hudson's Bay Copy Book of Letters: Commissions' Instructions Outward, 1688–1696*, London: Hudson's Bay Record Company, 1957, xiii. See also Margaret Lucille Kekewich, ed., *Princes and Peoples: France and the British Isles, 1620–1714*.

65. John Romeyn Brodhead, "The Government of Sir Edmund Andros over New England in 1688 and 1689," New-York Historical Society, 4 December 1866, Huntington Library, San Marino, CA.

66. See *A True and Faithful Account of an Intire and Absolute Victory over the French Fleet in the West Indies by Two East India Ships and Other Vessels at Barbadoes*, 1690, Huntington Library, San Marino, CA. In the same archive, see also *A Full and Particular Account of the Seizing and Imprisonment of the Duke of Tyrconnel, and other Great Officers by the Express Command of the French King to which Is Added an Account of the Inhumane Barbarities, Lately*

Committed by the French on the Protestants in Plundering the Husbands and Ravishing their Wives and Children in the West of Ireland, 1690. See also Monsieur de Pointis, *An Account of the Taking of Carthagena by the French in the Year 1697, Containing All the Particulars of that Expedition from Their First Setting Out, to Their Return to Brest*, London: Buckley, 1698, Brown University, Providence.

67.   "Memoir of the Marquis de Seignelay Regarding the Dangers that Threaten Canada and the Means to Remedy them," January 1687, in Clarence L. Ver Steeg and Richard Hofstadter, 328–33.

68.   John E. Pomfret, *The Province of East Jersey, 1609–1672*, 182, 184.

69.   *A Letter from a Gentleman in the Country to His Friend at Edinburgh Wherein It is Clearly Proved that the Scottish, African and Indian Company Is Exactly Calculated for the Interest of Scotland*, Edinburgh: Mosman, 1696, Brown University, Providence.

70.   Michal Rozbicki, *Transformation of the English Cultural Ethos in Colonial America*, Lanham, MD: University Press of America, 1988, 134, 141, 146–47. See also Abigail Leslie Swingen, *Competing Visions of Empire: Labor, Slavery and the Origins of the British Atlantic Empire*, New Haven: Yale University Press, 2015.

71.   Pomfret,*The Province of East Jersey, 1609–1672*, 292. See also *A Discourse Concerning High Treason or the Statute of the 25th, Edward the Third...also a Short Treatise of Treason Designed for the Introduction of the Ignorant*, London, 1683, Huntington Library, San Marino, CA. In the same archive see also *The Arraignment, Tryal & Condemnation of Algernon Sidney...for High Treason for Conspiring the Death of the King and Intending to Raise a Rebellion in this Kingdom...*, London, 1684.

72.   R. C. Dallas, *The History of the Maroons, From their Origin to the Establishment of their Chief Tribe at Sierra Leone, Including the Expedition to Cuba for the Purpose of Procuring Spanish Chasseurs...*, vol. 1, London: Strahan, 1803, 24.

◉

9. Apocalypse Now

1.   Philip Boucher, 218–19.

2.   Statute, 8 August 1688, in Richard Hall, ed., *Acts Passed in the Island of Barbados from 1643 to 1762*, London, 1764, 112–21, Barbados National Archives, St. James..

3.   Statute, 3 October 1688, in ibid., 121–23.

4.   *Act of Assembly Passed in the Charibbee Leeward Islands from 1690 to 1730*, London: Basket, 1734, Huntington Library, San Marino, CA.

5.   To the Lords of the Commissioners of Trade and Plantations, 15 March 1692, CO28/2, National Archives of the United Kingdom, London (henceforth, NAUK)..

6.   Report, 27 February 1693, CO28/2, NAUK.

7.   Statute, 3 November 1697, in Hall, *Acts Passed in the Island of Barbados*, 138–55.

8.   Report, 20 June 1696, CO28/3, NAUK.

9.   Report, 2 November 1697, CO28/3, NAUK.

10. Statute, 1 December 1703, in ibid., Hall, 157–159.

11. *Acts of Assembly Passed in the Charibbee Leeward Islands from 1690 to 1730*, London: Basket, 1734, Huntington Library, San Marino, CA.

12. Statute, 2 August 1692, in Hall, *Acts Passed in the Island of Barbados*, 127–28.

13. Statute, 27 October 1692, in ibid., 131.

14. Richard Beale Davis, *William Fitzhugh and His Chesapeake World, 1676–1701*, Chapel Hill: University of North Carolina Press, 1963, 356.

15. Minutes, House of Assembly Journal, 23 June 1696, 1b/5/1/2, Jamaica Archives and Records Department, Spanish Town.

16. Minutes, House of Assembly Journal, 27 June 1696, 1b/5/1/2, ibid.

17. Charles Leslie, *A New History of Jamaica: From the Earliest Accounts to the Taking of Porto-Bello by Vice-Admiral Vernon*, London: Hodges, 1740, 252. See also *A Full and Exact Collection of all the Considerable Addresses, Memorials, Petitions...Relating to the Company of Scotland Trading to Africa and the Indies, Since the Passing of the First Act of Parliament, by Which the Said Company was Established in June...*, Edinburgh, 1700, Massachusetts Historical Society, Boston.

18. Statute, 1695, *The Laws of Jamaica Comprehending All the Acts in Force Passed between the Thirty-Second Year of the Reign of King Charles the Second and the Thirty-Third*, vol. 1, 67, National Library of Jamaica, Kingston.

19. *Acts of Assembly Passed in the Island of Barbadoes from 1648 to 1818*, London: Basket, 1721, CO30/4, NAUK.

20. Minutes, House of Assembly Journal, 2 July 1696, Jamaica Archives and Records Department, Spanish Town.

21. Entry, in A. Van Dantzig, 54.

22. Report, ca. 1688, *Journals of the Assembly of Jamaica*, vol. 1: *From January the 20th 1663–1664*, Jamaica: Aikman, 1811, CO140/2, NAUK.

23. Report, 28 May 1692, CO140/5, NAUK.

24. Bill, 6 May 1699, CO140/2, NAUK.

25. Report, 8 August 1669, CO8/1, NAUK.

26. Report, 3 November 1698, CO8/3, NAUK.

27. Lucia Raatma, *Queen Noor: American born Queen of Jordan*, Minneapolis: Compass Point, 2006. See also Nancy Bowen, *Ralph Nader: Man with a Mission*, Brookfield, Connecticut: Twenty-first Century, 2002; Marlo Thomas, *Growing up Funny: My Story and the Story of Funny*, New York: Hyperion, 2010.

28. See, for example, Sarah Phillips Casteel, *Calypso Jews: Jewishness in the Caribbean Literary Imagination*, New York: Columbia University Press, 2016.

29. Minutes, House of Assembly, 16 November 1698, Jamaica Archives and Records Department, Spanish Town.

30. *Acts of Assembly Passed in the Charibee Leeward Islands from 1690 to 1730*, London: Basket, 1734, Huntington Library, San Marino, CA.

31. Statute, 1696, *The Laws of Jamaica Comprehending All the Acts in Force*, 71.

32. Proposed bill, 19 September 1688, CO140/2, NAUK.

33. Governor of Leeward Islands, 10 November 1707, MS 1016–18, National Library of Jamaica, Kingston.

34. Whitehall to "My Lord," 28 January 1707, MS1016–18, ibid.

35. Statute, 1698, *The Laws of Jamaica Comprehending All the Acts in Force*, 75, ibid.

36. R.C. Dallas, *The History of the Maroons*, vol. 1, London: Strahan, 1803, 33, 36, 38.

37. Statute, 19 December 1699, in H. R. McIlwaine, ed., *Executive Journals of the Council of Colonial Virginia*, vol. 2: *August 3, 1699–April 27, 1705*, Richmond, VA: Public Printing, 36.

38. Report, 19 December 1695, CO5/787, Massachusetts Bay Minutes of the Colony (henceforth, MBMC), NAUK.

39. Report, 24 November 1698, CO5787, MBMC.

40. Report, 14 December 1699, CO5/787, MBMC: Petitioner's spouse sailed from Marblehead to Bahamas in 1696 and after months apparently disappeared. Petitioner wanted to be declared single so as to remarry. Another woman said her spouse sailed to Nevis and has not been heard from since and also wanted to be declared single so as to remarry.

41. Report, 2 July 1696, CO140/2, NAUK.

42. Report, 5 June 1696, CO5/787, MBMC, NAUK.

43. Report, 9 July 1696, CO5/787, MBMC.

44. Report, 15 July 1696, CO5/787, MBMC.

45. Report, 16 October 1696, CO5/787, MBMC.

46. Report, 19 December 1696, CO5/787, MBMC.

47. Report, 7 June 1697, CO5/787, MBMC.

48. Report, 16 September 1697, CO5/787, MBMC.

49. Report, 10 July 1697, CO28/3, NAUK.

50. Report, 10 June 1698, CO5.787, MBMC.

51. Report, 29 December 1698, CO5/787, MBMC.

52. Report, 3 July 1699, CO5/787, MBMC.

53. Report, 19 June 1699, CO5/787, MBMC.

54. Report, 27 June 1698, HCA 1/98, NAUK.

55. Report, 6 July 1699, CO5/787, MBMC.

56. Report, 16 April 1700, CO5/787, MBMC.

57. Elaine Breslaw, *Tituba, Reluctant Witch of Salem: Devilish Indians and Puritan Fantasies*, New York: New York University Press, 1996.

58. Report, 29 May 1700, CO5/787, MBMC.

59. Report, 9 July 1700, CO5/787, MBMC.

60. Samuel Sewall, *The Selling of Joseph*, Boston, 1700, Boston Public Library. See also Nigel Tattersfield, *The Forgotten Trade: Comprising the Log of the Daniel and Henry of 1700 and Accounts of the Slave Trade from the Minor Ports of England, 1698–1725*, London: Jonathan Cape, 1991.

61. Gregory E. O'Malley, *Final Passages: The Inter-Colonial Slave Trade of British America, 1619–1807*, Chapel Hill: University of North Carolina Press, 2014.

62. Susan Alice Westbury, 25.

63. Graham Russell Hodges, *Root & Branch*, 40.

64. Wendy Warren, *New England Bound*, 191, 196. 226.

65. Sydney V. James, *Colonial Rhode Island: A History*, New York: Scribner's, 1975.

66. Affidavit of Dudley Digges, 1693, Charles City, Mss3C807a, Virginia Historical Society, Richmond.

67. Report, 24 March 1709, in William P. Palmer, ed., *Calendar of Virginia State Papers and Other Manuscripts, 1652–1781, Preserved in the Capitol at Richmond*, Richmond, 1875, Rockefeller Library, Williamsburg.

68. Letter, 24 August 1710, in R. A. Brock, ed., *The Official Letters of Alexander Spotswood, Lieutenant Governor of the Colony of Virginia, 1710–1722*, vol. 1, 16, Richmond: Virginia Historical Society, 1882.

69. Letter from Alexander Spotswood, 15 December 1710, in ibid., 42.

70. Ibid. Douglass R. Burgess, Jr., 44, 125, 133, 136, 145, 147, 149, 154, 167,171.

71. Gerald Horne, *Confronting Black Jacobins: The U.S., the Haitian Revolution and the Origins of the Dominican Republic*, New York: Monthly Review Press, 2015.

72. Gerald Horne, *Black and Red: W. E. B. Du Bois and the Afro-American Response to the Cold War, 1944–1963*, Albany: State University of New York Press, 1986.

73. Gerald Horne, *Blows Against the Empire: U.S. Imperialism in Crisis*, New York: International, 2008.

Index